© Nicky Joh

As an experienced business and life coach, management consultant and facilitator, Keren Smedley has been working for over 20 years with individuals, groups and organisations. She is *Woman's Weekly*'s agony aunt and Saga's life coach. She runs her own business, Experience Matters, a consultancy specialising in coaching and consulting on age-related issues. The mother of three adult sons, she lives in north London with her second husband.

Praise for WHO'S THAT SLEEPING IN MY BED?:

'Keren Smedley writes with honesty, insight and compassion. This is a practical, authoritative book covering a comprehensive range of issues'

Julie Peasgood

'Keren Smedley's book gives readers caring and commonsense in equal measure to professional advice. In Keren the generation of Baby Boomers has got itself a lot more than just an experienced life coach, more even than an articulate agony aunt; in Keren they have a friend'   Irma Kurtz

Praise for Keren Smedley's previous book, WHO'S THAT WOMAN IN THE MIRROR?:

'Show me any woman and I'll show you someone who doesn't feel secure about getting older. Here's the book to offer all women practical help and advice'

Gloria Hunniford

'In the introduction to her excellent book, Keren has used a quote from George Burns: "You can't help getting older but you don't have to get old." In every elucidating chapter, Keren argues that you are "never too old for anything" and to substantiate her claim, she offers simple and straightforward case studies with various options and alternatives. She also offers one of the most substantial lists I've ever seen of helpful websites. Keren's book is a must for the over-50s and, for my own benefit, I wish it had been around years ago'

Jan Leeming

'Once you've read Keren Smedley's book you need never look in a mirror again. It's all in the words. A must to keep by your bed!'

Lynda Bellingham

'Keren Smedley sees only opportunity and possibility when she looks at her 56-year-old reflection'

Woman's Weekly

'A practical, candid guide through the minefield of often painful and confusing experiences encountered by women in middle age and beyond'

Mature Times

WHO'S THAT SLEEPING IN MY BED?

The Art of Successful Relationships for Grown-Ups

Keren Smedley

headline
springboard

By Keren Smedley
and available from Headline Springboard

Who's That Woman in the Mirror?
Who's That Sleeping in My Bed?

First published in 2009
by HEADLINE SPRINGBOARD
An imprint of HEADLINE PUBLISHING GROUP

First published in paperback in 2009
by HEADLINE SPRINGBOARD

1

Cataloguing in Publication Data is available from the British Library

ISBN 978 0 7553 1881 0

Typeset in Times by Palimpsest Book Production Limited

Printed in the UK by CPI Mackays, Chatham ME5 8TD

Headline's policy is to use papers that are natural, renewable and recyclable products
and made from wood grown in sustainable forests. The logging and manufacturing
processes are expected to conform to the environmental regulations of the
country of origin.

HEADLINE PUBLISHING GROUP
An Hachette UK Company
338 Euston Road
London NW1 3BH

www.headline.co.uk
www.hachette.co.uk

Dedicated to Martin, Ben, Tim and Matthew.

Acknowledgements

I couldn't have written this book without Richard Barber's magic words, guidance and support; Kathleen Reddington's unwavering hard work and friendship; and the wonderful supply of meals, great videos and encouragement from my husband. Special thanks to Chris Kell and Jacky Spigel, who listened to me and never doubted that I could do it even when I did.

Many thanks to Bill Miller, Philip Lightowlers, Nigel C, Kevin Foster, Dermott Ryall, Martin Williams, Ros Constable, Diane Stallwood, Julie Cartwright-Finch, Chris Arciszewska and Erika Langen who gave up their time to talk to me about their relationships and their hopes and fears for the future now they are 50-plus. Thanks also to all my friends, who I have talked to over the years about getting older and our relationships; and my clients who have shared their lives with me. Huge thanks to Val Hudson at Headline, who really believes that the baby boomers need to have their voice heard and be supported as they travel forward into uncharted waters. Many thanks to Amanda Preston, who has believed in me and the topic right from the start. Thanks to Jane Butcher who, without a complaint, painstakingly copy-edited the book.

Credits

Contents

Introduction   9

Section one – Opposite Sex   14

Section two – Same Sex   71

Section three – Singles   112

Section four – New Relationships   161

Section five – Blended Families   199

Section six – Significant Others   238

Last Thoughts   277

Resource List   279

Bibliography   295

Index   301

Section One: Opposite Sex

1. I know you're not supposed to do this, something that a woman is more likely to do than a man, but I read my wife's diary and my suspicions were confirmed: she's been having an affair.   14

2. When we were young, my partner and I had a very varied sex life. We tried lots of things and sex was a big part of our lives. We now seem to be having difficulties, probably age-related. Does it have to be like this?   21

3. I've been married for 36 years and I haven't been happy for most of them. My husband can be a really lovely man, but, throughout our whole marriage, he's been physically violent. I've heard that physically abusive men stop when they get older. Do you think this will happen? I'm thinking I should leave him.   29

4. I've been married for 25 years. I just don't want sex any more and I don't even have many sexual fantasies. I'm worried she'll find someone else. How do we deal with this?   37

5. I have just had a dreadful shock. I was on our computer and I wanted to find a site I had been on a few days ago. I went into 'history', and there were to my horror loads of porn sites looked at daily for weeks. I can't believe it.   44

6. I have been married for 27 years. It's OK but certainly not great. How do you contemplate what might be another 27 years when you're not in love, when there are no longer children at home to distract you and there is likely to be illness and possible dependency?   48

7. My partner has just been diagnosed with early Alzheimer's. I'm 57 and she's 56. It's not fair and I'm terrified. I had so many things I wanted to do with my life and now I won't be able to.   56

8. My wife and I have started to talk seriously about getting older and dying and how we imagine it will be. We seem to have very different ideas. For example, I fantasise about a sky burial and she a religious one. What are the things we need to consider and how do we reconcile these differences?   64

Section Two: Same Sex

1. I've been married for 32 years. Our sex life has always been infrequent, even at the start of our relationship. Recently he told me he was bisexual, possibly gay, and has had a couple of relationships with men. What can I do?   71

2. I'm a woman in my mid-fifties and recently fallen in love with a woman who has up till now been heterosexual. All my friends are warning me off her as they say older heteros often want to try out a lesbian relationship; it's on their list of 'things to do before they die'.   78

3. My partner has recently retired and is depressed. He is ten years older than me and has always been the successful one. I'm still working and he doesn't seem to do much in the day. I don't see why he's so depressed. How can we stop the feelings of resentment we both have for each other?   85

4. We are a lesbian couple and we have asked a gay couple we know if they would father a child for us. One of the criteria they have stipulated is that we have a civil partnership to show our commitment to being there for the child. I am not keen.   89

5. I'm in my early fifties and I have been with my partner for 22 years. I still say 'have' but I should say 'had', as he died last year from bowel cancer. But, now he's gone, I'm lonely. I'm too old to rejoin the 'scene' at my age. It's not easy being gay when you're older and on your own.   96

6. I've been part of a lesbian community for years. My ex-partner and I split up after 20 years but we've remained very good friends. I've recently met someone new and I really like her. I don't think she understands about remaining friends with former partners because she says it feels like our new relationship is going on in the shadow of the old one. How do I keep both? 104

Section Three: Singles

1. I've been on my own for a while and had a few lovers. The sex hasn't been great, though. Is that what I should expect at my age? (I'm well into my fifties.) 112

2. I've been single since I was in my mid-forties. I made a conscious choice that I didn't want to live with anyone. I just can't get this into some of my close friends' heads. How do I help them to understand I'm not incomplete or frightened of being sad and lonely when I'm older? 120

3. My husband and I split up about four years ago. I'm very content with my single status; he's dated, but nothing serious until recently. He wants to bring her to events like our grandchildren's birthday parties and he's planning to take her to his family functions rather than me. I hate it. What can I do? 127

4. I'm single again and I don't want to be. I had an affair and my husband left me. My family are all appalled at me and have rallied round him. I feel lonely, hurt and cross. How do I pick myself up? 135

5. I am a member of a singles group. I have met a really lovely woman and we get on very well; she says I understand her. However, I know I can't keep up with her intellectually. Am I mad to want to pursue this relationship? 143

6. My last relationship's ending was seriously unpleasant and the one before was pretty grim. I felt so rejected and hurt each time that I can't bear the thought of going through that again. I know it's limiting my chances of finding a new partner.   150

7. I'm 57 and I've met a new partner. He is everything I've been looking for, except he has a job at the other end of the country. I don't want to give up my life here or him. What can I do?   158

Section Four: New Relationships

1. I met a new man and moved in with him. Early in our relationship I found out that he liked to wear women's clothes. At that time it was only at home. Since then it has slowly become more important to him and he spends a lot of time dressed as a woman. He is now considering changing his gender as he wants to live as a woman.

     161

2. I'm 58 and I'm having a great time sexually since I came out of a long-term relationship. I'm heavily into cybersex. It suits me fine as I can stay at home, don't have to be judged physically and can have safe sex with lots of people. The drawback is I'm still on my own when the screen goes off. Is this an addiction and is it bad for me?   167

3. I'm in a newish relationship and I'm feeling rather anxious about the sex. My partner is much more sexually experienced than me. Sex with my new partner has been all right so far but he keeps asking me what I'm into and I just don't know what to say. I've no idea what you can do. Am I too old for that kind of caper?   174

4. My new partner wants to have anal sex. This is something I've never done. I have always been negative about it, but recently I've been wondering maybe I'm not very adventurous? I just wonder if I am missing out. I don't even really know what happens and how to do it.   180

5. My marriage split up about nine months ago and I've had several lovers. Some I met on the internet and others at clubs. I didn't think about safe sex; at 53, I thought I was too old. I've just been diagnosed with chlamydia and gonorrhoea. I'm distraught.   183

6. I started a new relationship a few months ago. My partner's great: we get on well and chat easily. However, there's a bit of a problem with sex. I know there are things that would make the sex better but there are also some things I just don't like and I feel embarrassed to raise them with him. How do I discuss this?   190

Section Five: Blended Families

1. I separated from my wife twelve years ago. We've been divorced for seven of those. She's still smarting and spitting. My daughter told me last week that she was thinking about not inviting me or her mother to her wedding, as she didn't want the tensions between us to spoil her day.   199

2. I brought up my children as a single mother. They've now left home and I've just moved in with another couple as an equal partner in their relationship. We've been very good friends for a while and we practise polyamory. My daughters are appalled. Should I give up my life because they disapprove?   207

3. I have tried every which way to stop feeling so bad about my divorce and my ex-husband. Everyone says I should get help. I'm sure they are right, and in truth I think they are a bit fed up with me. I just don't know how to go about it.   214

4. I'm a 53-year-old woman. I lost my mother just under two years ago after a long battle with breast cancer. My father is 77 and he has just announced he plans to get married. How can he do this?   218

5. I'm a desperate stepmother. I have three children of my own and three step children. I've recently remarried a man whose wife died two years ago. I'm trying to do a good job but I'm really struggling. What can I do to be a better mother?   223

6. I'm no good at this. My wife and I divorced very acrimoniously nine years ago. The children split their time more or less equally between both of us. My wife and I still don't speak. I hate it when my kids spend time with their mother and her new partner. How do I manage my feelings?   230

Section Six: Significant Others

1. My son and his wife split up a few months ago. The children are living with their mother. My daughter-in-law is refusing to let me come round as she's so angry with my son. How do we find a way through this?   238

2. My father died a few years go and my mother fairly recently. It was a huge strain on me. I now don't know what to do about my brother and sisters. Should I reinstate the family get togethers or is it OK to let those relationships just drift apart?   245

3. Life isn't how I expected it to be. My father-in-law is ill and in hospital. He has lived on his own for years and been totally independent. Now that will no longer be possible. My husband is an only child and he thinks that we should ask him to move in with us.   249

4. I am 62 and I have four adult children. We downsized. We now have two back living at home and our eldest child wants to come home, too. There's no room. I feel dreadful that we can't have them all. What can I do to keep everyone happy? I'm the one that gets upset and feels guilty.   257

5. When my marriage ended, several of my close friends rallied round my husband so I lost people who'd been dear to me; others I saw frequently. Now I'm in a new relationship and I don't have as much free time to see them. How do you balance friends and partners?

263

6. My parents split up many years ago and both married again. All four parents are elderly and frail and need care. I now have to discuss this with my own siblings as well as my stepbrothers and sisters. Am I supposed to look after my step-parents as well? 270

Introduction

Y ou may be wondering why another book on relationships. Surely there are enough! I probably would have thought that, too, if I hadn't received so many questions from baby boomers wondering how to manage this next stage of their life and confirming there was little or no specific information out there for them. This book is for all of us, men and women of all sexualities and whether in couples or single: the issues raised affect us all.

In my working life as a consultant and coach for Experience Matters as well as an agony aunt and relationship coach for *Woman's Weekly*, Saga and various radio stations, I've been struck by the variety of issues that affect people of our age and how important it is that we feel good in our relationships whether they are with lovers, family, friends or colleagues.

A belief that many of us hold is 'all you need is love' and then everything just falls into place. I wish it were as simple as that. From my experience, both personally and professionally, it takes a lot of hard work to maintain a relationship and to feel that you're growing and developing within it. However, it's true that, if our personal relationships are going well and we feel satisfied and self-confident, the rest of life seems more manageable.

Since the early 1900s, the number of people over 65 in the UK has grown tenfold, along with a realistic expectation of a good life. Baby boomers are the first generation not predisposed to putting on their carpet slippers when they reach the age of 50 and sitting at home with a mug of cocoa waiting for life to pass them by. We have every chance of making it to 90.

We're also the pioneers in developing ways to handle sex and relationships well, however old we might be. We were the ones, after all, who put sex on the map in the sixties!

The area of relationships is of interest to all men and women, whether single or in a couple, gay or straight. Recent research into the sex lives of baby boomers by both the University of Chicago in 2006 and Parship.co.uk in 2007 revealed that we're continuing to reap the benefit of the sexual revolution which began almost fifty years ago. We were the first generation to take the contraceptive pill, challenge marriage, campaign for women's and gay rights, and continue to want to be considered sexual for as long as we want.

It's clear that being 50 does not mean you give up on sex and love. However, it does bring with it different challenges for those facing the next generation. Happily, men are increasingly more willing to discuss issues of the heart. Relate, the counselling, sex therapy and relationship education service, recently reported that there has been a 40 per cent increase in the number of their male clients admitting they're no longer interested in sex and seeking advice because of the problems this is causing in their relationships.

It's easy when you get to 50 or 60 to be seduced by the media into believing that your days of heady sex and fun are over. As Joel Block points out in his book, *Sex over 50*, sex may change as we get older but that's the good news! How many of us stumbled our way through our youth not sure what we were doing, feeling too shy to ask and assuming we should somehow know? Most, I expect. But here we are still healthy and, in spite of the odd creaky joint, not only still fit enough to enjoy good sex but confident enough, too, to ask for what we want. Women become more assertive as they age, less in need of reassurance from their partners and more able, therefore, to get their needs met. Men, by contrast, become more able to nurture and more comfortable with intimacy. Whether we're in the same relationship or a new one, these attributes will enable both men and women to enjoy sex to the full.

For all though, that we're children of the sixties there are still many questions about sex we are too shy to ask. This book is emphatically not a sex manual so you won't find any advice on techniques (although the Resource List does tell you where you can find that information). What it does contain, however, is many of the answers to things you may have wondered about, while also I hope helping to dispel concerns you might have had but which you've been too embarrassed to articulate in public.

We're not on the scrap-heap at 50. Rather, most of us are keen to maintain our vitality and energy and want to take an active part in all aspects of our life, both in our personal relationships and in wider society. We may, due to the inevitable changes in our bodies, need to do this in a different way but with no less enthusiasm.

By this stage of our lives, we should have learnt a lot. For many, their love life will not have run as smoothly as they might have hoped and they will not be in the relationships they may have fantasised about when they were younger. The challenge is often greater if you're lesbian, gay, bisexual or transgender. Many of the issues are, of course, similar but often aren't discussed alongside those of heterosexuals. Figures released by the Office of National Statistics (ONS) in 2008 revealed that the trend in long-term marriages ending in divorce shows no sign of abating and that the greatest percentage increase in failed marriages turns out to be in those of over thirty years' standing.

The consequence is that there are now more and more single

individuals in their fifties and sixties either looking for a relationship or learning to be single again. There are an estimated 15 million singles now living in Britain (source: ONS 2006) of which just over half (a staggering 7.65 million men and women) are looking for a long-term relationship.

You may be in a long-term relationship needing the spark put back into it after years of child-rearing; you may be having to work out how to go it alone after a divorce or bereavement; you may be trying to find the strength needed to come out of an abusive relationship; you may even be coming to terms with a change in your own or your partner's sex preference or gender. Many of us feel we have to face up to our changed circumstances alone, trying to work out how to negotiate a path through the minefield because of the myth that, by this age and stage, we should know it all. But it's just not true.

Many of us also have to help adult children and elderly parents come to terms with the changes in their lives and their relationships. An unprecedented number of people in their eighties and nineties will need care and support from adult children who may well be going through significant life changes themselves. This group of 50+ men and women don't want to give up on romance and passion and dedicate the rest of their lives to simple pastimes, looking after their grandchildren and sometimes even supporting their children financially, rewarding though this can be.

Doing it differently from previous generations brings with it inevitable challenges. This book is based on questions asked of me by readers, listeners and clients and I hope it will offer you the opportunity to solve your own dilemmas through the experience of others. The more we understand one another, the better our communication. We often have difficulties relating to people because we can't put ourselves in their shoes. By reading about a variety of situations and answering some questions about yourself, you'll be better placed to find solutions and more able to support your friends and family with their problems.

This book offers the 50+ answers to many of the questions that concern them but are rarely voiced. We are a generation who, in spite of flower power and free sex, carry many of our parents' inhibitions with us and find ourselves caught between two approaches for dealing with life. At times, we feel inhibited and guilty about airing our feelings; at others, we want to share our thoughts and experiences with anyone who will listen.

For more and more people, being 50 is literally to be middle-aged with years still ahead to enjoy fulfilling relationships with friends, partners, lovers and children. It's also a time when many will have to face the prospect of losing elderly parents, becoming the new older generation in the process.

I've divided the book into a number of different sections. That doesn't mean, of course, that certain types of problem only affect some people: problems tend not to be segregated by gender or sexuality. So don't limit yourself to just one section in the belief that your 'category' is unique. You'd be surprised at the area of overlap in lives apparently totally dissimilar from your own.

In the end, and whatever your situation, this book is for you.

Section One
Opposite Sex

Q1 **I know you're not supposed to do this, something that a woman is more likely to do than a man, but I read my wife's diary and my suspicions were confirmed: she's been having an affair for a while now with the husband of one of our friends. I don't know what to do. I still love her and we get on well. I feel so betrayed and don't see how I can ever sit down to supper with the other guy again even if she and I work it out. I've now told her I know. She says she loves me, too, and didn't want to hurt me. I feel anxious and so low I would really appreciate some advice on what to do.**

You must be feeling really bad. Discovering that your partner has been unfaithful is one of the most painful experiences anyone can go through. Infidelity creates intense emotional pain. I expect you're experiencing a number of different emotions: disbelief, anger, hurt and betrayal. Infidelity shakes the marriage foundations to the core and leaves you wondering whether it can weather the storm.

Before we go on to look at how you might cope, the alternative outcomes and the ways in which you could respond, let's take a moment to think about the diary. First, and you might say it's because I'm a woman, I don't think women look for clues any more than men do if they have suspicions that their partner is having an affair. (For anyone in a similar position, it would be better to discuss this with your wife rather than searching for evidence behind her back.)

An affair is often indicative of the fact that talking about your feelings and relating to each other have gone out of the window. So although I understand you felt you had no choice, reading someone's diary is an infringement of their privacy. You need to stop now even if you are in a heightened anxious state. It's common for many of us when we're hurt to blame ourselves for the problem. I wonder if it's less painful to blame yourself for being a 'spy' rather than focus on the issue in hand? I think you should put the matter of the diary aside, both in your own head and when you're discussing with your wife what's happened. From what you say, you wouldn't have snooped if you weren't suspicious.

There's very little research on the frequency of infidelity and the reason people have affairs. People rarely answer honestly, sometimes exaggerating and other times denying anything in case they're caught out. There is, though, one useful piece of relatively recent research. In the data collected from the National Survey of Sexual Attitudes and Lifestyles, 'Sexual Behaviour in Britain: partnerships, practices and HIV risk behaviours' (*The Lancet,* December 2001), it states that 14.6 per cent of men and 9 per cent of women had overlapping sexual relationships that year. The survey also revealed that, in spite of the liberalisation of sexual behaviour, most people saw affairs as not acceptable.

There is, however, a wealth of information gained by therapists on how to survive infidelity and some excellent books on the subject of how to move forward (see Bibliography, especially Gottman, John 1999 and Kirshenbaum, Mira 2008 and Resource List).

Affairs can happen in any relationship: opposite sex, same sex, married couples and co-habitees, anyone in fact, in a committed long-term relationship where being monogamous is part of the contract made between the two people involved.

I'm defining an affair when one or all of the following apply:

- The person who is having the affair has a strong sexual attraction to someone who isn't their partner.

- Their relationship with the other person is kept secret.

- They feel emotionally connected and closer to this person than they do to their partner.

Interestingly, a new type of affair has arisen with the increased use of the internet and chat rooms. Studies have shown that more and more people are using these sites and not telling their partners; and, without meeting their 'lovers' in person, they're conducting intimate relationships.

So why do affairs happen? There are, of course, as many reasons as there are people but we can make loose categorisations. Usually, there's a problem in the relationship which is being resolved externally rather than internally within the marriage. There are those who have an affair to expose the fact that something is wrong and unconsciously leave evidence around; there are those who want to leave a relationship and use the affair as their escape route; there are those where boredom and lack of passion in their full-time relationship makes them seek an affair in order to feel alive again; and there are those who see an affair as a way of maintaining their marriages by getting those needs that aren't fulfilled within the marriage met elsewhere.

John Gottman in his book, *The Seven Principles for Making Marriages Work* (1999), says that most affairs aren't about sex but about 'seeking friendship, understanding, respect, attention, caring and concern – the kind of things that marriage is supposed to offer'. We often forget the importance of this when we're focused on managing our busy lives: looking after children, holding down jobs, dealing with elderly parents and so on.

Clearly, I have no idea why your wife had an affair but you say in your question that you get on well. So my hunch is that it started because it met some of her emotional needs that are not being met in the marriage. I expect a lot of her needs *are* met, though, which is why you had thought everything was all right. In these circumstances, very often the person having the affair is using their lover as a 'painkiller', enabling them to stay with their partner. By having both husband and lover, her life is complete.

I don't want it to sound as though I'm excusing her. Breaking a contract in any relationship is not acceptable. I'm just trying to explain what might have been happening. Also, painful as it is, she has chosen someone who is also in a marriage so the likelihood of him leaving his partner and setting up home with your wife is much reduced. I know a number of women who, rather than going to marital counselling (the sensible route, to my mind) have managed unfulfilling relationships by finding external support in the shape of an affair.

You ask what you should do. Sadly, there isn't one definitive answer and you alone have to make the decision. I'm going to pose a few questions, for you to think about. Some may make you raise your eyebrows and ask 'Why should I do anything?' The answer is that it takes two to make a good relationship when things go awry and both of you will need to change your behaviour even though it's your wife who has broken the trust.

I. What would it be like if I never raise the issue again?

2. What am I hoping to gain from raising it?

3. Do I want to remain married to her?

4. How would I like our relationship to be?

5. What have I done that has led us to this place?

6. What am I going to do differently to improve the relationship?

7. What do I need from my wife in order to feel able to begin to repair things?

8. What do I need her to do immediately?

Having answered these questions, you should know the direction in which you want to go. As I've said in other answers, it's often very hard to sort these things out on your own. Counselling really can help. Find someone who'll help you mend your relationship, if that's your and your partner's goal. Go to someone who's a registered marital couple counsellor and who is used to working with infidelity. Please take a look at the Resource List.

There are, however, things you can do and things that you can think about on your own and as a couple. First, remember that, although it might feel like your marriage is over, it almost certainly isn't. Marriages can recover from affairs and go from strength to strength. Although there's no blueprint for this, there are a number of steps you can take. You may well find yourself going back to some of these steps several times and taking them in a different order. That's fine: you need to do what's best for the two of you.

- Agree with your wife that you both want to repair your marriage. This will take time but it needs to be a joint goal.

- If you and your wife are going to get through this, she has to agree that she'll stop seeing the other man with immediate effect. It's impossible to rebuild mutual trust while her lover is still in her life. This may well be very hard for her but it has to happen. If she wants to see him to end it, she needs to tell you when she's doing so. One meeting is enough and she must tell you when it's done. No long endings. You mention how hard it would be ever to have a meal together again with this man and his wife. Why would you want to? You certainly don't have to.

- You may well need to find out why she had an affair. You don't have to agree with her reasoning but let her explain. If you want to ask questions, that is your right but think about why you're asking them. Is it to help move things forward or to have more reason to be hurt and angry?

- Express your anger, hurt and disappointment: she needs to know how you feel. Say what you need to say now. I know this will be hard but the less resentment you bottle up, the easier it will be to move on. I worked with a client whose husband had an affair and, although she said she wanted to move on, she found herself unable to finish any sentence without referring to it. She came to see me when she realised she was the one creating the wedge between them and that she needed help to forgive, which can be very hard.

- Talk about what's lacking in your relationship from both your points of view. She may feel that you'd stopped talking to her or that you were tired when you got home and not interested in hearing about her day. Or perhaps you never got home till late so she went out with other people. Similarly, either you may have felt that she had little interest in you which is why you concentrated on your work or you tried to show her you cared by working hard to provide for your family.

- You need to feel that she is truly sorry for what she has done and she needs to take responsibility for her behaviour. There were other ways to deal with difficulties than by cheating on you. You have to be convinced that you can forgive her over time.

- Agree what you need in the short term. This might include her letting you know her movements – what she's doing and with whom. It's reasonable for you to want to know but do so sensitively, otherwise she may feel you're policing her life.

- Discuss how you'd like your life together to be. Find ways in which you can connect with each other. Think of things you could do. Re-start activities you used to enjoy doing together.

- Introduce some physical intimacy. One of the blocks that often occur when you rekindle this part of your relationship is the concern that your sexual practices and proficiency will be compared with your rival's. This is a normal response. The important thing here is that you and your wife talk about it. You may want to start just by cuddling and touching each other. For some, it takes a long while for this part of their relationship to be healed; for others, it's the first area tackled although the sense of trust may well take a while to return.

- Don't imagine that this will be resolved in one conversation. It will take time, maybe months. You'll find yourselves going back to different stages on numerous occasions before you're finally on an equal footing once more.

Perhaps you think that your marriage will never be the same as a result of your wife's affair and, in some ways, that's true. But, equally, that doesn't mean it can't be good again. Once through this really horrible patch, you may well have a stronger relationship, both physically and emotionally. I do hope so.

Q2 When we were young, my partner and I had a very varied sex life. We tried lots of things and sex was a big part of our lives. We then went through a quieter phase when we had our family but we always imagined our earlier sex life would resume once the children were grown. We seem to be having physical difficulties, probably age-related. Does it have to be like this? Have you any advice?

Of course you can have good sex at any age. The only thing that stops us is when we believe we can't. Our brains are amazingly powerful organs and we need to have them working for us not against! As baby boomers, we've redefined middle age and are refusing to get old in the way our parents did. And yet, it's too easy to think of ourselves as too old or with too many problems to enjoy sex. While you cling to this belief, you won't do anything positive to overcome your difficulties and, therefore, it will become a self-fulfilling prophecy that you're too old for sex! If it's any comfort, you are by no means alone.

I'm going to answer this question more from a physiological than a psychological point of view, focusing on the things that can happen to our bodies as we get older and how we can manage them. You don't give your gender but you do raise issues that afflict men and women. This answer should be read in conjunction with this section Question 4 and Section 3 Question 1 where I talk about sex at 50+ and its emotional and psychological implications.

The ageing process affects our whole body so it's bound to have an impact on our sexual organs and practices. It isn't surprising that we know little about this stage of our lives as most sex education focuses on the young, puberty and early sexual relationships as well as on pregnancy and post-natal sexual experiences. Until recently, very little research in this area has concentrated on the older person. Many of us seem to have regressed to how we were as teenagers and become almost monosyllabic on the subject!

I was talking with a group of post-menopausal women recently and they all said they'd been avid readers of books about sex when they were young women and during their pregnancies and that they'd also bought books to educate their children about sex and puberty. However, only a couple had books on the menopause and only one had a book about sex for the older person. I expect that would be true for most groups of older women and men. It's as though we want to bury our heads in the sand.

Little wonder we have problems in this area! We don't seem to have caught up with the changes that have occurred in society or to our bodies. Unlike our parents' generation, there are many single, divorced and widowed men and women looking for a relationship, while those in long-term relationships are looking forward to thirty more years together and don't want it to be devoid of sex.

There's no doubt that, as we age, we get tired more easily and we become prone to illnesses that need medication – drugs for high blood pressure, for example, or for high cholesterol. A combination of these factors will have an effect on our sex drive. When we're exhausted, we're less likely to summon up the energy for sex; and medication can adversely affect our libido.

Two hormones have a direct effect on our sexual desire and performance – oestrogen and testosterone – and, as we get older, we produce less of each. For women, the changes start at peri-menopause, often in their late forties and continue into menopause, which occurs on average between 51 and 55. At this time, there's a decrease in the levels of oestrogen and progesterone produced but usually there is not much change in the level of testosterone. (This male hormone is also present in women but not often talked about.) The change in the production of these hormones is very significant for a woman.

The effect of oestrogen levels dropping is that it:

- Reduces the growth of new cells in the vagina causing the walls to thin and become less elastic. This is known as vaginal atrophy and can cause irritation and tearing, and loss of firmness in the vaginal lips leading to discomfort in lovemaking.

- Causes the vaginal walls to become less lubricated which leads to dryness and soreness when having intercourse.

- Reduces the flow of blood through the arteries making the vagina and surrounding tissue less engorged, which can lead to a reduction in sensitivity.

- Causes nerve-endings to become less sensitive with the result that it can take longer to become aroused or have an orgasm.

- Causes a burning discomfort, soreness and redness of the vulva that can make intercourse very painful.

The effect of progesterone levels dropping is that it:

- Changes the menstrual cycle in conjunction with the reduction in oestrogen levels until menstruation ceases altogether.

- Results in the uterine wall no longer thickening each month as ovulation ceases.

Although the testosterone levels don't alter much, some women report an increase in their sex drive as the proportion of the different hormones changes. A number of symptoms may occur. All of these can be reduced and many cleared up completely. I'm going to give you some basic management information here; more can be found from the Resource List and Bibliography.

I. Vaginal dryness

- Talk to your GP about this. It can easily be solved and no one needs to suffer. Sometimes, your GP will prescribe oestrogen vaginal pessaries or a cream.

- Water-based lubricants such as K-Y jelly can be bought over the counter and these often do the trick. If you feel embarrassed going to a shop and asking for something like this, you can buy it by post or via the internet.

- Another solution is more sex! This helps regulate oestrogen levels and increases production of the hormone.

- Make sure you keep well hydrated and avoid drinks such as coffee and alcohol and foods such as melon and watercress that act as diuretics and dehydrate you.

2. Vaginal atrophy

- All of the above are useful.

- Try masturbating using a penis-shaped vibrator or dildo to help your vagina to get back into shape.

- Do Kegel exercises, also known as pelvic floor exercises, to strengthen the pelvic floor muscles.

3. Loss of libido

- Have your oestrogen levels checked by your GP.

- Think about your life and whether you're stressed, anxious or over-tired. If you are, get some counselling help.

- Examine your beliefs about sex as an older person and, if stuck, find someone to talk to.

- Discuss this with your GP as testosterone replacement therapy may be appropriate for you.

4. Difficulty with orgasm

- Talk to a therapist who can help you to uncover what's inhibiting you; it often has an emotional basis.

- Pain at orgasm can be helped by hormone treatment.

- Incontinence at orgasm sometimes occurs in older women. Check that your bladder muscles are functioning well; if not, they can be repaired.

5. Vulvodynia:

- If you're suffering from soreness of the vulva, consult your GP who will refer you to a genito-urinary specialist as it may be caused by a virus or an inflammation due to irritants e.g. shampoo and soap. There is no need for you to be in pain.

Now let's turn to men. The effect of testosterone dropping is twofold:

- It reduces sex drive.

- It affects the quality of erection and erectile endurance.

In men, the reduction in testosterone has less impact on their sexuality than the hormonal changes do in women. Most men can maintain a reasonable level of sexual functioning well into their old age. But, psychologically, for many men the symptoms of ageing can have a huge effect and this then can impact on their sexual practice.

Most men of 50+ will have some deterioration in their arteries which can start as early as their twenties! This can cause blockage of blood to the penis, which can lead to erectile dysfunction. A drop in testosterone is sometimes the cause but this is uncommon. For those of you interested in finding out more, please take a look at the Resource List, www.ipm.org.uk and the other medical sites.

I. Erectile dysfunction

- Psychological – counselling is a very helpful way to get to the underlying problem; either consult your GP or a counsellor specialising in sexual therapy.

- Arteries – Viagra® and other drugs are effective in helping to achieve an erection. There are also other treatments your doctor might suggest including injections, penile pellets and vacuum devices. Rings placed around the base of a man's penis will slow the flow of blood from the erect penile tissue, thus maintaining the erection for longer.

- Diabetes – improving control of the diabetes as well as the use of Viagra® and other drugs such as Uprima and Caverject help a large number of men. Your doctor will recommend the appropriate drugs.

- Alcohol and smoking – too much can reduce the ability to have an erection, so drink and smoke less!

2. Premature ejaculation

- One of the pluses about getting older is that this is less common – however, exercises taught by a therapist and practised with a partner can be effective.

3. Inability to climax

- The average time to reach orgasm for a 50+ man is longer than for a 20-year-old and this just needs to be accepted.

- Fantasies and sex aids can help to reduce the time it takes to achieve an orgasm.

- Talk to your partner so both of you are aware of the problem, as this will stop it escalating. Think of different ways to be stimulated, some of which can be outside your partner's vagina especially if they're suffering from dryness.

- Check with your GP that any medications you may be taking are not affecting your ability to get an erection. These can often be easily changed.

4. Soreness and pain

- The skin in the penis becomes thinner and more easily damaged as you get older and therefore can become sore. Use lubrication.

5. Less semen and less powerful ejaculations

- This is just a fact and nothing to worry about.

These conditions – as with those that affect women – can all be treated and managed. We often apportion blame when things aren't right. It's really important to realise that none of these are your fault or the fault of your partner. I think one of the problems is that we often start from the wrong place when we're thinking about sex. When we fantasise or muse about our past, we tend to idealise our past selves as either sexy and virile or stunning and sensual! This is really not very useful as it can only lead to disappointment now and may well never have been the case. What you need to do is take stock and reassess who you are, what gives you pleasure and how you can achieve it.

I recently read an article by a young woman who got me thinking. She was comparing the pleasures of having sex with a 25-year-old and someone of 50+. She said that her choice would be an older man as they are patient, have a quiet confidence and are in no hurry. The whole encounter, she concluded, can be sensual and full of his sexual experience with little pressure and performance ego to cope with.

Its not just women who fancy older men. I have a female client who is 54 and has a male 28-year-old lover. Older women have always figured in younger men's fantasies. The secret, if this is what you want, is to keep yourself fit and in good shape. You may not be a Mrs Robinson but you certainly can be alluring! Of course, most of us have no desire to bed a younger person but we do need to feel good about ourselves. This is the way we'll have satisfying sex with our partners, whatever their age, something which we all have the right to look forward to in our more mature years.

Q3 **I'm 58. I've been married for 36 years and I haven't been happy for most of them. My husband can be a really lovely man – everyone likes him – but, throughout our whole marriage, he's been physically violent. It goes in waves so for a while it's fine and then something triggers it off again. He's always sorry afterwards and promises it won't happen again although he often says I provoked him. I've heard that physically abusive men stop when they get older. Do you think this will happen? Now our two children have gone to university, I'm thinking I should leave him. But I've never lived on my own so, whenever I think about being on my own, I feel sick to my core, and I've no idea where I'd go. I probably wouldn't meet anyone else; I don't think anyone else would have me. I feel as though I've had the stuffing knocked out of me. What should I do?**

I'm so sorry. Being in an abusive relationship is seriously unpleasant and painful but, as you say, very difficult to walk away from. I think you know I can't tell you what to do. What I can do, though, is explore with you some of the issues involved and, I hope, point you in the right direction so you can get help and begin to make choices that aren't based on fear of the unknown.

I think it's really important that we spend a little time looking at the nature of an abusive relationship. If, as with many victims, you haven't talked about it to anyone else and have endured it because you thought you had to, you'll know little of the research that has been done in this area. It's easy – and, believe me, you're not alone – to make light of the situation and just shrug and say that's how it is. This is totally understandable because, without going into denial, the pain is too hard to bear.

The government defines domestic violence as, 'Any incident of threatening behaviour, violence or abuse (psychological, physical, sexual, financial or emotional) between adults who are or who have been intimate partners or family members, regardless of gender or sexuality.'

Domestic violence occurs across the whole of society. It has no regard for age, gender, race, sexuality, wealth or geography. It occurs in the full range of relationships: heterosexual, lesbian, gay, bisexual and transgender. The figures show, however, that in the main it's violence by men against women. Research indicates that 45 per cent of women and 26 per cent of men had experienced at least one incident of interpersonal abuse (Walby and Allen 2004).

However, when there were more than four incidents – in other words, ongoing abuse as you describe – 89 per cent of the victims were women. In any one year, there are 13 million separate incidents in the UK of physical violence or threats of violence against women from partners or former partners (Home Office 2004). It's not just in the UK, though, where the figures are high. The Council of Europe in 2002 reported consistent findings over ten countries with one in four women experiencing domestic violence in their lifetime and 6–10 per cent of women suffering in a given year.

The available figures, of course, are a gross underestimate, as the majority of cases are never reported to the police. The numbers quoted in the research estimate that between 24 per cent (Walby and Allen 2004) and 35 per cent (Home Office 2002) are reported. Even so, the police receive one call about domestic violence every minute in the UK (Stanko 2000) and the National Helpline in 2006–2007 answered an average of 387 calls a day.

As you can see, you're not alone. It is, however, something that most victims feel unable to discuss. And it's especially difficult when, as in your case, your husband is clearly not expressing this side of his character to others. It must be very easy, in the circumstances, to believe that you must be part of the cause.

Domestic violence is rarely a one-off occurrence. Rather, it should be seen as a pattern of abusive and controlling behaviour through which the abuser seeks power over their victim. It can involve more than one family member but, in your case, it sounds as though it's just you. Very often, children can be involved, too. However, even if they're not direct victims, children are almost always aware of what's going on in the household so they are indirectly abused as witnesses to violent scenes or, at the very least, conscious of the cause of their mother's bruises and cuts. (You don't mention how your children have responded to this but you clearly felt you needed to maintain the family unit while they were still living at home.)

Domestic abuse is not confined to physical attacks; it includes verbal abuse when you're constantly being put down, criticised, ignored or lied to. Money can also be used as a weapon in that it can be withheld as a means of curtailment and control. The victim can be stopped from going out on her own and making new friends. Threats can be made as to what will happen if you leave. You can be forced to agreeing to have sex because you're afraid of the consequences if you refuse.

And, throughout it all, you can be made to feel everything is your fault, that you've brought it all on yourself. Often, victims feel as you do – worthless and useless. It's not surprising when you've been told it so often. Moreover, many people, like you, then find themselves believing they're unlovable and, if they summon up the courage to leave their abusive partner, doomed to a lonely, sad life on their own.

I can't emphasise enough here that the person responsible for the abuse is the abuser. Never lose sight of that; never believe that you've contributed in some way to the abuse you suffer at his hands. He has a choice, as we all do, as to how he behaves. You said that your husband is lovely some of the time to you and always to others. He is, therefore, fully able to control his behaviour, whatever he may say to you. Blaming you is his way of absolving responsibility. The sad thing is that, if someone says it enough, we begin to believe it.

It is very easy to become so used to our life's troubles that in effect we become anaesthetised and we no longer know either what we want or whether what we have is so terrible. Take a look at the exercises in Question 6 in this section and weigh up the positives against the negatives in your relationship. We all need more positives than negatives; one negative to four or five positives is the sign of a good relationship (nothing is perfect!). If there are more negatives than positives, than your relationship is really not doing you any good. Even if it is equally balanced, I think you need to do a lot of thinking.

Once you have done this, now answer the following:

- What do I want from an intimate relationship?

- What would my partner need to do for me to have this?

- What must change in our relationship in order for me to get this?

- How might I go about implementing these changes?

You raise the question of whether your husband will change as you both grow older. Interestingly, there's very little large-scale research on domestic abuse and the older woman. Our age group of 50–70 has been missed out. Most of the work done has been on women of childbearing age and on much older women abused by carers, both family and non-family members. The self-completion questionnaires on domestic abuse from the British crime surveys of 1996 and 2001 were not given to women over 59. This won't happen the next time round as it's now recognised that baby boomers are still living very active lives and shouldn't be lumped together with those over 80!

The reasons given for this were that older women are less likely to experience domestic violence as younger men are more violent than older men; also, that younger women have more relationships so are more likely to encounter a violent man and older women are less likely to report domestic violence. It's thought this may be because the incidents started early on in their relationships and have been worked into the fabric of their lives. Interestingly, research done in Australia indicates that a third of all current victims of domestic abuse are older but over 60 per cent didn't ask for help (source: *Two Lives, Two Worlds: Older People and Domestic Violence* Volumes 1 and 2, Morgan Disney and Associates

2000). For these purposes, older women were defined as those over 50.

Research into abuse in older women is relatively recent. There have been three small-scale studies in the UK: Marsha Scott et al (2004), Imogen Blood's report for Help the Aged (2004) and Jacqui Pritchard's study (2000), based on confidential interviews with women who had been abused throughout their marriages, often financially. Many stayed because they didn't know how to get help.

The studies talked about three different categories of abuse in the older person: 'Domestic violence grown old', that is, when it's endured for over thirty years; 'Enter into domestic violence', when someone begins an abusive relationship with a new partner; and 'Late onset domestic violence' that begins as people get older and often occurs when the tensions and strains that have always been there just below the surface erupt and the relationship deteriorates as people age. When it starts in older age, it's invariably linked to life changes such as retirement, financial difficulties, disability, sexual problems or changes in roles of family members. The research does not support the myth of the stressed 'care-giver' (Lisa Manuel (2004) *Does caregiving lead to abuse?*, newsletter on older women abuse). None of the research to date supports the view that domestic abuse stops as people get older and certainly not in our middle years.

Many of us in our fifties and sixties embarked on long-term relationships thirty to forty years ago when there was little information and few options available to help abuse victims. In the main, we went into marriages with a feeling that whatever happened we had to put up with it. Domestic violence is now on the political agenda and has been recognised as a cross-government priority. There has been a lot of progress since 1997.

There's no single criminal offence of 'domestic violence'. However, many forms of domestic violence *are* crimes – for example, harassment, assault, causing criminal damage. Being assaulted, sexually abused, threatened or harassed by a partner or family member is just as much a crime as violence from a stranger, and often more dangerous.

As baby boomers now move into their fifties and sixties and we continue to live our lives differently from our parents, we begin to see that there are many more alternatives than staying in an abusive marriage (see this section, Question 6 about divorce in the over-fifties). That said, it's very hard if you've been abused not to feel ashamed and embarrassed and also to wonder what others will think about why you stayed so long. It's so easy for outsiders to know what they'd do when thinking about it from their non-abusive point of view. Being judgmental isn't helpful. Ignore these people and try to do what's right for you.

Your children are now old enough to pass comment. So, talk to them and listen, although remember that ultimately it's your life. Be prepared for a number of different responses. They may have worked hard over the years to keep their parents together and feel sad or disappointed you're letting them down. They may also feel it's your job to hold it together for them and worried they'll now have to look after their father. On the other hand, they may have begged you to go and will be relieved and supportive if you make the decision to leave.

I suspect you've been asking yourself whether you should leave for many years. As you say, you've never lived on your own so this would be a huge new challenge. You may also be financially dependent on your husband and anxious how you'll support yourself. There will also be lots of reasons for staying: you may still care for him; you may feel ashamed of what other people will think and so on. You may be frightened the violence will continue even though you're no longer together. It sounds as though he has very effectively destroyed your self-esteem. But just remember: it isn't lost for ever and with help you can start to feel confident again. I think it would be useful for you to read Section 3 Question 5 as it has tips about how to improve your self-confidence.

All the research shows that being abusive is a behaviour pattern. So, lovely as it would be to think that your husband will 'grow out of it', it seems very unlikely unless he agrees to attend a Perpetrator Programme (see www.respect.uk.net). This of course means he has to acknowledge his own abusive behaviour. Whatever he does or doesn't decide to do, it sounds to me as if you need some help to think about your options.

Have you considered couple counselling? There are conflicting views on this. Some say this is not an effective way to move things forward as it's very hard to be open about the situation without fearing the consequences once you get home. But it does work for some women especially when their husbands have been enthusiastic about seeking help.

Throughout the UK there are telephone helplines and counselling services available which offer support and will help you to understand the issues more fully, gain the confidence to make an informed choice and point you in the direction of available resources. Go somewhere where there are women of your own age, both as the professionals and the other women using the service. This way, you will see you're not alone and you'll be able to share your experiences with contemporaries who'll understand. If things get really bad there are women's refuges that provide emergency and temporary accommodation.

At this point, I don't expect you can imagine that there could ever be life after abuse but there is. Many women go on to build very healthy, happy new lives, establishing both intimate and non-intimate relationships. You still have a lot of life to live.

One final thought: we tend to regret those things we didn't do rather than those things we did. You *can* break the mould. If you believe in yourself, you can do anything.

Q4

I've been married for 25 years. Our children have now grown up. When they were young, my wife often said she was too tired to have sex, which I found difficult. The tables have turned and she is now keen and I just don't seem to have the interest. It isn't that I don't love her; I do. I just don't want sex any more and I don't even have many sexual fantasies. I'm worried she'll find someone else. How do we deal with this?

You may have wondered when you asked this question whether your problem was unique. I can assure you that it isn't. Many couple counsellors have reported that low sexual desire in men is a common reason couples seek therapy.

So why isn't it talked about more? Most men – or so we're always told – have grown up with sex on their brain. It's how they were taught to define their masculinity, it seems. I remember many years ago, when I ran a sex-education project for young people, a young man saying that it felt as though his penis went first into a room and then he followed! He was concerned about the inappropriateness of his erection. Although we all laughed, we weren't surprised as men are supposed to be obsessed with sex. Women, on the other hand, do not associate their femininity with their desire to have sex so it's easier to talk about, as it's not what is known as a core identity issue.

What's changed is that as a society we've become better at talking about sex and our intimate relationships with the result that it's probably now easier for people to raise these issues openly with their partners and friends. Talking about sex is something we have had to learn. Most of us were brought up by parents who didn't talk about sex. I wonder how many of you can remember the TV being turned off if anything about sex came on, or had a father who hid behind the newspaper when it did! No wonder we aren't very good at talking about it. We didn't have the sex education our children have had or exposure to an increasingly explicit media and internet. I'm not for one minute saying all the material to which they are exposed is good, only that it is very much more comprehensive.

A really significant part of your question is where you acknowledge that you and your partner have changed roles. Before we look at this, I think it would be helpful to understand what having a low sexual desire means, and why people are affected by it, and then look at how you can address and perhaps alter this. The fact you're asking about it and don't want your partner to find a lover is a very good place to begin as, with some understanding, change really is possible.

Low sexual desire is defined by the American Psychological Society as a lack of interest in sex or lack of sexual thoughts that continues for a length of time and which can create a problem in a relationship. It's not an illness nor is there something wrong with you. However, as in your case, it's something that has caused a difficulty in your marriage for a while and needs sorting out.

There's no such thing as the correct amount of sex. Magazines and the television are full of articles and programmes about sex that leave many of us feeling we're over- or, more usually, under-sexed, never mind deficiencies in our technique. Your sex drive is normal if you and your partner are happy with it. Twice a day, week, month or year are all fine, if it's right for both of you. It's when there's a mismatch between partners that a problem is created.

Our sexual desire will ebb and flow depending on a number of external and internal factors. The reality is that the person with the lesser desire is usually the one who controls the sexual pattern. Therefore, if it's going to change, it's you who needs to be the one to take action to begin the process.

It sounds as if for a long while your wife controlled the sexual activity in your relationship and now the roles have reversed. I'm sure you know – from when the boot was on the other foot, so to speak – that every time your partner said 'no' what you heard was, 'I'm not attractive enough. She's fallen for someone else,' leaving you feeling upset, hurt, angry or resentful.

Let's take a moment to think about what sex does for a couple. As well as being a biological urge, it brings an emotional connectivity, it increases intimacy, it gives pleasure to your partner, it relaxes you and it helps you go to sleep thinking about things other than your next day's meetings at work. It can also put a full stop to a row you may have been having.

I wonder how far the lack of intimacy in your marriage has gone? Do you no longer sit and have a cuddle on the sofa, give each other a peck on the cheek, walk hand-in-hand along the street? If so, you need to think of ways to reconnect if you're going to get your relationship back on track.

There are lots of reasons why your sexual desire may be reduced. It would be useful to explore these as more understanding will give you ideas about how to improve things for both of you.

Some reasons are biological and caused by a change in hormones. Low testosterone in men (which can happen at any time but most usually as they age) and hormonal changes in women after childbirth and at the menopause, can kill sexual desire.

39

As they get older, some men – although by no means all – can experience erectile and ejaculation problems and fear they will lose their sexual desire or drive. A doctor and/or an alternative health practitioner can treat all of these factors. If you had an ear infection, you'd go to the doctor and sort it out so, even if it is a bit embarrassing, you owe it to yourself and your wife to have yourself checked out. Be sure to ask your GP to check that there's no medical reason for the diminution in your sex drive but my hunch is it's something else.

There are a number of psychological reasons that affect libido. Being depressed will reduce your desire for sexual activity. You're likely to have less enthusiasm, sleep less well, and generally want to withdraw from company. Again, this might be something you need to get help with. But a word of warning: the drugs given for depression can in themselves reduce sexual desire as can alcohol, recreational drugs and some medications for hypertension. If you're on medication of any sort, it's worth checking out the side effects.

Other factors that could affect your libido include feeling stressed, being tired from work or looking after children and poor self-image, something that's common after women have children and for both men and women as they get older; they no longer see themselves as desirable and would rather hide away than be seen or touched.

I don't think we give enough thought to what it means to be a sexual being as we get older. Many of us imagine – and we may be right – that our parents stopped having sex when they had us! It was certainly not something ever talked about. We were brought up to believe that sex was for the young. So some of us may feel it's wrong to still have sexual desires.

Nowadays, or so it seems from reading the papers, we're all meant to be as sexually active as we were in our teens or twenties. Ageing pop stars – think Mick Jagger – always have gorgeous young women on their arms and we assume they're having rampant sex, something a lot of men no longer want. It can make you worried about whether you are normal. These conflicting images – either we're too old for sex so it's inappropriate to want it or we're inadequate compared to the still sexually voracious rock stars – will undoubtedly affect men's libido.

I believe we're never too old for sex (see Section 3 Question 1). As to whether the fantasy fed to us about the sex lives of so-called celebrities is true, I think it's a red herring which we should try to ignore. There are lots of other aspects of their lives you wouldn't be the slightest bit interested in following and the same should be true of their purported sex lives.

The most important explanation for the change in sexual desire has to do with the relationship between the two of you. Take a quiet moment to consider the following questions:

- How do you feel about your partner?

- Are you angry with them for something they said or did?

- Are you resentful they didn't want sex when the children were young?

- Do you feel any pressure in being the breadwinner?

- Do you feel unnoticed and under-appreciated for who you are?

- Do you feel you're the deposit for your partner's disappointments?

- Do you feel they have limited your ambition?

- Do you still feel hurt they didn't have sex with you when you wanted it?

If more than two of these ring true, I expect you're harbouring resentments and there's nothing that's more of a turn-off. Why would one want to have sex or be intimate with someone, for example, who you think stopped you taking the promotion you wanted because they wanted to stay living near their mother – or whatever might be the reason for your resentment?

One thing I know for certain is that, if things are going to change, you're going to have to do something about it. The first and most important in my mind is that you put the problem openly on the table:

- Tell your wife what you told me: that you love her and want the relationship to continue.

- Tell her that you're aware that you're rejecting her sexual advances and that you know this is causing a problem.

- Say that you want to sort it out and you need her to help you so that you can both have a good time again.

- Remind her without accusing her that she, too, has been through a phase of not wanting sex.

- Ask her to try to get in touch with how she felt at that time because that's how you're feeling right now.

- Tell her you're aware how your rejection of her must feel.

If things are going to move forward, you're going to have to deal with grievances and conflicts. If you feel you can do this yourselves, that's great; if not, discuss this with your wife and look for some help together. (There are some suggestions of helpful contacts in the Resource List, and in Question 5 in this section, I look at how to have difficult conversations.)

It sounds to me as if you and your partner have experienced what I call the 'elastic band effect'. One pulls out and the other pulls in. Others call it the 'seesaw effect'. When one of you goes off sex, the other wants it. The more one wants it, the less the other does. Sometimes, when we switch places in a relationship, it signifies that there's an unspoken, or even unconscious, knowledge of a problem. It's as though one person needs to be the custodian of the problem. In your case, both of you have had a period of carrying the burden of the problem and now it's time to get it resolved.

Michele Weiner Davis in her book, *The Sex–Starved Marriage*, suggests that, rather than talking about the problem, try having sex again! You may find that, once you do, you'll really enjoy it. Some of us don't become sexually turned on until we're stimulated. She suggests 'that you allow yourself to be responsive even if you're in a neutral mood'. You may be surprised how much fun you have. We can get into a habit of turning away when someone touches us. A bit like Pavlov's dogs, this can become an automatic response. If you're going to break the mould, you'll have to consciously change your behaviour.

Remind yourself of when you did want sex. What was it that turned you on? For example, what time of day was your favourite for making love? And where was your favourite place? What did you find stimulating? If it was having a bath together, then give it another whirl. In other words, do the things that used to make you feel sexy.

You said you want to maintain this relationship so why not see the resumption of a sexual relationship as a gift to her that shows her you love her – like mowing the lawn! Once she no longer feels rejected, you'll find it easier to negotiate what is best for you both and feel content with the sexual balance. And remember: as long as you and your partner feel satisfied, it doesn't matter where, when or how often you make love.

Q5 **I've just had a dreadful shock. I was on our computer and I wanted to find a site I had been on a few days ago. I went into 'history', which I've never done before. To my horror, I found loads of porn sites looked at daily for weeks. I can't believe it. It has to be my husband because he's the only one besides me who uses the computer. I don't know what to do. Do I talk to him? Do I throw him out? Do I call the police? I didn't look at much of it although what I did see certainly wasn't child porn so I expect it's legal. We've been married over thirty years and our sex life has dwindled. I thought it was just because we were older and too familiar with each other but now I wonder. This is too embarrassing to talk about to any of my friends so I need some clear advice, please.**

I understand that it must have been upsetting to find pornographic material on your computer and that it made you anxious about your husband's behaviour. I want to spend a few minutes, before discussing your dilemma, looking at what pornography is. I think it will make it easier for you to know if his viewing is legal or not.

Pornography is a surprisingly young word in the English language: 'pornographer' is first recorded in English from about 1850 with the word 'pornography' appearing by 1857. These words derive from the Greek 'pornographos', which translates as writing about harlots, from 'porne' (harlot) and 'graphe' (picture or writing). It originally referred primarily to ancient Greek and Roman texts on the subject. It wasn't until the late nineteenth century that it came to refer to newly written works. Pornography became more visible in the 1960s and 1970s and has become commonplace since the arrival of the internet.

The Oxford Dictionary definition is 'printed or visual material containing the explicit description or display of sexual organs or activity intended to stimulate sexual excitement'. There are many interpretations of the term, which will depend on your values and beliefs, and much discussion about what is classed as 'art' and what is obscene.

Interestingly, the UK is the 'pornography capital' of Europe. In the UK alone, it's estimated to be worth £1billion according to Adult Industry Trade Association (2008). Porn is, whether we like it or not, available everywhere. A quarter of all searches on the internet are to seek access to one of the 1.3 million porn websites and the most common Google search word is 'sex'. Pornography has fuelled the internet's development. Men use these sites much more than women do.

That being said, it doesn't mean you should like it, look at it or feel OK about your partner using it. You mentioned the possibility of your going to the police, but having access to adult pornography isn't illegal. However, it is illegal to own abusive images of children or adults who look like children and pictures showing adults engaging in 'extreme' sexual activity. It is also against the law to look at internet pictures of abusive images of children and to send pornography through the post. If your husband is not doing any of those things, he isn't breaking the law and therefore the police would not become involved. If, however, the pornography is illegal, it's important that you don't see this as something you could learn to tolerate. You need to report it immediately (Internet Watch Foundation – see the Resource List for this section).

Pornography is an issue in many relationships. Its easy access through the internet has brought the potential to every home. It can be accessed passively and purely anonymously as you don't, as previously, have to take it up to a till and pay for it in a shop. Relationship agencies have reported that as many as 40 per cent of couples with problems believe pornography has contributed to their difficulties.

Let's turn now to you. Can you identify what has made you so upset/angry/hurt?

- Does it make you feel unattractive, not sexy enough, undesirable?

- Do you feel devalued and disrespected?

- Do you feel he is being unfaithful? (See Section 4 Question 2 on cybersex.)

- Is it because he is using images of someone else to pleasure himself?

- Do you feel rejected?

- Do you mind he has been doing this without your knowledge?

The reason I'm asking you to think about these things is because you're going to have to talk to him. I know you suggested walking out as one course of action and, even if that's what you decide to do in the long run, you can't just leave home without explaining why. The clearer you are about what it is that upsets you, the more effective you'll be when talking to your husband. This is unlikely to be the last discussion you have on the subject so don't expect it to be resolved immediately but having clear goals can guide you through to a place of agreement – even if it's just to talk again tomorrow.

Discussions such as these are often difficult. The following tips may help:

- State your feelings clearly and honestly.

- Listen to what he has to say – that doesn't mean you have to agree.

- Try to keep your voice firm, relaxed and calm.

- If either of you gets over-emotional, stop the conversation, agree when to resume talking and take a break.

- Keep talking about it – don't let it go back into the closet.

- Suggest you seek a counsellor to talk to (see www.basrt.org.uk and the general Resource List).

- Talk to a trusted friend – a problem shared is a problem halved. Tell your husband you are going to do this. It is important that your behaviour is not secret.

The following are tips on things to avoid:

- Don't keep this to yourself: talk to your husband.

- Don't blame yourself.

- Don't look any more at the material – it won't do you any good.

- Don't police the computer and check on him daily.

- Don't embarrass him by talking about this to others in front of him.

- Don't delay getting help. If he's unwilling to see someone, you can go to a professional on your own.

If your marriage is going to be able to move forward, you have to find an open and honest way to talk to each other. Be prepared for it being difficult at times but, with the right help, I'm sure you can find a way through this so that you feel comfortable with whatever choice you make.

Q6 **I have been married for 27 years. It's OK but certainly not great. Over the years, I've thought about leaving and those feelings have intensified recently. But I worry about the effect it would have on my family. My marriage isn't intolerable so I'll probably stay put but I'm aware that I'm settling for something because it's familiar. I also know that lots of people are divorcing in their fifties and sixties. Is it fear of the unknown that prevents my leaving? How do you contemplate what might be another 27 years when you're not in love, when there are no longer children at home to distract you and there is likely to be illness and possible dependency?**

You raise a very common question for both men and women of 50+. Who knows? – it is likely we will live till we're 80 or 90 as a result of improved social conditions and significant medical advances. There are now available to us operations to repair knees, hips, feet, even hearts, as well as drugs to reduce blood pressure and cholesterol so that we can continue to lead active lives. We're working longer and retiring later.

Many of us find ourselves in relationships that have revolved around our children and their lives so we've had little time to focus on our marriages or ourselves. Once the children leave, we're suddenly alone with our partners, unsure what we talked about and how we spent our time together when it was just the two of us. We may like our partners well enough while feeling we have little in common except our children and some mutual friends. The old spark is no longer there.

For some, this becomes intolerable and they no longer feel able to stay in their marriage, as the divorce figures testify. Others feel, as you suggest, they have to resign themselves to another twenty or thirty years of non-intimacy, not a prospect many of us would look forward to, especially when there's likely to be some illness and dependence (I cover both these aspects in this section Questions 7 and 8). It's what many of our parents endured but we're the generation that has done it differently from the start. We haven't followed the rules. We've created our own style and, for some people, this has included not staying in relationships when we feel they've run their course.

Figures recently published by the government's National Statistics Department show that, in 2007, the 'provisional divorce rate' in England and Wales fell, with the divorce rate at its lowest level since 1981. However, this trend is not the same for the older person. In 2005, 8,086 husbands and 4,671 wives over 60 petitioned for divorce compared to 5,454 husbands and 3,199 wives in 1991 (source: Saga). Since 1997, the average age of divorce in England and Wales has risen from 40.2 to 43.7 for men and from 37.7 to 41.2 years for women.

I'm assuming from what you say that you want to stay in your marriage but that you'd like to rekindle some of the passion you felt when you fell in love. If that's the case, then it's well worth looking at how to achieve this. We often talk as though our relationships are static, that they'll remain as they are now for ever. Nothing could be further from the truth.

But, before we start discussing the issues, try these two exercises:

MARRIAGE REVIEW

Take a few minutes on your own to think through your relationship with your husband from the first moment you met.

1. Where was it? What was it like? What drew you to him initially? Concentrate hard on recreating as accurate a picture as possible.

2. What were his qualities that made you continue to date him and to marry him?

3. What were your hopes and dreams?

4. How were the first few years pre-children? What were the good bits and what were the hard bits?

5. What was it like when the children arrived?

6. When did you begin to fall out of love? See if you can pin down the event or period.

7. What did you do about it? How did you react?

8. What did he do and how did he react?

9. How have you managed over the years since then? What has kept you together?

10. How would you like it to be?

If you answer the questions above as honestly as you can, you'll be aware that your relationship has ebbed and flowed; it's never been static.

The following exercise looks at this in a bit more detail so you can begin to understand the factors that affect your relationship:

RELATIONSHIP TIMELINE

1. Draw a line in the top half of a piece of paper representing the time from when you met your husband till the present day. Put in all the significant events such as getting married, buying and moving into your first home, having your first child and subsequent children, moving house, getting a job, promotion, retirement, illness or death of your parents, illness in your own family and so on.

2. Now draw another line under it which plots your feelings at the times of these events, i.e. a high peak if great and a low if miserable etc.

3. Take a separate piece of paper and draw two columns – in one write all the good events and times you felt good, and in the other the times you felt bad.

4. Take a look and see how the 'good' and 'bad' columns balance. Is there more good than bad? Or does the bad outweigh the good?

5. Are there things you could do to improve the balance?

Dorothy Tennov, an American psychologist, did some work on the first stages of a relationship – the falling in love bit, the part we all remember and idealise. She coined the term 'limerence' to distinguish this phase of a relationship from the other stages. (She charts the five stages in her book *Love and Limerence*.)

1. Eyes meet and, even if you don't immediately go weak at the knees, you like what you see and feel there's a special connection.

2. 'Limerence' kicks in and all the physical manifestations like weak knees, butterflies in the stomach, loss of appetite leave you feeling elated.

3. If reciprocated, your thoughts are only for the other person.

4. Your feelings intensify; your life revolves around the other person; all other friends and family are put on hold.

5. You oscillate between elation when the two of you are together to despondency when he doesn't call! Your self-esteem becomes enmeshed in his response to you.

Dorothy Tennov suggests that this high state of 'limerence' lasts for six months. Andrew G. Marshall in his book, *I Love You but I'm Not in Love with You*, claims that this initial state of elation can last up to three years. It can't last indefinitely although you can relive it when thinking about the early stages of your romance and marriage, and after times of separation or after a difficult patch the joy of getting back together.

One of the reasons we often feel we've lost true love is that we're hoodwinked by all the books, magazine articles, songs and films that dwell on the subject and which idealise it. They don't include all the boring bits like doing the washing up and taking the kids to school so they leave us with the belief that long-term sustained love should last forever at this heightened pitch. But that's a dangerous illusion which clouds our judgment and prevents us from seeing our situation for what it is.

Having said that, there's no doubt that relationships need to be fed, otherwise they wither and die. Marshall describes two states of a stable relationship: one is enjoyable (most of the time) which he calls 'Loving Attachment'; the other is 'Affectionate Regard', a category that could well cover the current state of your marriage.

So what makes a good relationship where we have 'Loving Attachment'?

1. Sharing, telling each other bits about our day, both good and bad.

2. Listening properly. We multi-taskers think it's all right to carry on while listening which may be true for us but it's not for the other person who, understandably, can feel low on our list of priorities.

3. Touch and cuddles – being tactile with each other.

4. Giving something to your partner. This doesn't need to be a physical gift but can be doing both the cooking *and* washing up if you know they're stressed; in other words, putting yourself out for them.

5. Being there for them when they want you there – coming to the office party, for instance, or going out with friends of theirs.

6. Sharing a laugh and a joke.

These are all things we do for our friends, children and other family members but stop doing with our partners when we're stressed or have been hurt by them and either forget or choose not to behave in a loving way.

'Affectionate Regard' is the other state Marshall describes. It's when we care for someone: we don't dislike them, we don't want to hurt them but our life isn't inextricably linked with theirs emotionally. It exists independently from them. The relationship has become unremarkable, routine. It is devoid of passion. I think this is where you are in your marriage right now. It's not intolerable but it doesn't fulfil you.

No one would suggest that you stay in a relationship that is harmful for you or where you are really miserable. John Gottman in his book, *Why Marriages Succeed or Fail: And How You Can Make Yours Last*, says the difference between a contented couple and an unhappy one is that the former have achieved a healthy balance between their positive and negative feelings and actions towards each other. He claims a ratio of 5:1 is the magic number. So, as long as there is five times as much positive feeling as there is negative feeling, the marriage is likely to be stable. Is that true for you? If not, then you need to find ways to improve things, otherwise you may well find yourself in a relationship heading for a real crisis. Take a look at your columns and see where things are for you.

Marshall also suggests – and I wholeheartedly agree – that the most important factors in a relationship are love, respect and a sense of value in your history together. If you spend your time undermining the other person or they you, it's hard to feel a loving attachment. If you never feel considered and supported and you can barely be bothered to support your partner, emotionally speaking it will be hard to feel genuine affection. I don't think you've reached that state yet but you could if you're not careful.

Wherever you are in your relationship I suggest that you find a piece of paper and do the following exercise:

IF I COULD HAVE MY IDEAL MARRIAGE

Fill in the sentences below:

1. I would like my marriage to be . . .

2. I'd like my husband to . . .

3. I like to do . . . with my husband.

4. I'd like to give my husband . . .

5. I'd like to resolve issues by . . .

6. I like us to talk to each other in a . . . kind of way.

So now you know what you want but it takes two to make a good relationship so, if it's going to get better, you need to talk to him. Find a time when you're both relaxed and not stressed. Suggest that you go out for a walk or a meal and then tell him your concerns about life post-children; tell him what you think is good about your relationship and how you want it to be good between you again; ask him how he's feeling and how he would like it to be. He needs to want to stay in the relationship and, ideally, for it to be more intimate, too, for things to change.

Even if he can't answer immediately, ask him to spend some time thinking about the state of your marriage. You owe yourselves this. Invite him to do the above exercise, too. Don't expect him to do it there and then but do suggest you talk about things again and agree a time. Remember, it's taken a while for things to get to this situation. There's no major rush so pace your conversations; you don't want them to become another stress trigger.

Once upon a time, you knew what made your relationship good. Start doing those things again as well as using the skills discussed above in 'Loving Attachment'. For example, really listen to him: you'll be amazed the effect it has and more than likely he'll start mirroring your behaviour. My hunch is if he, too, feels the same way, you'll be able to bring back the spark together.

It's often very difficult to have these kinds of conversation with our partners, particularly when we've been in the habit of avoiding them. If you're finding it difficult, there are lots of places where you can get help. Don't for one minute think you have to do this on your own. The ideal, of course, is that you go to couple counselling but, even if your husband is initially unwilling, you can find someone to talk to and get some objective support. The Resource List will give you some ideas as to where you can go. Good luck!

Q7 **My partner has just been diagnosed with early Alzheimer's. I'm 57 and she's 56. It's not fair and I'm terrified. I don't want to be a nurse and I don't want her to be like the people in all those articles I've read. It makes us**

seem so old and I feel ashamed and embarrassed to tell people. I'm also worried it might be hereditary: we have two children. I had so many things I wanted to do with my life and now I won't be able to. I don't know what to do.

We can't choose the cards we're dealt in life but we can choose how we play them. This is of course a hand that none of us would choose and will undoubtedly have a big impact on your life. Having said that, it doesn't have to be all bad and you certainly don't have to let go of all your dreams. It's just that you will probably have to manage them differently.

According to the Alzheimer's Society there are currently 700,000 people with dementia in the UK but only 15,000 people with early-onset dementia, which affects people under the age of 65. Early-onset Alzheimer's is therefore relatively rare but, as it's normally a disease that afflicts the elderly, it doesn't surprise me that it makes you feel old. The novelist Terry Pratchett was diagnosed last year at 59 with a rare form of early Alzheimer's. He has been very open about it and has certainly put the condition on the map. One of the things he said that struck me was, 'It seems that, when you have cancer, you're a brave battler against the disease but, when you have Alzheimer's, you're an old fart. That's how people see you. It makes you feel quite alone.' He also said that he was envious of his father who died at 86 from cancer and was completely lucid with his brain functioning fully until his death. Alzheimer's is scary precisely because we're all frightened of losing our mind.

It must feel as if this is happening to you in the 'wrong' generation. Generally, if we do get Alzheimer's, and not all of us will, it will probably be when we are in our late seventies or eighties. Some of your friends' parents may be suffering from dementia but they'll be having to cope with this from a very different perspective. It is predicted that there will be over a million people with dementia in the UK by 2025. (See www.alzheimers.org.uk for further information.)

Alzheimer's and dementia are the poor relations in terms of the amount of money spent on them. The Alzheimer's Research Trust points out that only £11 is spent on UK research into Alzheimer's for every sufferer, compared with £289 for each cancer patient. Even accessing drugs is difficult. I think we should be joining in the fight to increase the research budget into this disease so that people like your wife can have the best medical care possible. More money would also increase the chance of a scientific breakthrough that will either reduce the likelihood of us developing the disease or help slow its progress. The baby boomers can make a big difference and it's in our own best interests to do so.

I'm only going to touch briefly on the illness itself as there's a wealth of written information you can obtain from the Alzheimer's Society and other organisations. Early-onset Alzheimer's symptoms are similar to those of late-onset. They include memory loss, confusion, restlessness, trouble performing everyday tasks, changes in personality and behaviour, loss of motivation and emotional apathy.

The difference between early- and late-onset dementia is that, by the time the disease has been diagnosed, the person may well have had the illness for a while and therefore there are already quite pronounced changes in the brain. It's often very hard to get a diagnosis and people sometimes have to go through a series of misdiagnoses such as depression, stroke and sleep apnoea before finding out what's wrong. As your wife has just been diagnosed, I imagine you've been going to numerous hospital appointments and tests, which in themselves can be very stressful.

But you are now at a place where you can take stock and begin to plan your life accordingly. It's no wonder that you're frightened and anxious about the future or that you're concerned about telling people. Sadly, it's a disease that doesn't follow any strict rules so it's difficult to predict either how it will progress or how it will affect your daily life. Apart from her specific Alzheimer-related symptoms, your wife may be fit which can lead to a feeling of powerlessness and frustration when there are things that she's unable to do.

It's really important for you to manage this situation positively – easier said than done, I know. Life is by no means over and it is vital that you both continue to do the things you enjoy. Even if up till now you've not been keen on this, joining a support group can be extremely helpful. Don't rule anything out. Don't feel you have to manage this on your own: get some help and support (see the Resource List). There are some amazing professionals in this field and also volunteers who can help you through. Your wife may still be working and you may well have financial and family responsibilities. The two of you need to talk practically about finances, household management and the children; and, most importantly, about your feelings, your relationship, and about sex and intimacy.

Let's consider some of the areas of concern. You say, not unreasonably, that you don't want to be a nurse. You and your wife will have to decide what care you feel capable of giving and what help you'll need – and at what point. Your medical specialist and their team will be able to advise you of what they can offer and how to make contact with the local authority's social services.

Depending on where you live, the specialist might be a:

- Neurologist (a doctor who specialises in diseases affecting the nervous system)

- Geriatrician (a doctor who specialises in the healthcare of older people)

- General psychiatrist (a doctor who specialises in mental health)

- Psycho geriatrician (a doctor who specialises in the mental health of older people)

As well as having to care for your wife, you'll also need time for yourself to do the things you want to do. If there are things that you both fancy – travel, for example, to somewhere you've never been – each of you should sit down and plan how you're going to achieve them now. It might sound a bit morbid but making a list of the ten things you want to do before you die is a very good way to focus on what matters most to you. Living in the present rather than the past or the future is the essence of all spiritual teaching and there's no better time to start doing that than right now. Write your lists separately and then discuss them together. Your lists won't be identical and that's fine. If there are things your wife doesn't want to do, find people who will accompany you at some other time.

You'll need to put your house in order, so to speak, and make the necessary decisions. Things to think about include:

- Finances, and don't forget to find out about possible benefits you may be entitled to.

- Legal matters such as power of attorney (see this section Question 8).

- Writing a living will.

- Weigh up what effect her condition will have on both your careers before deciding on any changes that need to be made.

- Research what is available to you medically so you can make informed choices.

You may already have done this but you need to talk to your children about the illness. Not knowing what's going on but having a sense that something's amiss can cause real anxiety for children. However hard it is for them to know, it's important they're fully aware and involved.

I understand that you feel embarrassed and ashamed and it is easy for me to say there is no need. This illness is no different from any other serious illness and none of us chooses to have it. I think it is really useful for the sick person's partner whatever the illness to have professional support. Your local Alzheimer's Society will be able to offer all you need or direct you to the best place. You can find their details via the UK Alzheimer's Society website. Your GP will also be able to point you in the right direction for local services.

You will both need support from your family and friends. The more openly you talk to them, the easier they'll find it to respond to you in an appropriate manner. Your predicament, as well as being hard for you, will create a feeling of anxiety in your friends. I wouldn't be surprised if some of the people you mix with have only sketchy knowledge about Alzheimer's, making some over-solicitous and others nervous to be around you. It may be that you and your wife will have to start educating your friends and family so that you can go on enjoying their company and get the support you need.

This is a topic that has recently interested filmmakers. I've seen four films about people suffering from dementia. *The Notebook* and *Away from Her* both glamorised the illness, in my opinion, and didn't do any favours for those with the disease or caring for people who had it. Two others – *The Savages* and *Ashita no Kioku* (*Memories of Tomorrow*) where Japanese actor Ken Watanabe plays a patient with early-onset Alzheimer's – are more realistic. It might be a good idea to watch these with your friends and family so you have a common starting point for any conversation.

Sex and intimate relationships are another area that will change. You may well have found during the worrying time of pre-diagnosis that things became less good sexually as stress without doubt has an impact on sexual desire. The effect the dementia has on someone's sexual behaviour will depend on which part of the brain has been affected. It can mean more interest in sex or less, less sensitivity to a partner's needs, more aggressive behaviour and changes in levels of inhibitions.

Very often, even if no sexual contact is wanted, physical closeness or cuddling can be very pleasurable for both people involved. It's really important that you each feel comfortable with the physical side of your relationship. If things get difficult, seek help from your GP or a counsellor. This may be awkward if you haven't been used to talking about this side of your relationship but communication is a key way of your coping with this illness.

It's important to be clear and clarify when you're faced with a problem that's new and dementia-related. For example if you have always been irritated with your wife because she interrupts you when you talk, this is her trait, and not the illness. However, if she rarely forgot her keys and now she always does, this is a new situation and has to be managed.

You are concerned about this being hereditary. Genes do play some role in dementia but their specific effect varies enormously. Early-onset Alzheimer's does often have a genetic component. The only way you can know whether that's the case in your family is to talk with your GP who would put you in touch with the geneticists at a regional clinical genetics department. As with any fear, our imagination can run riot. The only way you'll know what's what is by getting the information. Although this can be hard, the end result will be the comfort of knowing where you stand and being able to make informed choices. So don't sit on your worry.

Don't neglect yourself. Caring can be hard work and you need to be healthy and happy. Decide what you can and can't do and get the necessary help: this will change as the disease progresses. Have some breaks by yourself, meet a friend, go to a class, organise to have a weekend away and build up your own social network. Don't feel guilty about taking some time out: it's essential and will become more so over time. Keep an eye on your dreams and make sure you're as near to fulfilling them as possible.

There's no doubt this will put a strain on you and your relationship. So it's important that you continue as much as you can to run your life as you've always done. If you're someone who did a lot on your own, then you need to continue to do so. If you're part of a group or have always enjoyed certain social activities, don't abandon them. I hope you'll take a leaf out of Terry Pratchett's book and not keep this from the people you know. Feeling ashamed and embarrassed and hiding yourself away are not going to help either of you.

I appreciate that what's happening is making you both feel very old but that kind of thinking needs to stop. Sadly, Alzheimer's and dementia can affect any of us. Make sure that each day you do something for yourself so you feel nourished and emotionally strong – and able to cope with whatever lies ahead. To start with, you and your wife will be able to do things together. As the illness progresses, she will need company when you go out. Again, the services mentioned will be able to help you. I do believe that if you can feel good about yourself you will be better placed to help your wife. I wish you the very best of luck.

Q8 My wife and I have been together for many years and managed our ups and downs fairly well until now. We've started to talk seriously about getting old, how we imagine it will be, the role we want our children to play, living wills, burials or not and we're struggling. We seem to have very different ideas. For example, I fantasise about a sky burial and she a religious one. What are the things we need to consider and how do we reconcile these differences?

I was at the Retirement Show in London last summer and I was struck by the number of stands that focused on alternative ways you could be buried, information on living wills, ordinary wills and power of attorney, everything, in fact, about putting your house in order before you die. You are wise to be discussing these things now because, if *we* don't make the decisions about our own lives and how we want them to end, someone else will and that really isn't fair on our children and our family.

A number of things have changed in relation to dying since we baby boomers were born. Many of us will still have parents alive when we're well into our fifties and sixties so we've felt we've been able to avoid confronting the whole business of death. But there will inevitably come a point when we find ourselves as the older generation. On the other hand, sadly, many of us will have lost friends through illnesses such as cancer while others may be in the early stages of dementia (this section Question 7). Each time we're exposed to someone's death or illness, it reminds us of our own mortality and, sooner or later, it becomes impossible to avoid thinking about it.

You asked about the role of your children. I have a particular view on children's roles that I know not everyone agrees with. It is, like most views, based on my own subjective experience where, due to lack of planning, I didn't feel I had a choice in the part I played in my mother's sad and protracted dementia. It has left me with a very strong belief that decisions need to be made *prior* to an illness so that all individuals involved can state their needs and wishes and the best plan of action can be worked out. This should lead to agreed care being given freely and with love. If it isn't enough or as forthcoming as a parent might wish, it's to be hoped that it's not to do with the love their children feel for them but for other reasons.

These kinds of discussions give families an opportunity to talk about underlying issues that might affect the relationship at later stages of a person's life and hopefully sort them out in advance. If discussions take place early enough, emotions aren't raw and rational decisions and positive conversations can take place: a bonding experience for everyone involved if done with the right, light touch. Decisions made at the height of a crisis can lead to hasty solutions and cause distress all round.

As a society, there are certain things we aren't very good at and talking about death is one of them. It can appear morbid or tempting fate or, if you're part of the next generation, potentially greedy with one eye on your inheritance. Again, though, that shouldn't be an excuse for avoiding the subject. The one thing we all know is that at some point we'll die so it makes sense, where possible, to have a plan.

When individuals have lived together for many years, like the two of you, they usually find a way to manage their differences. Many couples I've worked with have said how volatile their relationships were at the start when they felt it was impossible to rationalise their differences. They had fierce arguments about whether their wedding should be religious or not, whether the children should be christened and so on. But, as they got into the swing of things, they learnt to manage their differences and found mutually agreeable solutions.

When death doesn't seem imminent, we tend to put off talking about it. And, of course, it's different from the other events I've mentioned as you rarely die together. Difficulties can arise, however, when you're being asked to do something that doesn't meet your needs and values. You have to ask yourself if you're willing to carry out your partner's wishes, even if they wouldn't be yours.

If you're unable to agree, a partner may have to appoint someone else to do his or her bidding. There's nothing in law which says that person has to be your spouse or your children. Just write down who you wish to appoint and the authorities will refer to them in the event of your death. Although this may sound a difficult thing to do, honouring each other's wishes is one of the greatest things you can do for your partner.

More and more people are beginning to take control of what they'd like to happen when they die. Every individual who's mentally capable has a right to decide on their medical treatment. Although we've made wills for centuries, detailing how we want our money and property disposed of, it's only recently that people have started making advance directives. Advance directives generally fall into three categories: living will, power of attorney and healthcare proxy. They don't have the same legal standing as an ordinary will but they certainly have a major influence on our medical treatment.

An advance directive does not permit a doctor to behave illegally (e.g. euthanasia) and, if the medical team think your request is excessive or inappropriate, they are not bound to carry out your wishes. But a living will can help prevent interventions such as resuscitation. It also gives your family a clear idea of your wishes so they don't have to have a debate about it at a stressful time. An advance directive is usually made with the help of your GP so you can ensure it both meets your demands and doesn't place your doctor in a difficult position. It needs to be signed, dated and witnessed, otherwise it will not be recognised as a legal document, and then kept with your medical notes at your GP's. Family members should also have access to a copy. The document should be updated every few years as your needs may well change as you get older.

You should also consider setting up a lasting power of attorney (LPA). This is a legal document that allows you to appoint someone you trust as an attorney to make decisions on your behalf if you become incapable of doing so yourself. This can be drawn up at any time and registered with the Office of the Public Guardian (OPG). There are two types of LPA. One is for property and affairs, which allows someone to make decisions on how your money is spent and your property managed; the other covers personal welfare and allows someone to make decisions about your healthcare, including making decisions about appropriate treatment. The property LPA can be used once registered at the OPG. The personal care LPA only comes into effect after registration *and* you have become mentally incapable of making a decision. These documents need to be filled in by you appointing one or several 'attorneys' (for instance, friends, children or a solicitor) and also a further form needs to be filled in by someone who has known you for some time, ideally a solicitor or doctor.

There is information on this and the advance directives in the Resource List.

Of course, I can't tell you what kind of burial you should have and I don't think you're asking that. What I can do is point out some of the alternatives so you can make timely decisions. You mentioned a sky burial, a common funerary practice in Tibet, a country mainly above the tree line, so burying is difficult and there's little wood for cremation. Most Tibetans are Buddhists who believe in reincarnation. They regard the cadaver left behind as an empty vessel. The practice involves bodies being cut up and put on a mountain top to be eaten by eagles and other birds of prey; the bones are smashed into a powder. This form of a green burial still continues although the People's Republic of China, which has dominion over Tibet, will not always allow it.

There are a number of other unusual (to us) burials including air sacrifice in Mongolia, spirit offerings in South-East Asia and cave burials in Hawaii. You can find out more in travel books or on the internet. Sky burials as practised in Tibet are not permitted elsewhere so I assume when you mentioned it you were thinking of a green and non-denominational funeral versus a more formal religious ceremony. The normal practice is for an interment or a cremation, although sea burials are possible and any sea captain has the authority to conduct a burial service. Both can be religious ceremonies or not. Therefore, you and your wife could have different funeral services and be buried side by side or cremated and your ashes scattered in the same place, or one buried and the other's ashes put in the burial site.

A green burial is one that occurs in as natural a way as possible. The body is not embalmed as that process uses chemicals that contaminate the ground. The body is laid in a biodegradable coffin (cardboard, for example) or in a cotton, silk or woollen shroud. A number of green burial sites have been created (see the Resource List). The body decomposes more easily and you are truly recycled! Very often, trees or flowers are planted on the site in honour of the deceased, thus creating a beautiful place without unwieldy headstones, which often decay and require maintenance.

In some sites, there's a place for a wooden plaque to be put up in your memory. Others plant a broad-leafed tree for every coffin or casket of ashes. In time, you will contribute to the vegetation grown above you. People choose all sorts of different locations: woodland and meadows, scenic views, bluebell woods, moorland and even the sea. Any type of service can be held either on the site or before burial and the body or ashes then brought for burial.

One coffin-maker who specialises in beautiful willow coffins suggests that you buy one now and use it as a piece of furniture – for example, as a coffee table or blanket box, but that may not suit every taste. At your death, it will be used to transport you to your burial place and you will be wrapped in a woollen shroud and placed in your grave. The coffin is then returned to be used as a piece of furniture again! The advocates of this type of burial suggest that, as cemeteries become more and more crowded, this is a good use of land as well as reducing pollution since cemeteries require a lot of maintenance and often pesticides and weedkillers are used.

Cremation is an alternative to burial and at present 70 per cent of people who die in the UK choose to be cremated. With our general increased awareness of pollution, concern has grown about the chemicals used and the toxic emissions created. Crematoriums are aware of this and are currently modifying the process and adding filters to reduce airborne omissions. Disposal of the ashes has always been up to the family although there are now companies specialising in transporting ashes to far-flung places, such as the Sierra Nevada in Spain or the Sahara Desert in North Africa (see the Resource List). This could be a practical solution to your request for a sky burial!

✎ Section Two ✎

Same Sex

Q1 I've been married for 32 years. I met my husband when I was 23 and we married two years later. Our sex life has always been infrequent, even at the start of our relationship. I got pregnant very early on in our marriage and we have four children and three grandchildren. When they were young, we were holding down two full-time jobs, which kept us busy and tired so sex wasn't an issue. When our last child left for college last year, I imagined that we'd spend more time together and that our nearly non-existent sex life would improve. None of this happened and recently he told me he was bisexual, possibly gay, and has had a couple of relationships with men. It felt like the worst thing that anyone could say to me. We still love each other but I don't know if I should stay or go. I think he'll continue to want sexual encounters with other men. What can I do?

This is a devastating and difficult dilemma and something that happens more often than many of us might imagine. There are very few relevant figures available in the UK because we're not asked about our sexuality in the census although there is talk about its being added to the 2011 UK census. However, according to the American Straight Spouse Network *www.straightspouse.org* (the only organisation set up for straight spouses with gay or bisexual partners), it's estimated there are up to two million mixed orientation couples in the US.

Meanwhile, the Family Equality Council, an American organisation *www.familyequality.org* (see the Resource List), has compiled the following statistics:

- 20 per cent of all gay men are in a heterosexual marriage.

- 50 per cent of all gay men have fathered a child.

- 40 per cent of all lesbians are married to a male partner.

- 75 per cent of all lesbians have children.

I'm going to answer this question from the perspective of the woman facing this dilemma. Of course the male partner can be the straight spouse and their partner lesbian or bisexual so, if that is your situation, read it from that perspective.

The revelation of your partner's true sexual orientation will have come as an enormous shock. Your feelings will follow the grief cycle (as described in this section Question 5) as you have lost both a relationship and possibly a future together. Added to this will be other painful emotions directly related to the situation. You're likely to be feeling sexually rejected. Women who've been through this talk about the fantasy that, if their partners had gone off with another woman, they'd have been able to lure them back. Of course they may well be wrong but they say they wouldn't feel as powerless as having a man as their rival.

Your own sexual esteem will have taken a knock and you may initially blame yourself and think it's your fault and be asking yourself where you went wrong. You'll also experience a strong sense of loss of trust as well as real anger at being lied to. Your belief system will have been blown apart leaving you feeling desperate and confused. You may also feel anxious about your children and grandchildren and their relationship with their father. You may even worry that you've been exposed to a sexually transmitted disease (see Section 4 Question 5). Now, your uncertainty about whether you want the relationship to continue will be confused by a fear of being alone.

Very often, because this disclosure is seen as socially unacceptable, women withdraw into themselves. Like their husbands, who have hidden their secret, they feel ashamed. In effect, you've gone into the closet with your husband. This is a common reaction but sadly it's the most unhelpful thing you could do because what you need is support and to talk to other people. I've listed in the Resource List some organisations you can contact. These are run by people who are professionals in this field and will be able to help you.

You also need your own friends' and family's support. Choose people who are likely to be kind, caring and sympathetic, not anyone who you know is going to give you a hard time. Also make sure you can trust them to keep this confidential; there could be people your husband is not yet ready to tell. Let him know who you're talking to; although he's not in a position to choose, it's reasonable to put him in the picture.

Now you have to decide what it is you can and can't live with. Amity Buxton from the Straight Spouse Network says, 'When a gay, lesbian or bisexual person comes out, a third of the couples break up immediately, another third stay together for a short period to work out what to do and then divorce and the remaining third try to make their marriages work.' Of this last group, 18 per cent divorce after three years and, of the remaining 15 per cent, only 7 per cent maintain a long-term relationship.

No solution is the right one unless it's good for you. What's essential is that you maintain your own power and make your own choices. As well as finding emotional support, it's also important that you get physically checked out. Going to a sexually transmitted disease clinic is strongly advised. This may be your first experience there, so take someone with you if you think it might be easier for you.

Keep in mind at all times that no one can turn a person gay: it is *not* your fault. If it's your habit to blame yourself for things, you need to address that, otherwise it will just lead to your feeling down and depressed. Get some counselling help with this if you find yourself unable to shake off this mood.

Telling your children will be hard; in your case, they're older which may make it easier in some respects. It will be up to them what they tell your grandchildren, if anything at all at this stage as I take it that they are still quite young. How the children are told will affect their future attitude towards their father and therefore it's essential it is well thought out. You may want to get some helpful advice in advance (see the Resource List).

Bear in mind that your husband will continue to care for your children as much as he did before he came out. His sexuality doesn't change how he feels as a father and grandfather. Your children need to continue to have a relationship with him. But, even though they're grown up, they will still require reassurance that they're not responsible for this, especially your child who has just left to go to college. Often, youngest children feel that if only they'd stayed things would be all right.

Although this is really painful for you, it's your husband's right to choose when he tells his children, something you must allow him to do in his own time. On the other hand, he may wish that you tell your children together. In Carol Grever's book, *My Husband*

Is Gay, a number of the women she talked to decided this was the best way. If you can demonstrate acceptance and respect, your children are likely to follow suit.

You'll also have to decide whether you want to stay in the marriage or not, a decision you don't have to make immediately. I'm assuming from what you've said that you are both living together at home at the moment.

Before making your decision, take a moment to consider the following questions:

- Does your husband show you he loves you by actions and not just words?

- Are you content with your present sex life?

- Would you trust him if he said he'd be faithful to you from now on?

- Do you believe he can maintain that for the next 20+ years?

- How will it make you feel if he continues to have other sexual encounters?

- Will this fit within your value system or will you always feel uncomfortable?

- Are you going to be content in this marriage and feel fulfilled?

- Do you want to stay for appearances' sake and because it holds the family together?

- Would you want the freedom to have other sexual relationships yourself?

- What if you or he fall in love with someone else?

- Does he want to be with you as much as you do him? Are you both prepared to put in the emotional hard work?

- Is he your best friend and are you his best friend?

Your success at maintaining a good relationship will depend on a number of factors:

1. How well do you get on as a couple? Are you a solid team, one that's able to communicate about things? Those couples who have been in your situation report that talking to each other and expressing their feelings – including fury and hurt – was essential to their survival.

2. How knowledgeable are you about situations such as these? Find out more: go on the internet, read books, talk to other people who have been in similar situations. The more you learn and understand, the more informed your choices will be. It's really important that you don't leave yourself open to other surprises.

3. How are you going to manage the sexual side of your relationship? A marriage without intimacy is hard to maintain but it's possible to have a close loving relationship without sexual intercourse.

4. How open-minded are you to him having external sexual encounters? Having been in what you thought was a monogamous relationship for 32 years, are you now able to

accommodate your changed circumstances? Patricia Cheney, a coach who specialises in lesbian and gay relationships, says that an alternative to seeking external partners, which has its own risks, is to change your sexual practices and become more creative by using toys, erotic videos, even cross-dressing. This may well be another area where you want to take advice.

5. I know he won't feel like your best friend at the moment, but if you think back prior to his coming out, how would you have described your relationship? Would you say you had mutual respect and love? I'm not talking about sexual love but being loving and close with each other. This is really important. You need solid foundations on which to build when the trust between you has been so dramatically shaken.

6. Are you able to honour his sexuality and not try to make him into someone he isn't? Now that he's finally been open and honest with you, don't do or demand anything that forces him to start pretending again. It won't work and it isn't going to be good for either of you.

7. Does it feel all right to you to continue with as little sex as you've been having or possibly none at all? This may be absolutely fine but you do need to be clear in your mind.

8. If you both have either a religious or moral conviction that marriage is for life, then you'll both be committed to its continuing and making the relationship work.

9. Agree with each other about what's acceptable and what's not. If the relationship is going to work, you'll need to draw new boundaries as things are different now.

10. Make sure you both independently take responsibility for your own happiness. Develop your own interests: it's good to have independent interests and also important if things don't work out that you have a strong support network of friends.

Remember, marriage takes two people pulling together to be successful. You both need to focus on your needs, goals and interests and be kind to each other. Give each other the space and permission to question your altered circumstances and try to be as flexible as possible.

One last thought: don't let this betrayal take away the good memories you have of your marriage and the things you've done together. And, even if you don't choose to stay living under the same roof, there is nothing to stop you being the best of friends.

Q2 **I'm a woman in her mid-fifties who has recently fallen in love with another woman who has up till now been heterosexual. We've got as far as discussing moving in with each other. All my friends are warning me off her as they say older heteros often want to try out a lesbian relationship; it's on their list of 'things to do before they die'. They say she will leave me and I need to be careful. Is it risky to have a relationship in these circumstances?**

It's so hard when 'well-meaning' friends start telling us what the pitfalls might be in a new relationship. It immediately makes us feel anxious. I think this is particularly common among female friends, whatever your sexuality. I'm sure they believe they're doing the right thing 'to save their friend' when what they are in danger of doing is leaving you feeling vulnerable. The result? We end up making precisely the mistakes they are trying to warn us against.

So we feel bad and our friends feel justified. (Please remember this when one of your friends starts a relationship you're not sure about.)

That said, your friends are probably acting in your best interests. Try this exercise which will help you understand their concerns.

WHAT MAKES MY FRIENDS WORRY ABOUT ME?

- What are their real concerns?

- Is this what they always do, a familiar way of behaving when someone starts a new relationship?

- Are you someone easily blinded by love?

- Have you had your heart broken recently or too often?

- Are they feeling left out?

- Does it rattle their beliefs because it involves someone previously of a different sexuality?

- Are they anxious they won't know how to relate to her?

Let's spend a little time thinking about your friends' motivation.

1. They themselves may have been hurt by a 'mostly heterosexual' woman and they're hoping to protect their friend from the pain they experienced.

2. Because it's your lover's first lesbian relationship, your friends may well see her as bisexual rather than lesbian and wonder how serious a bisexual woman could be about

her relationship with another woman. They may wonder if she's just having a break from men for the moment. Can she see herself in a long-term relationship with a woman? She may be attracted to you but would she identify herself as 'mostly heterosexual' and end up hurting you?

3. Whatever the relationship, and whatever their age, women tend to abandon their friends when they start a new relationship. Are you sure you aren't doing that and it is this they are reacting against?

4. Are they protecting you from possible hurt? Have you been hurt before and find it hard to get over relationships?

So now you have an idea as to what might be going on for *them*. What can you do? For a start, talk to them and ask what's behind their comments. Are they missing you? Perhaps you've neglected them. Then ask them if they're happy to have this conversation with you and her together as their talking to you about her is making you anxious. Maybe if they knew her better, they'd feel differently.

I think it's also important for you to talk to her, in private, as something about what your friends have said is clearly resonating with you which is why you're responding as you are. But you mention just your friends and not hers. Ask her what some of her heterosexual female friends are saying. They will certainly have opinions. Perhaps they think she's going through a phase or are worried she's distancing herself from them. She could be worried, meanwhile, about raising her friends concerns with you. She may also be concerned that your friends are causing you anxiety. Discussing your individual friends' reactions together can only be useful and will create a sense of trust and sharing.

Nobody can predict how a relationship will develop and that's true whatever our sexual orientation or history. What I do know is that talking about our feelings, sharing our concerns, finding joint ways to manage how we react to one another makes for stronger and healthier relationships.

I want to spend a little time thinking about the woman who has come out in mid-life. What do you think is going on for her? Carren Strock was 44 and had been married for 25 years before she realised she was a lesbian. In her book, *Married Women Who Love Women*, she discusses this delayed reaction which is common among women who have suppressed their true orientation. She interviewed a hundred women and their families. Over half reported that, when they got married, they had no idea they were gay.

Some women really don't know they're lesbian until something happens to trigger this change, such as falling in love with a woman. Others know that their heterosexual physical relationship is not good but put up with it, assuming that's their lot. Some have known they're lesbian for many years but are only able to express it and explore their true sexuality when their children have grown up. (See Section 1 Question 6 on late divorce.)

You may be reading this as a woman who has come out in mid-life and who knows little about the 'political' issues that can make lesbians, as in any minority group, feel anxious when someone new wants to join. Perhaps you do not see your sexuality in a 'political' way and are uncomfortable with some of the thinking about women's sexuality and thus oppose the views held by the lesbian community. If challenged – as could happen – you may believe you'd be ill-equipped to enter into the conversation with any real conviction. If that's the case, have a look at the Bibliography as well as some websites detailed in the Resource List.

Being lesbian is usually defined as a woman with a sexual orientation towards other women. One of the issues that could trouble your friends is that being 'lesbian' means to them so much more than being attracted to people of the same gender; it has its own subculture. And, while you may not like or feel comfortable with everyone who is part of that group, it gives a foundation to your beliefs and a safe place to come back to. In their eyes, though, a bisexual woman can never truly belong in their world and could be seen as a threat. For them, bisexuality blurs the boundaries, muddies the waters and potentially weakens the political stance of the lesbian movement, not an unusual feeling for a minority group. They may not see you as being as committed to the lifestyle as you once were.

Those of us who were born in the late 1940s and 1950s were young women in the seventies at the height of the feminist movement when books such as Germaine Greer's *The Female Eunuch* influenced our thinking. There was a radical change in beliefs about women's roles, the effects of which continue to shape how we are today. The theories were based on the premise that all identities are socially constructed and that the dominant power, in this case men, created not only their own identities but also those of everyone else. It was during this period that many wrote about lesbian identity and being 'out' in society became more acceptable.

A recent book, *Sexual Fluidity: Understanding Women's Love and Desire* by Lisa Diamond, challenges the view that we have a fixed sexual identity – in other words, that we're heterosexual, homosexual or bisexual. She questions this premise and then asks how important is sexual attraction, desire and love in shaping our identities? Through her study of a hundred young women over a period of ten years, she suggests that sexual fluidity is the hallmark of many women's experience of sexuality throughout their lives: strict definitions are false and can stereotype people.

She gives examples of women for whom the attraction and love they feel for someone is not inevitably gender-related. It's not only to do with biology; social and economic status also play their part. She talks about women moving from same-sex attractions to opposite-sex attractions and back again. This is not done, as is being suggested by your friends, as some sort of experiment, but because we fall in love with different people at different times.

Now let's turn to you and your lover. I think what you need to decide here is what you feel about her. Forget whether she's heterosexual, bisexual or lesbian. Do you have a good relationship? Falling in love is the easy bit. Do you have enough going with her to make a long-lasting relationship? The period of passion will vary in relationships but usually lasts between eighteen months and two years. As this wanes, it's really important that you have a mutual respect for each other and that you're compatible.

Here are some tips on how to build a long-term satisfying relationship:

1. Communication. Talk! Talk! Talk! I can't say this too often. Discuss everything. Don't hide your feelings and hurts so they grow into mountains. Tackle things as they arise. Difficulties invariably occur because we let a minor issue develop into a major crisis. But, if issues can't be resolved, the earlier in the relationship you discover this, the better.

2. At your age, you'll both have your own lives, friends and families. You don't mention this but many women in their fifties will have children. It's important to keep all these relationships going. You need time alone with these people and also time with all of you together. Don't push the introductions; they'll happen slowly as you start to feel

83

more secure. Let the other person choose how quickly she wants to introduce you to her family. It will be hard for them as they'll have to accept that she's now with a woman. Support her in this in whatever way is best for her.

3. Don't become jealous of these other relationships or anxious that she'll leave you for a man. Talk about it and, if necessary, find some outside help to deal with it.

4. Don't allow your friends to influence your thinking. Be clear what you want and need from this relationship.

5. Make time for each other – easy at the start when you want no one or nothing else but slowly the outside world creeps in. When that happens, still plan some time just for the two of you.

6. Do new and exciting things; don't get stuck in a rut. Develop new interests and hobbies together so you can enjoy shared activities.

7. Compromise. Remember that you won't always get exactly what you want but that's one of the trade-offs for having someone sharing your life.

8. Do stay connected with your lesbian community. Don't cut yourself off simply because your new partner wasn't originally part of it. It's important to get support and not feel isolated.

If, in your heart, you feel this is the right relationship for you, go for it. As the old adage has it: It's better to have loved and lost than never to have loved at all.

Q3 My partner has recently retired and is depressed. He's ten years older than me and has always been the successful one. I'm still in my job and meeting new work colleagues and he is behaving as though his status has evaporated. He's envious of my money although he has a pension and he isn't doing any more of the chores than he did before even though he has so much more time on his hands. How can we stop the feelings of resentment we have for each other?

Do you mean depressed or fed up? Everyone feels a bit low at times but we can usually shake it off, a bit like getting a cold. Sometimes, though, it lingers and we may need some help to get over it. We tend to use the word depressed to cover a lot of emotions from feeling a bit down in the dumps all the way through to clinical depression, a recognised condition than can disable us from getting on with our lives.

When someone is fed up with their partner and feels, as you do, that they're not pulling their weight, it's sometimes easy to miss that in fact they're really having a tough time and not just being difficult for the sake of it. Indeed, they may need some external help. Embarking on retirement can be a very difficult chapter in life and I'm not surprised your partner is unhappy.

There is a continuum of feelings which stretches from being totally happy through feeling all right, a bit down and right through to a full clinical illness. It's important for you and your partner to identify where he is on that arc as it will affect what happens next. Below are some questions for you to discuss with him to establish his state of mind:

- Does he start his day with a feeling of dread or lethargy?

- Does he wake in the night, unable to get back to sleep?

- Is his eating significantly less or more than usual?

- Does he feel exhausted all day?

- Does he feel totally pessimistic?

- Is he anxious, tearful, and short-tempered?

- Will nothing change his mood?

If this sounds like him, it may be that the depression has gone on too long and turned itself into physical symptoms, in which case he should consult his GP or a counsellor.

If he only says yes to a few of the above questions, he's probably feeling low but isn't clinically depressed. It's not unusual to feel depressed when you can't see a way out of things, or when you've lost something important to you like your job. Very often, people with this kind of depression are suffering from low self-esteem and end up feeling bad about themselves for not functioning well and not achieving much. A counsellor can help him to reacquire his confidence and to see that how he's thinking is having a detrimental effect on you and on other people who are fond of him (see Section 5 Question 3 re finding a therapist).

As well as getting external support, there are things the two of you can do to improve the situation. You mentioned that your partner is behaving as though he's lost his status. Isn't that putting it a bit harshly? Perhaps you haven't really considered what retirement means to a person. It takes time to adjust to life without regular work. A job isn't just about money; it covers lifestyle, self-image, a role in the world, friendships and much more besides.

It's also somewhere to be creative and to experience personal fulfilment.

Many of us spend long hours at work and therefore don't develop hobbies and interests. If a job suddenly comes to an end (that's always how it feels, even if you've known about it for months), you can be left without an identity. I wonder if your partner is someone who if asked at a party 'What do you do?' would answer 'I am a . . .' or 'I work at' . . . The word *'am'* is a giveaway as it tells us that it is a core part of the person and without it they lose part of their core identity. Not a very nice feeling and one that does nothing for our self-worth.

Being retired is not the same as being on holiday. There's no end in sight other than old age, illness and death – not a very alluring prospect. And if you see his retirement as a time when you can give up the household chores and be looked after, no wonder he's feeling a little glum! In Japan, where a fifth of the population are over 65, psychiatrist Dr Nobou Kurokawa coined the term 'Retired Husband Syndrome'. A growing number of Japanese women are presenting with stress disorders, complaining that they now have to look after their retired partners or *sodai gomi*, as they're known, which literally translates as a large type of waste! I know this doesn't quite apply to you but it's worth pointing out that you could be exacerbating your partner's feelings.

So what can you do about it?

- Talk to each other. I can't say this enough. Ask him how he feels.

- Listen to how he's finding retirement. Ask him what he'd like to do.

- Explain how you believe you've fallen into the trap of thinking he's there to do the chores and that isn't the case. You're still a partnership and he and you need to make joint decisions about your lives together.

- Negotiate how to organise things now he's at home more. You may yet decide together that he does more so you can spend more quality time with each other.

- Agree some new things you can do together that you may not have had time to do before. Exercising, whether at the gym or outside, will both increase your wellbeing and improve your emotional state.

- Discuss finances; you said he felt envious about your money. Maybe now one of you isn't earning, you need to change the financial arrangements? It would be a good idea to talk to a financial advisor.

- Make sure when you return from work you don't immediately launch into what you've been doing all day, leaving him to feel he's got nothing to add. One tip I was given many years ago that has held me in good stead is that the returner, be it from a day's work or a trip away, asks the person at home what they've done first before talking about themselves. It immediately ups the other person's status.

- Very often, when we leave our place of work, we also lose a lot of our social connections. Although he might not want to keep in touch with all his work colleagues, it is important to stay in contact with his mates. Encourage him to go out, too, and meet new people so he has a network of friends.

- Many people want to travel when they retire but perhaps he feels he can't go because you're working. Come to some agreement about this. If he waits till you retire, he'll be 75 and possibly not be as willing to consider an adventurous trip and so miss out.

If I may say so, I think it's really important that you change your attitude. It's easy to see work as the be-all-and-end-all and those who don't have gainful employment as not making as useful a contribution to society. You may not be guilty of this, but try to see his retirement as a new time for both of you. Could you rearrange your work schedule so you got a bit of time off or take a sabbatical so you could have some fun together? All your partner probably needs is a bit of a boost.

Q4 **I've been with my partner for 12 years and we've lived together for 10. We're a lesbian couple and we've asked a gay couple we know if they would father a child for us. They're keen, as they really would like to be parents. They'd be the secondary parents, more like close uncles, and we'd be the primary ones. My partner who's younger than me would be the biological mother. One of the criteria they've stipulated is that we have a civil partnership to show our commitment to being there for the child. But we're very happy with the way we are and the fact we couldn't marry was certainly not an issue for me. Lately, several of our older friends have gone down the civil partnership route and my partner now wants us to. I'm not keen, which she says is a commitment problem. I don't know what to do.**

Let's start with civil partnerships before dealing with rights and responsibilities of parents and then move on to your personal concerns.

The Civil Partnership Act became law in the UK in December 2005. The Act enables same-sex couples to form a civil partnership. Once registered, civil partners have the same rights as a married couple in relation to wills, inheritance law, capital gains tax, pensions, housing and immigration. It also provides next-of-kin rights for the couple, while each partner has a duty of maintenance for their partner and any children. Each partner has the responsibility to be assessed for child support in the same way as in a heterosexual marriage.

As in a marriage, a civil partnership can only be ended by dissolution and a court order and not before a year post-registration. The court has the same powers as in the dissolution of a marriage and can make orders in relation to financial matters and children.

It's important for you to be really clear what the difference is between co-habiting and having a civil partnership. There is a common myth that, once you've been living together for a year, you become common-law partners. There is no such thing. The truth is that couples who are neither married nor have a civil partnership have few automatic rights and can be left in a very vulnerable position. As I'm sure you know, from either your own experience or from others', the end of a relationship is never imagined when things are going well. If you're a co-habitee, you need to be aware that your rights are very few and should make all necessary provisions legally so you're protected at the end of the relationship, whatever the reason. This is especially the case when a child is involved.

Let's now focus on the effect of a civil partnership on parenting. As civil partners, the one who's not the biological parent will automatically be classified as the step-parent. In your situation, the biological father would be the other parent and his partner (if they've been through a civil partnership) would be the official step-parent.

Only the biological parents have automatically what is legally known as 'parental responsibility'. The father in this case, as he wouldn't be married to the mother, would only have parental responsibility if his name was on the birth certificate.

Parental responsibility is defined as 'all the rights, duties, powers, responsibility and authority which, by law, a parent of a child has in relation to the child and their property'. It gives the parent the right to make major decisions about the child's upbringing, consent to medical treatment, full involvement in the decision of where a child will live, what religion they follow and what school they attend. The step-parent can also have parental responsibility; you just have to sign a legal parental responsibility agreement. It's also possible to have parental responsibility via a Shared Residence Order which requires a court application.

Your scenario is complicated as there are in effect four parents: two biological and, if both of you undertake civil partnerships, two step-parents. My understanding is that, if the two biological parents agree, all four of you could have parental responsibility. It is, however, something that you should find out about it advance so you have a clear idea of who you think should be primary and secondary parents. Once you have parental responsibility, you have the same duties as any other parent.

It's worth mentioning here that gay and lesbian couples are now legally able to adopt a child as joint-parents. Local authorities will take note of whether a couple has undertaken a civil ceremony in just the same way as they would if a heterosexual couple is married. This won't stop a successful application but may have a bearing on the eventual decision. If the child's father is unknown, as is the case when an artificial donor's sperm has been used, the non-biological partner can apply to adopt the child.

In your situation, you've obviously decided with your partner that you want the father to be known and it sounds like the father similarly wants to play some part in the child's life. It's interesting that the gay couple feel it's important for the welfare of the child that you're in a legal partnership. Obviously, in their opinion, it's a sign of committing to the long-term responsibilities of bringing up a child. Only you can know if you are committed to this although, from what you say, my hunch is that you are. I don't think your reason for not wanting to enter a civil partnership is to do with your lack of intention to stick around. What you don't mention is whether the gay couple are in, or plan to be in, a civil partnership themselves. Is this one of your criteria or doesn't this matter, as they're to be 'secondary' parents?

Reading your question made me think. Although civil partnerships were welcomed by the gay and lesbian community and by many others, too, new laws obviously bring with them some restrictions and for you it is being faced with decisions which up till now were not relevant to you.

The question of whether to get married, especially when there's a child involved, has hitherto been confined to the heterosexual population and has without doubt caused problems for some couples. Those potential dilemmas have now spread into the gay and lesbian communities.

You ask whether you're frightened of commitment but also reveal that you've lived with your partner for ten years and now want to bring up a child together. I wonder what commitment means to you and your partner. Are you worried about the effect of a civil partnership on your relationship? Frankly, I think you're asking the wrong question. It seems to me that you've already displayed how committed you are but that you're less secure about the prospect of a civil partnership. However, just in case I'm wrong, why not try my commitment test?

COMMITMENT QUIZ

Tick the column that most accurately fits your thinking:

	True	*Not sure*	*False*
1. I am willing to support my partner through everything			
2. I feel that being in a long-term relationship will stop me achieving my goals			
3. It would be a worry if my partner became dependent on me financially			
4. I can't imagine life without my partner			
5. I look forward to seeing what the future holds for us both			
6. I don't like sharing my life			
7. I love spending time with my partner more than anyone else			
8. I like to know I can up and go whenever I want			
9. I have difficulty trusting my partner			
10. The success of my relationship is my highest priority			

Scoring

Give two points if you've said 'True' to questions 1, 4, 5, 7 and 10.

Give two points if you've said 'False' to questions 2, 3, 6, 8 and 9.

Give one point to any where you said you weren't sure.

Interpretation

0–5 You're not at all committed and I don't know why you're thinking of having a child.

6–10   You have some serious issues and you need to take advice and do some long-term thinking before you make any decisions.

11–15 You're feeling wobbly and unsure and need to talk this through with your partner – it may be a good idea to see a relationship counsellor.

16–20 You don't have a commitment problem so stop worrying about that and look at your true concerns.

If, as I imagine, you scored pretty highly, I think what you're suffering from is the fear of the formalisation of your partnership. It even has a name – gametophobia – derived from the Greek 'gamete' meaning wife and 'gamein' to marry. For some people, marriage can be a real phobia and the person suffering becomes anxious just thinking about it. If that's the case, then talking to someone about it is really important. Gametophobia usually denotes fear of living with another person, fear of parental responsibility and fear of failing as a sexual partner, none of which seem to apply to you. Fears can, of course, be useful if they alert us to a danger or perceived danger but I wonder what the 'danger' is here for you? It's important that you work out what it is that's concerning you because, if the whole notion of a civil partnership is being clouded by fear, you'll be making your choice from a position of weakness rather than strength and that's never a good idea. Think about the following questions:

- Are you worried about falling out of love and not having enough to talk about? That can happen whether you're legally bound or not.

- Are you concerned that a civil partnership is a journey into the unknown which will make your relationship different and not necessarily as good?

- Is it because you feel you may not live up to her expectations? You obviously have up until now.

- Is it that someone else has told you to do it? I wonder if that's a problem. If so, I think you should stop worrying about their criteria and focus on what the pros and cons might be for you.

I've started the list for you but I suggest you and your partner sit down and have a look at this together and agree between you what's best for you both and why:

Pros

- The same inheritance rights as a marriage

- Avoidance of inheritance tax if one of you dies

- Easy joint parental responsibility

- Benefits automatically paid to the surviving partner

- Relationship recognised abroad

- Greater protection from domestic violence

- Transfers of money between you are not liable to capital gains tax

Cons

- Less freedom, more legal requirements

- Increase in the number of people with parental responsibility

- If the relationship ends, it has to go through a legal process

It isn't my place to tell you what to do but I'm willing to stick my neck out a little here and suggest you take a look at the situation from the child's point of view. Your child will be born into a relationship that is different from many. Nothing wrong in that but what he or she won't want to feel is that one of their mothers can't make the same decisions as the other. For example, if the child had an accident at school requiring medical treatment and your partner was out of town, you couldn't sign the consent form unless you had parental responsibility via a civil partnership. So bear the child in mind when you're making your decision. As long as you and your partner feel good about what you've decided, I think you'll go on to make great joint parents.

Q5 I'm in my early fifties and I have been with my partner for twenty-two years. I still say 'have' but I should say 'had', as he died last year from bowel cancer. We went through a civil ceremony last year which meant all the

financial side was sorted. But, now he's gone, I just don't know what to do and where to turn. I think my family and friends aren't sure how to help me. Sometimes, I don't want to be on my own and want to be in a relationship; then there are times when I do want to be on my own. I'm too old to rejoin the 'scene' at my age. It all goes round in circles in my mind. It's not easy being gay when you're older and on your own. Please help.

I read this elegy a while back. It was written by Paul Monette an American author who wrote and talked openly about gay relationships when others were in the main still in the closet. This poem about grief applies to us all whatever our sexuality.

> Grief is madness – ask anyone who's been there. They will tell you it abates with time but that's a lie. What drowns you in the first year is a force of solitude and helplessness exactly equal in intensity to the love you had for the one who's gone. Equally passionate, equally intimate. The spaces between the stabs of pain grow longer after a while, but they're empty spaces. The clichés of condolence get you back to the office, back to your taxes and the dinner table – and, for everyone else's sake, you collaborate. The road of least resistance is paved with the gravel of well-meaning friends, rather like the gravel that cremation leaves.
>
> Paul Monette, *Last Watch of the Night*

Losing someone you love, whether expected or not, is always traumatic; and never more so than when it's the death of a long-term partner. If, as in your case, there's been a long illness, your period of grieving and loss will have been protracted. When the illness is first diagnosed, it will begin to impinge on your life, not only with hospital appointments and a change in lifestyle but discussions about the future. Many couples will find this draws them together while also changing the nature of the relationship with one taking on the role of carer.

With death, when your loss is all too real, there will come a huge change in your life. You may have come to rely on medical and nursing support which will now no longer be there for you, forcing you to begin to find a way to cope alone. Families and friends all rally round for a while although some will have found the pain of watching you hurt too hard to bear and will have tried to push you through this phase. It's important that you let them know what you need; if people have an expectation of you that you can't meet, this can lead to the confusion you describe. In the end, though, most people will assume you're all right and they have lives of their own anyway.

Elisabeth Kübler-Ross, a psychiatrist working with death and dying developed her 'grief cycle', which describes the processes people go through. Firstly shock – we can't believe that this has happened. Then denial – this can cause us to sometimes carry on as if nothing has happened or become more energetic and active. Then a period of resistance – we hold on to our original beliefs as strongly as we know how, e.g. by saying to ourselves 'I am still part of a couple.' Next anger and blame – this can be internally and/or externally focused: we blame anything and everyone including ourselves. Then follows the start of the healing process and acceptance – we begin to accept things are different and start to work out how to manage. This is followed by awareness and recognition of our strengths – we begin to control, to know we can do something and our self-esteem grows. We now have the energy to explore, possibly discover what is available to us and move to meet new challenges. We move through the cycle at our own pace, sometimes sticking at one place and sometimes going backwards before forwards and hopefully we finally move on. It can take time to complete the cycle and some people get stuck and need help to find their way through.

There are a number of things which I think are helpful to remember when going through bereavement:

- Allow yourself time to mourn. It's an inevitable process you have to go through. If you put it off, it will either come out emotionally, through depression or anger, or in a physical way, or make you ill.

- Resume as much as you can of your former life. Go back to work, even if it's only part-time. The more your life gets back to normal, the easier it will be to get into a new routine.

- Understand that you'll go through many phases and feel many different emotions. Don't worry if your moods fluctuate from day to day or hour to hour. It's OK if at times you find yourself 'going round in circles.' It is part of the process. The problem is when it goes on too long – then you need to seek help.

- Don't be frightened by your feelings; their depth and range may make you feel out of control but you aren't. It's normal to feel 'wobbly'.

- I expect you are right about your friends and family. We are in the main very bad at dealing with death. I suggest you talk with them and say that you know they are trying to help and are unsure how to, but that's OK. Tell them you like them being there for you, but you also want permission to tell them when you need time alone.

- Keep yourself physically healthy. Do some exercise. As well as becoming physically stronger, you'll also be stimulating production of endorphins that will make you feel better.

- Make sure that you do the things that are vital, like paying the bills. If you really can't face it, get help from someone else. Don't build up more troubles for later.

- Although grief is a process, you need to work at it. If you find you're stuck, seek help. There are lots of counsellors out there (see Resource List).

In order to move forward successfully, it's obviously necessary to reorganise and reconstruct your life and adjust to the fact that you're single again. In order to do this, people often need help from a counsellor so they can position themselves in the world in their new role. There are a number of questions that are likely to occur to you. How long do I define myself as a widower? How do I adapt in a healthy way to my new state? Do I start being truly single again when I meet someone new? Could I bear to ever go through the pain of losing someone again?

As part of my research for this book, I talked to a number of 50+ gay men about getting older. What struck me was the difference in their views. Some never expected to get to this age and that being able to say they'd had a partner for twenty-two years would be a real achievement. Others felt the complete opposite. Yes, they did know men who'd died from AIDS but it never crossed their minds that they wouldn't make 'old bones'.

Michael Shernoff, a gay psychotherapist who himself sadly died from pancreatic cancer in 2008, wrote several papers about being a gay widower and also edited a book *Gay Widowers: Life After the Death of a Partner*. I suggest you take a look at this and also the Resource List. Gay widowers were not researched or discussed prior to the onset of AIDS. (In fact, most of the research on 'widow(er)hood' has been undertaken about older women as, traditionally, they survive longer than their partners.)

For everyone, the death of a partner means the transition from the married status (used loosely here for co-habiting partnerships) to the non-married state. Socially, it's an awkward and difficult time, while emotionally it's excruciatingly painful. Gay men have had few role models in this respect since, prior to AIDS, many older men had not 'come out'. There was, therefore, no group wisdom. Living as you do in the UK, and having had a civil partnership, you'll be seen by most as being entitled to fully mourn your loss. There will be some, though, who have not 'come out' and are therefore being supported by people who don't understand why they're so distressed about a 'lodger' or 'friend' who's died. Others may suffer a homophobic reaction from families which will only add to their distress and impede their ability to move forward.

Most gay baby boomers have lived through radical changes in societal views and values about homosexuality. It's incredible to think that, as recently as 1967, the Sexual Offences Bill was passed legalising gay sex in private for consenting adults over the age of twenty-one and only since the 2004 Civil Partnerships Act that all of us in the UK can have the same rights. I know that doesn't mean there's no homophobia and perhaps you have come across it yourself but at least you're not fighting the law or your partner's family to be allowed to stay in your own home.

Let's now focus on the other part of your question: whether you're ready to start another relationship and go back to the gay scene. I remember a comment made to me recently by a gay man whose relationship had broken down. He said that, for the last thirteen years, 'he'd been living a straight life in a gay world' – he meant that he'd been in a monogamous relationship – and now he was faced with going back into the gay community and he didn't know how to do it.

If you don't fancy the gay scene, don't go there but you need to be clear what it is you don't like about it and, indeed, if it's still like it was. You may be surprised to find how it's changed over the last two decades and more. There are now many more gay social events based on activities that have nothing to do with just having sex. It would be worth finding out what's going on in your area. Start talking to your friends and see if they can point you in the direction of suitable venues (see Section 3 page 119 on where to find a partner).

But, beforehand, it's important to ask yourself a few questions:

AM I READY FOR A RELATIONSHIP?

Answer either 'Yes' or 'No':

1. Am I running away from grief?

2. Am I frightened of being alone?

3. Do I know what I want from a new relationship?

4. Do I feel ready to have fun again?

5. Would I be able to love someone new without feeling guilty?

6. Could I see someone new for who they are without making a comparison?

7. Am I looking for a man to share my life?

8. Am I fun to be with?

9. Am I strong enough to choose what's right for me?

10. Am I looking forward to being able to share something with someone?

Scoring:

Give yourself one point for 'No' in questions 1 and 2, then one point for 'yes' answers for the rest.

Interpretation

8–10 You're pretty much there.

5–7 You're on your way – start getting out and trying new activities.

0–4 You have not completed the grieving process – don't isolate yourself but don't get involved until you're ready.

Whatever your score, you can still prepare yourself for a possible new relationship. The following steps will point you in the direction of the kind of partner you want and where to go to find him. (And, if you don't want a guy who likes the gay scene, then don't go there!)

Steps to take:

1. Create a clear picture of who you're looking for. Is it a new life partner, or someone to have a date with? Be aware of your goal.

2. Accept your age and what goes with it. As we grow older, we want different things. What makes you passionate and what makes your life meaningful? Once you decide that, you'll know what matters in a partner.

3. Manage negative thinking. Clear from your mind all the thoughts that stop you getting what you want – for example, 'I'm no longer attractive' or 'I need to be loyal to my late partner.' Enjoy what you have to offer. Remember, you have experience in making successful long-term relationships; you know how to be intimate.

4. Think of some friends who can support you. It's good to have someone to talk to. Coming out of a long-term relationship may mean you've got out of the habit of sharing intimately with friends. Well, now's the time to start again!

5. Write a list of all the places where you might find your kind of person and then start going to them.

Once you know the type of person you're looking for and where you'd be likely to find them, you're two-thirds of the way there. My sense is that little by little would be good for you. Start by setting the goal for just meeting new people before you even consider having a date or jumping into a full-on affair and moving in together. I wish you every success in establishing a new relationship as enriching as the one which endured for twenty-two years.

Q6 I live in a smallish town where there are a couple of gay women's groups that meet regularly both for activities and socially. I've been part of this lesbian community since I moved here as a young woman nearly forty years ago. Most of my close friends are part of this group. My ex-partner and I split up after twenty years but we've remained very good friends. I've recently met someone new at work and I really like her. I don't think she understands about remaining friends with former partners because she says it feels like our new relationship is going on in the shadow of the old one. I don't understand the problem but I don't want to lose either of them or have to leave the community.

Your question made me think of a poem written by L. J. 'Tess' Tessier in the 1970s which highlights the issues you raise about lesbian relationships and ex-partners.

FAMILY AFFAIRS

I am your lover
and your ex-lover's one-time lover
and your ex-lover's lover's lover
and your ex-lover's ex-lover's part-time lover

I have called you the wrong name
Four times in the last month

I have forgotten your birthday
and your favourite colour
and the shoes I bought you
are the wrong size

I don't remember if the conversation
I had last night
was with you

And I don't know how to tell you this
But I love you

If that poem is anything to go by, no wonder you're finding it difficult! I appreciate it exaggerates the situation but it does raise the fact that it's common in lesbian relationships for ex-partners to remain friendly. This is very often more pronounced in small communities and with minority groups where everyone knows each other; it's not uncommon to find several people in the group have been intimate with each other. A lot of research into lesbian relationships indicates the tendency for lesbians to remain in contact with former lovers. Many lesbian relationships will have developed out of very close and intimate friendships with best friends becoming lovers. When the relationship ends, there's still a very close bond of friendship that is extremely important and valuable which neither partner wants to lose.

I want to start by looking at lesbian mid-life relationships. In a book edited by Marcy Adelman *Midlife Lesbian Relationships: Friends, Lovers, Children, and Parents*, Jacqueline Weinstock has a chapter entitled, 'Lesbian Friendships at Mid-life: Patterns and Possibilities for the 21st Century'. It addresses women born between 1935 and 1961, the war babies and the baby boomers. This group of women to which we belong has seen enormous changes in the way society now views lesbian relationships compared to when we were young. During the seventies, in particular, views and attitudes radically changed. Weinstock's research was carried out on white, middle-class lesbians in the USA. I expect that the findings would be echoed in the UK and other Western societies where same-sex relationships have been accepted and are allowed to flourish.

Although things have certainly changed over the years and there are now many mid-life lesbians who have children, the majority of those who have been lesbian all their lives don't have children. It's often those who have been previously married and came out later who have families. It's also the case that older lesbians are less likely to have children than younger ones, as cultural changes have meant that it's now much more acceptable for lesbians to have children either in a partnership or on their own. Even with this new, more tolerant climate, lesbian culture doesn't revolve around reproduction and a child-centred existence.

Although most lesbians don't tend to settle into long-term partnerships when they're younger, this tends to become the norm later on. There are a number of reasons for this. One is that pressures from their birth family recede as lesbian women grow older and their partners become more readily accepted. Gradually, their parents who may have previously objected and been pressing them to get married and have children become more accepting once the childbearing years have passed and are content to see their daughter settled with someone they love. It's important for parents as they age to see their children settled and comfortable.

Some people find it easier to accept the relationship because of the fantasy that women move beyond sex as they grow older. Nieces and nephews grow up and find it easier to relate to their aunt as an adult and often seek out relationships with another adult who isn't their parent. Aunts can play a very important part in their lives especially if their nieces or nephews are going through relationship issues themselves or their home life is a bit rocky.

As both we and our parents get older, lesbian women may reconnect more closely with their family and feel once again that they belong. Even if there have been periods of little contact and certain issues are still unresolved, they're drawn back to the family as their parents age and power shifts in the family (see Section 6 Questions 2, 3 and 6). Of course, there are lesbian women who continue to have close relationships with their family of origin and this doesn't change as they reach their forties, fifties or sixties.

Those who have not had supportive family relationships through their life often create their own 'family space' and the place they've found that support is within their very close and intimate circle of friends. You say you moved to your present town when you were a young woman so I'm assuming you were away from your roots. It's not surprising, therefore, that you became part of the local lesbian community and that this is where you made friends, found lovers and were nurtured and cared for. We all gravitate to people who are like ourselves and have similar interests and values and the lesbian community is where you will have found this.

It sounds as though your current partner is new to the community so she may not have close friends within the group. However, it's very unlikely that any of us in our fifties or sixties will come to a relationship without having an ex or two somewhere in the background. Often, the ending of a relationship is fraught with difficulties and it's less painful to sever all links. (Of course, if you have children, that's another story which I discuss in Section 5 Questions 1, 3 and 6.)

It's vital that you talk this over with your new partner to find out what her fears are. The two of you must work out how you're both going to manage this situation. You'll need to help her accept and respect the relationship you have with your ex-partner while also helping your ex-partner accept your new one which is, after all, now your primary relationship. Jacqueline Weinstock suggests that the concept of friends as family is very helpful when negotiating this so that, rather than being seen as a threat, the ex-partner comes to be regarded as part of your extended family. The relationship with her also becomes safe, much as the relationship with a sister or brother.

It's especially important, as we get older, to have a group of close, caring people around us. There's a societal assumption that we'll be cared for by our children and extended families in our dotage, one that I personally am not sure is an appropriate expectation (see

Section 1 Question 8 and Section 6 Question 3). In this respect, the lesbian community is ahead of the heterosexual community in looking at how they can support themselves through the friendships created through their life. This is no more than an extension of the very close emotional ties they've established with other women.

In my discussions with mid-life lesbians, several revealed they'd already started the process of combining their resources with others and setting up communities where they can live either in one large property or very closely so they can support one another as they get older. They're doing this now while they're still relatively young and fit so everything will be in place before they need it. It's a model the rest of us would do well to consider.

Now let's return to you and your specific situation. I wonder if your new partner worries that your former relationship isn't completely over and is threatened by the place she holds in your affections. It's worth you spending a few minutes thinking about this so you're really convinced it's over and able to convince her.

PAST LOVERS

1. When you think about your ex-lovers how would you describe them?

2. Do you still have sexual feelings for the woman you were with for twenty years?

3. Are you still wondering if things could be different?

4. Why are you no longer together?

5. Is there some unfinished business that ties you to each other?

6. Do you sometimes contact your ex rather than sharing a problem with your new partner?

7. Do you talk about your ex and have mementos of your relationship around the house?

8. If you could only see one of them which would it be?

9. Who would you like to grow old with?

10. What makes your present relationship special?

It's important when answering these questions that you're true to yourself. If you do have any leftover feelings, your new partner will pick them up in exactly the same way you've picked up her insecurity and possible jealousy. If you think there's any unfinished business, then you need to sort it out. If you identify how you might be doing things that fuel the situation, then you can change them.

Once you're absolutely clear how you feel and that being with this new woman is what you want, then tell her so. In relationships, we often don't understand why someone's behaving the way they do about something. Of course, you can't control how someone feels but be aware that she'll have her own history and experiences and these will colour how she sees the world. What do you know about her past experiences? Perhaps she has been hurt by an ex coming back into a partner's life or seen someone else hurt in this way.

It's understandable for her to feel jealous and anxious, especially if the model of remaining friends isn't one she has experienced before. After all, your ex has shared many intimate moments with you, seen many of the things you've seen, been part of the same local community and nursed you when you were ill. As a result, she undoubtedly knows you better than your new partner does.

The important thing is for your current partner to know that you're with her now, that you've chosen her. Unless you talk this through and find a resolution, this will continue to be a problem that will destroy your relationship either with her or with your ex and the lesbian community. In Section 5 Question 6, I also discuss jealousy about former partners. I think it would be helpful for both you and your new partner to read it, albeit in a different type of relationship.

Section Three

Singles

Q1 I've been on my own for a while and had a few lovers. The sex hasn't been great, though. Is that what I should expect at my age? (I'm well into my fifties.) I'm not lonely and I have lots of friends. I'd like to be in a relationship so, if I'm going to have a partner, I want it to be good sexually. How do I go about it?

The quick answer to your first question is no, absolutely not! After a period of no research into the sex lives of the over-fifties, things have changed. Over the last four years, there have been a few studies undertaken. The world has finally woken up to just how many of us there are, the baby boomer is becoming of interest to both the scientific community and the commercial market. An in-depth survey in 2004 of 8,000 people in the UK in their fifties undertaken by Complan Active revealed that just over 82 per cent were involved in a sexual relationship with 54.9 per cent saying their sex life was better than when they were younger. The main reason as identified by over a quarter of the people questioned was that they'd learnt what they do and don't like, sexually speaking. What's more, 77.2 per cent thought they would still be having sex in 10 years' time. Many people also said that the bedroom was not their preferred place for making love: the living room followed by the bathroom were also popular.

In 2006, a Global Study of Sexual Attitudes and Behaviours (funded by Pfizer) addressed the sexual activity and problems of 27,500 men and women aged between 40 and 80, in 29 countries around the world. In the UK, 1,500 individuals took part in the survey. Overall, 69 per cent of men and 56 per cent of women reported having sexual intercourse during the past year. The UK ranks low among western nations, with around 65 per cent reporting they are satisfied with their relationships and a slightly healthier 75 per cent reporting they have good sex lives. In Australia, 83 per cent of men and 74 per cent of women had engaged in sexual intercourse during the previous 12 months with 38 per cent of all men and 29 per cent of all women engaging in sexual intercourse more than once a week. The study also revealed that, although a number of people experience minor sexual problems, very few seek medical help (see Section 1 Question 2).

There are so many myths about sex and they don't stop just because we become older. Why not try this sex quiz based on some ideas from *Sex over 50* by Joel Block. Then perhaps we can put some of these myths to bed!

SEX QUIZ

Please answer all the questions before you look at the answers, otherwise it's no fun!

Answer 'True' or 'False':

1. A man's sexual peak is in his teens?

2. A woman's sexual peak is in her thirties?

3. Orgasms in our youth are more intense?

4. The quality of sex decreases as we age?

5. Erection problems are inevitable as men age and always need medical help?

6. The sign of arousal is an instant erection for men and vaginal lubrication for women?

7. Women go off sex during and after menopause?

8. If his partner doesn't visually excite a man, he'll find it hard to make love to her?

9. Men and women with heart or other health problems should abstain?

10. Sex without intercourse isn't really sex?

11. Oral sex is only for the young?

12. All sex has to end in orgasm?

Answers

1. False. Men achieve an erection more quickly in their teens than at any other time of their life. This change can be a relief as the shame of an erection at the wrong time for an adolescent boy is something many men over 50 can still remember with embarrassment! Young men also have harder erections. If a peak is judged on speed and hardness, the young have it; however, for most of us, the peak is more to do with enjoyment. This comes from how a man uses his erect penis and it usually takes an older man to be able to control when he ejaculates and to please his partner.

2. False. While for most women sex does get better in their thirties, some find that, as they get older and more confident, it actually continues to improve.

3. False. Many women report that their orgasms become more intense as they become more confident lovers and the ability to have multiple orgasms also continues into older age. Men report that they feel the orgasm throughout the genital area as they get older and not just in their penis, so this gives them increased enjoyment.

4. False. It's different, and different doesn't mean worse. As we grow older, both men and women are able to control their responses more easily and are much more sensitive to each other's needs. Increased sexual confidence means that we are able to express our desires and teach our partners how to pleasure us. Most of us will have learnt more about our own bodies through masturbation and sexual experience. So, contrary to what we've been taught to expect, the quality of sex should increase as we age.

5. False. Not all men have erectile problems. If men compare their erections to how they were when they were 18, they may think it's a problem but it isn't!

6. False. The amount of vaginal lubrication produced by a woman will alter as she gets older because of hormonal changes not desire. Older men may not get an instant erection; they're just as likely to be stimulated in other parts of their bodies and an erection will then follow.

7. False. Many women are delighted to no longer have the anxiety of becoming pregnant and therefore feel freer in

their sexual relationships. The reason some may have less desire will often be related to a hormone imbalance or non-sexually related issues. Of course, if you believe that, as you age, you're no longer an attractive sexual being, it may become a self-fulfilling prophecy.

8. False. Young men are more easily stimulated by a visual image and this alone can give them an erection while the older man (and this change often occurs in their late thirties) needs tactile stimulation. As men age, they often become more psychologically in tune with their partners and therefore the emotional side of the relationship has an effect on their desires. Research has shown that an ageing body doesn't put off either men or women.

9. False. According to the British Heart Foundation, sex doesn't put undue strain on the heart. It's no more strenuous than many ordinary activities and exercise. If you can climb two flights of stairs without getting chest discomfort or becoming breathless, sexual activity should be fine. Heart attacks during intercourse count for less than one per cent of all coronary deaths and three-quarters of those occur in extra-marital liaisons where the stress level is likely to be higher. Making love is good for you as it induces a sense of wellbeing – and remember, that doesn't mean it has to be intercourse. One last word: wait to be given the all-clear for sex from your doctor if you've had a heart attack. The same goes for any other illness.

10. False. It has become Western practice to decree that sex 'has' to include intercourse. Many of us were brought up on the idea that foreplay was to get us into the mood for intercourse or that it was all that was allowed in premarital

sex and therefore wrongly we don't think of it as sexual activity.

11. False. In a 2007 American survey undertaken by Stacy Tessler Landau at the University of Chicago of 3,005 people aged between 57 and 85, more than half of those aged under 75 said they gave or received oral sex, as did about a third of 75 to 85-year-olds. Older, more experienced lovers tend to be less inhibited.

12. False. Sex can be very enjoyable without an orgasm. Touching, kissing, stroking, licking and so on are all satisfying activities and pleasurable in themselves. Making orgasm the goal can add a pressure and also mean that you miss out on some of the other pleasures along the way.

For more information see Section 1 Question 2.

How many did you get right? I hope by now you can see that sex can be very good, whatever your age. Maybe you just haven't yet found the right person. You need to adapt your expectations, the most important being that you shouldn't compare yourself to a 20-year-old! We tend to do this in relation to our physical selves. I'm sure you can't run as fast as you once did and I expect you've got a wrinkle or two. But there are so many emotional and practical ways in which you're vastly more sophisticated and able than you once were. It's time we accepted that things are different now that we're older and, for the most part, pretty good.

Let's now move to your concerns about finding a good sexual relationship.

- First, stop looking to recreate the past and resolve to change your expectations.

- Spend a bit of time reconsidering your body so you know what pleases you most.

- Communication is the key. Practise telling a partner what you need. You can do this through role-play at home. Set it up so your pretend future lover is sitting on the sofa. Tell him what you want sexually. Then go and sit in his chair and imagine what it felt like to listen. Was it a bit aggressive or too apologetic? Now go back to your original position and try again. Continue until you feel comfortable with what you have to say and your imaginary partner seems comfortable with hearing it.

- Remember that it isn't just intercourse: oral sex and manual stimulation are also very pleasurable.

- Keep some lubricant to hand so you can ensure you're comfortable.

- Think of different positions that would suit you. If you have arthritic hips or knees or a bad back, some positions may be less comfortable than others. If it's hurting, it won't be good sex.

- Don't forget about romance: make it a pleasurable experience in a nice place or an unusual environment.

- Finally, don't expect instant gratification. Give it time and let things grow.

Now all you have to do is go and find the right man! Here are a few tips:

- Think about what you did when you were younger and wanted to find a partner. Would it work now?

- Write a list of qualities and attributes you'd like to find in your ideal partner.

- Prioritise the list – you may not be able to get everything but you want the ones that really matter.

Now decide where you could find this person:

- The internet

- Newspaper adverts

- An activity which interests you – for example, rambling club, tennis group or an evening class, in art for instance

- If you feel comfortable with the idea, tell your colleagues and friends you're looking for a relationship. They may know someone, and have never thought of introducing you

- Remember to go to places on your own so you have more chance of meeting someone

- If one activity doesn't bear fruit, then try another

- New friends are always good as they have friends you might not know

Armed with this knowledge and as long as you keep yourself healthy and fit and have a positive frame of mind, I don't think there'll be any stopping you – however old you get! (There are also a number of sites in the Resource section and books in the Bibliography worth exploring. In my first book, *Who's That Woman in the Mirror?* I discuss this at greater length.)

Q2 I've been single since I was in my mid-forties after a longish relationship. I'm now 56. Over the years, I've had a couple of relationships where I co-habited but I decided that neither was for me. I made a conscious choice that I didn't want to live with anyone, the same way as I made a choice not to have children. I have lovers at times and I'm very happy as I am. I just can't get this into some of my close friends' heads. They were all right for a while but now it's becoming a problem. What is it about couples that make them feel insecure if you're happily on your own? At this rate, I'll lose some of them because I'm sick of being 'paired up'. How do I help them to understand I'm not incomplete or frightened of being sad and lonely when I'm older?

It is interesting how hard many people find it to believe that being single is a positive choice and not something that a person puts up with whilst they are waiting for a partner. It is as though you are incomplete unless you have an 'other half'.

Most of us born in the 1940s and 1950s were brought up in a household that comprised two parents. Of course, there were divorces but relatively few. Even if you were in a single-parent household or in care, the message was that being married was the ultimate goal. Men would go to work and provide for their family and women would stay at home and care for their children.

If we look at how things are fifty or so years later, it seems hard to believe that we were conditioned into that way of thinking. Clearly, your married friends still subscribe to that view. Many who are divorced, separated or single also hold those beliefs and do believe that being in a couple is a goal they want to achieve which is why they continue to search for someone. Others, like you, are equally clear that being single is good and are comfortable with their choice.

It seems to me that many of us have not taken stock of the changes in society and our beliefs are a bit outmoded as a result. The England and Wales Population Census 2001 (the latest to be published) reveals some interesting figures:

- Over 30 per cent of the adult population are single

- More than half the adult population (50.9 per cent) is married or remarried

- Over 10 per cent of adults are separated or divorced

- Widows and widowers make up over 8 per cent of the population

- For the first time, there were more people aged over 60 than there were children aged under 16

The figures are even higher in the USA. Their latest census, published in 2006, revealed there were 92 million unmarried Americans aged 18 and older – that's 42 per cent of the population.

With those types of figures, you'd think that we'd be perfectly comfortable whatever someone's marital or co-habiting status. And yet, there's a common belief that single people are having a less good time than those in couples. Bella dePaulo, author of *Singled Out: How Singles Are Stereotyped, Stigmatized and Ignored, and Still Live Happily Ever After*, is in her mid-fifties and has never married.

Even so, there are certain things, she said, that still make her feel uncomfortable about her status. She notes the look of pity on people's faces when she reveals she's single. At work, it's automatically assumed that she'll be available to take on an out-of-hours task as she won't have any other demands on her time. She also notices that, although she gets invited to a couple's house during the week, it doesn't happen at weekends and she never gets invited by couples to go with them to the cinema or theatre.

She decided to check this out with other single people – and heard much the same story. Together with her colleague, Wendy Morris, she undertook research into the attitudes held about single people by all groups in society. They found that single people were viewed more negatively than married couples. They were seen as unhappy, lonely, and self-centred compared to their married counterparts (although they were thought to be more independent). It was also felt that single people were discriminated against by landlords, for example, or hotel chains which often charge a single person's supplement.

DePaulo cites a study by Walter Grove and Hee-Choon Shin (1989), 'The psychological well-being of divorced and widowed men and women' that shows there's little difference between the happiness rate scored by married or single people. Another study 'How Stable Is Happiness?' (2007) undertaken by Professor Richard Lucas and Brent Donnellan of Michigan University showed that, except for occasions such as getting married or a relationship breaking down, an individual's rate of happiness is pretty consistent throughout their lives with some people always more content than others.

Now let's look at the behaviour of your friends who are couples and try to understand their attitudes and beliefs. We're all attracted to people who are like ourselves. They won't be exactly like us but they'll have enough similar traits, interests and experiences to make us feel comfortable in their company. I wonder if you've ever been in a situation where you've met someone and within minutes you feel as though you've known them all your life. This is because they remind you of someone you know well – yourself!

The other experience, which I'm sure you'll have had, is when someone to whom you feel very close invites you to meet a new friend. They tell you that you'll adore them but, when you meet, you sit there with your mouth open thinking, 'This isn't possible!' The other friend has connected with parts of your friend that you haven't even noticed exist. And it can come as a real shock if this other friend holds such contrary views to you and what you assumed were the beliefs of your mutual friend.

The other thing that seems to happen is that, because some married people believe they'd be distraught if they were on their own, they think they know better than you and therefore feel perfectly within their rights to invite someone you've never met to their house at the same time as you and expect the two of you to walk off together into the sunset! All of this is unbelievably annoying for the single person. But, from the perspective of the caring friend, it seems the right thing to do.

Everyone likes their friends to be interested in their lives and it helps if you're going through similar experiences because then there'll be more common points of interest to talk about. Relationships can be tricky and it's helpful for friends to unburden on one another. So it can be awkward if a friend wants to discuss their partner, or their children, or downsizing their home and these problems are outside your experience. From their perspective, it would therefore be lovely if you were in the same place as them because they could then share more about their lives.

Another interesting phenomenon is that single men seem to be invited more readily to couple events than single women. Again, I think this is because the woman is still, in many relationships, the person who makes the social arrangements and she believes, based on both her experience and what her partner says, that men are more at ease in social situations. Only rarely – although often it's what the single person believes to be the case – does the person extending the invitation worry that you and their partner will run off together. That's only likely to happen if the husband has been unfaithful or has said he fancies you.

So why aren't your married friends listening to you? I think one of the reasons we find it so hard to get our friends to hear what we're saying is because when they start beating 'the couples are best' drum, it revives those unconscious childhood messages of marriage being the ideal. This can be unsettling, leaving you feeling slightly less sure of yourself and your personal ambitions so you'll tend to retreat rather than assertively discussing your point of view.

How, then, are you going to change things? First, don't fall into the trap of your friends and try selling them the single life. Your aim should be not to convert them but to help them understand that you're happy as you are. If my premise is right that we like people who are like ourselves, then in order for them to truly hear you, it's important to find common ground and show them how similar you are in everything except your marital status.

It's important for close friends to have shared values: these are the foundations for our attitudes, actions and the way we behave. They're what matter most to us. My hunch is that, if you share common values with your friends but explain to them that you're very happy with your single status, they'll accept you at face value.

First of all, though, it might be worth your trying the following exercise so that you're absolutely clear in your own mind what matters most to you. Once you are clear about your own values, you will be able to see where they match your friends' and where there may be differences. Remember: being different is OK – you just need to understand their perspective.

WHAT'S IMPORTANT TO ME?

- Having close friends, seeing new places, trying new experiences?

- Having my own home, financial security, a pension?

- Having support and understanding from friends and sharing activities and fun with them?

- Having close relationships with your family, your friends and their children?

- Having a good meal, flowers on your table, a massage to help you feel pampered?

- Having a good relationship with someone who listens to you, someone who tells you about themselves and their life?

- Having an interesting job, going on holiday, the sun shining – all reasons to get up in the morning?

- Having a new skill or enjoying a new activity to feel stimulated?

Finally, ask yourself the following three questions:

- What makes you more uncomfortable about how people view you – thinking you're unhappy because you're single, or trying to change you?

- What are your feelings about your sexual activity? Are you happy with how things are? Would you be happy being celibate?

- What are the values that shape the way you lead your life – for example, honesty, integrity, love, trust?

I've given you a few examples. You need to do this on your own and make your own list. You may want to add to the questions. Once you've finished and are clear about your values and what's important to you, talk to the friend who makes you feel the most uncomfortable and tell her that, while you care for her deeply, you're worried that there are some stumbling blocks in your relationship.

Ask her how she feels and why she wants to pair you up with someone. Really listen to what she says, as often when communication has gone wobbly it's because both parties aren't listening properly. Ask her to do the above exercise and suggest that you talk about it next time you meet. Share your answers. I think you'll both be surprised how similar they are. But don't forget that it's good to have some differences in a relationship so don't expect or want everything to be the same.

Kay Trimberger, in her book, *The New Single Woman*, looks at the six pillars she thinks are important to single women in mid-life. She talks about 'the pillars of support that allow her to lead a satisfying life', the first three being fundamental: making a home somewhere you feel totally relaxed; having a job that's fulfilling and brings in enough income: and having a network of friends and extended family. Belonging to a community is important, too, as is having a connection to the next generation and accepting one's sexuality.

None of us – whether married, single, divorced or widowed – will achieve all of these to a state of perfection. But, when Kay Trimberger completed her studies and started to share her thoughts with married women, she was surprised to find that these were the pillars for them, too. We really aren't that different!

I have listed some ideas in the Resource List where you can get more thoughts on being single today to help your discussion. Also direct your friends to *http://www.ivillage.co.uk* or send them a copy of their list '52 Reasons Why It Is Great to Be Single': it's a very useful aid. There may even be some you hadn't thought of!

Q3 My husband and I split up about four years ago. We have four children – all adults, two married, two not.

It was all very amicable and we've continued to spend time together, usually at family and friends' events. I'm very content with my single status; he's dated, but nothing serious until recently. Now he's met someone who he sees as a long-term live-in partner. I haven't met her yet. He wants to bring her to events like our grandchildren's birthday parties and he's planning to take her to his family functions rather than me. I hate it. I don't want her to be another grandmother and I don't want to be excluded from his family. I've known them for well over thirty years. What can I do?

I understand how hard this is for you but, as you imply, it's a situation that needs to be tackled. You sound very clear about two things: first, that you're happy as a single woman and second, that you don't want to rekindle your relationship with your ex-husband.

I wonder what you thought the scenario would be when you first split? Did you imagine you'd live in separate homes, lead separate lives but, when there were events in either of your families or with mutual friends, you'd appear as a couple as though nothing had happened? If I may be so bold, isn't that having your cake and eating it? You aren't alone in wanting the good things from a relationship but not the difficult bits. Sadly, as you're discovering, this just isn't how it's going to be.

It's absolutely normal and natural for your ex-husband to want to move on and find a new partner. I know you aren't in that place yourself but, from what you say, you've made a different and conscious decision to be single. It is, of course, understandable that you're reacting to the changes in your ex-husband's personal life and have feelings of resentment, hurt, jealousy, betrayal and so on. However well-managed a separation – and yours sounds as though it went as smoothly as it could – there will inevitably be unresolved feelings and regrets.

Your ex-husband's choice of a new long-term partner will signify to you and your family that your relationship with him is really over. You'll be experiencing again the sense of loss you felt when you separated. You may be feeling it even more acutely than you did then, particularly as you've managed to maintain many of the good parts of your relationship. You have over thirty years of history together and this has been important. You've lived through numerous events together, most happy, some sad, both with your immediate and extended family and now he's found someone else to do this with. No wonder you're feeling sad and angry; no wonder you want this new partner kept in a box and brought out only when you don't want to be there.

It sounds to me as though you haven't fully let go of your past relationship. One reason may be that you still believe that your ex-husband is there to meet your needs, something that undoubtedly happened throughout your marriage. For most people separating or divorcing, this changes at the point of parting but, for you, this has continued up till now. I think it's really important for you to identify what it is you're still holding on to with your ex-husband.

Ask yourself the following questions:

- What does he offer me?

- What do I expect him to do for me?

- What am I missing in my life right now?

- Where can I find that elsewhere?

- What skills do I have to improve my situation?

- Who can I get some support and help from to develop these skills?

- What do I need to do to really let him go?

Some of your answers may be totally practical – you need someone to put up shelving or unblock the sink, for instance. These are things you can easily find someone else to do although it would be unwise to involve your children. Just look in *Yellow Pages* or acquire some DIY skills.

Other answers may relate to more personal issues such as talking about your relationship with your now elderly mother or a rant perhaps about your boss who's been difficult for years. You may have been used to talking to your ex-husband about such matters but there will be others in whom you can confide.

Don't forget that there will always be one area you share together and that's the parenting of your children. Although they're young adults now and certainly don't need you in the way they did when they were little, there will be times when they'll turn to their mother and father for advice of some sort. The pleasures and, as is inevitable, times of difficulty they'll experience can continue to be shared with him. The difference now, though, is that he will also share these things – albeit differently – with his new partner. But you will always be your children's mother. No one else can fill those shoes.

I think it would be helpful to separate out which bits of your life you do still share with your ex-husband and which bits you don't.

SEPARATE LIVES

1. Take a piece of paper and divide it into three columns.

2. Head them, HIS. MINE. OURS.

3. Now write down all the things you consider being yours such as your home, your job, your sister, your nephew, the people or things that are directly to do with you.

4. Do the same for him.

5. Now do the joint column, listing your children, grandchildren and so on.

6. Now go back over the columns and look at where you've placed things.

Have you, as I think that's where they belong, put your former in-laws into his column and your family in yours? If not, think about why not. I understand that you have a close relationship with them and you can certainly maintain the friendship. However, you need to see them at separate times from your ex-husband's family events as you're no longer directly a part of that family. You gave it up when you divorced. His new partner is now becoming part of his family. Of course, there will be events at which you might both be present such as the funeral of an in-law. But that would be because you want to pay your respects.

I remember a client being indignant when both she and her ex-partner had remarried and her ex-mother-in-law died. She was asked to come to the funeral by her sister-in-law with whom she'd remained friendly. When she got there, there was not a place for her to sit with the family and she wasn't asked back to the house afterwards. She hadn't realised that, now there was a new daughter-in-law, she'd been replaced. It was painful as her children were obviously still family members but she wasn't. Sadly, this is an inevitable consequence of separating. It was the first time she'd really grieved the loss of that relationship with all its ramifications,

If you feel upset about the situation, it's important, even if your children are grown up, that you don't discuss your feelings with them. It will cause them difficulties, as they'll feel torn between you and their father. They'll be dealing with all their own feelings about 'Dad's new partner' and they may well talk to you; after all, you're their mum and that's what they do when they're feeling bad. It may be really hard for you to restrain yourself and just listen but helping them manage their feelings is essential. Make sure you don't spoil that special bond you have with them by adding your negative thoughts. Your children need to build a relationship with their father's new partner so allow them to do so without making it difficult for them. The fact they may like her doesn't mean that they don't love you. Much better, in fact, if they enjoy her company rather than having an awkward time whenever they are with their father.

That said, you need to find someone else in whom to confide, a close girlfriend perhaps; there's nothing like unburdening with a jolly good shout, a really effective way to get rid of your anger without letting it make you either ill or bitter.

As horrible as you say it feels, she *will* be another grandmother – of sorts. Your children will only ever have one mother but to your grandchildren, particularly those who are very young or still to be born, your ex-husband's new partner will be a grandmother. It's up to you to make it difficult or easy.

Now think back for a moment to your own life:

- What qualities do you remember in your grandparents?

- What made them good grandparents or bad?

- What are your favourite memories of them?

- Now think about your children's grandparents: what were their positive qualities that your children adored?

- Ask your children what makes a good grandparent.

Once you've identified the ingredients of good grandparenting, all you have to do is be a granny they can rely on, someone who gives them a good time (which doesn't mean buying the most expensive presents) and does special things with them. If you are a 'good' granny, they'll love you unreservedly.

Meeting your ex-husband's new partner is never going to be easy although there's no reason why you shouldn't like her. She's going to be around whatever you feel. Suggest you meet the first time away from an event. It's very hard to meet at a birthday party with everyone watching how you react. Arrange your meeting, with or without your ex-husband being there (whichever you are more comfortable with), at least a couple of days before the family event so you have time to recover if it throws you.

You sound as though you have an excellent relationship with your ex-husband so tell him that you're delighted for him that he's found someone new but it has made you feel a bit wobbly which is why you'd like to meet her before the party. You don't have to do it in either of your houses; you can meet for half-an-hour in a café just to break the ice. But make sure you look after yourself. Arrange to meet a friend afterwards so you can talk all about it and release any pent-up emotion.

It's important to plan beforehand, when we're going to do something we find hard so we get the outcome we desire. Although we can't ever be sure how others will behave, we can certainly behave in ways that are much more likely to get the response we want.

Ask yourself what you want to achieve with this meeting by trying the following exercise:

MEETING PREPARATION

1. What's your goal? How do you want to feel? And how do you want your ex-husband and his new partner to feel – warm, friendly, relaxed, thinking how nice I am?

2. Take a piece of paper and divide it into three columns. Head one column: My Feelings/Thoughts; the second: Their Feelings/Thoughts; and the final one: My Behaviour.

3. Now write down the first word in the left-hand column – 'warm', for example. In the far right-hand column, write down the behaviour you need to exhibit for you to feel this way – 'relaxed', for example – which may involve you arriving at the venue first.

4. When you've completed your column, do the same for their feelings; in other words, if you want them to feel warmly towards you, a smile will help.

5. Do this with all the words. Now look at the behaviour. If there's anything you know you're going to find hard to

do, practise in advance! You know how to make good relationships.

This exercise is also very useful whenever you want to make a good impression such as at a job interview or giving a speech. If you know what you need to do to have the audience eating out of your hands, then that's what you should apply to the situation.

As I've said, I know this isn't going to be easy for you but the better you do the first time, the better it will be for you in the long run. Although first impressions can be changed, it can take a long time so why put yourself and your family through that misery? As long as you make sure you feel good about yourself and your life, you'll find that this – like most difficulties in life – will fade into the past.

Q4 **I'm single again and I don't want to be. I had an affair and my husband left me. The affair was never serious but here I am alone at 52. We'd been married for 16 years; we don't have any children as neither of us ever wanted them. I still love him and want to be with him but he says he wants nothing more to do with me. My family are all appalled at me and have rallied round him. I feel lonely, hurt and cross. How do I pick myself up?**

I expect you've had more than enough of people saying that you brought this on yourself so I won't. I would suggest, though, that you take a look at Section 1 Question 1 so you get a better understanding of what was happening. When we start a new relationship, we very often behave in a similar way and fall into the same traps.

I want to answer your question in two parts – the first, looking at your family's reaction; the second, how to get over a relationship breakdown. It doesn't make it any easier if your behaviour has been part of the cause; the reality of any breakdown is that both partners need to take some responsibility. Neil Sedaka was right when he sang 'Breaking up is hard to do'.

The end of any relationship hurts us enormously because it turns everything upside down and leaves us feeling vulnerable. It often triggers childhood emotions, those that we had with our first carers – in other words, our parents. We connect with that early feeling of abandonment when they left us, however fleetingly. We've all seen children distraught when their mother goes off to the loo! It was perfectly normal behaviour but it still felt scary. For those of you who were left for longer periods – a parent having to go into hospital, for example – this feeling of abandonment may be stronger than for others.

Our brain is a highly complex organ. Paul MacLean, a neuroscientist, suggests in his book, *Triune Brain in Evolution* (1991) that the brain is divided into three parts. The reptilian brain, the inner and most primitive part, is responsible for all our vital functions such as blood circulation, breathing, sleeping and muscle control. The limbic system governs our emotions and instinct for survival, while the cerebral cortex controls our cognitive functions such as thinking, reason and speech.

The limbic brain stores all our memories. For example, when our feelings are hurt, the limbic brain is triggered, remembering all the past hurts we've known. It then sends this information to the cerebellum – that's the conscious part of our brain – and we're reminded of the pain we've felt before.

Memories, past feelings and beliefs all exist together and, when triggered by events in our conscious brain, pop up in no chronological order. The limbic brain has no sense of linear time so it sends all the information as though it were happening now. The result is that we find it difficult to work out what's relevant and what should be sent back to the storehouse because it belongs to the past.

For example, you might find yourself ranting at a friend who turns up two days after your birthday with a present because they forgot to send you a birthday card on the right day. As often happens halfway through a rant, you realise your reaction is way over-the-top. The explanation could be because this latest incident triggered the recollection of, say, your fifth birthday when your father was away working and he didn't remember to send you a card.

I think it would be helpful for you to separate out which of today's feelings are about your family not being there for you now and which are old scars from the past. Spend a few quiet moments asking the following so you will be identifying what relates to now, and what are habitual behaviours:

- Ask yourself if you've had these feelings before

- Make a list of when they occurred

- See if you can work out the origins of some of those feelings

- Address the feelings that are real and relevant today and put the others back until they're needed at some later stage

If you've done all of this honestly, it should now be easier to talk to your family about your current feelings. Whenever we're sad or feeling low or unwell, we instinctively reach out to our first carer.

When the chips are down, I'm constantly surprised by how many of my clients, even in their fifties or sixties, say that all they want is their 'mummy' or 'daddy', often using those childish words. If our parents aren't around, we turn to our close aunts and uncles and our siblings. We also seek solace in nursery food like hot chocolate or tomato soup. There's no shame in any of this so I suggest you comfort yourself like this if it's going to make you feel better.

The people you want and need don't appear to be around for you at the moment and that will be hard. They are, without doubt, cross with you. Let's stop and think why that may be. You've spoilt things, haven't you? They liked your life as it was with you settled with your husband. But that isn't, to my mind, a good enough reason for abandoning you. I suggest you give one of them a call and ask if you can come round and talk. Tell them that you know that you haven't behaved well and you're sorry. Explain that you need them now. You aren't saying they should take your side against your husband but they are your family, you're hurting right now and you want their love and support.

In the case of your mother and father, it sounds to me that you've all reverted to past patterns of behaviour with them being the critical parents and you being the naughty child. What you need to be now is an assertive adult woman and to discuss things in as unemotional way as you can. Don't berate them for their behaviour; that will just exacerbate the situation.

Also remember that it's not just our family who are there for us. Our good friends are usually very willing to help; but you do have to ask them directly. However, as in any split-up, friends are often challenged by not knowing who to support. If you make it clear you're not asking them to be there for only one or other of you, I'm sure they'll be supportive. If you have some friends who are yours alone – you might have met them at work – it might be helpful to seek their support as there's no possibility of divided loyalties.

Let's now turn to how you can get over the break-up. Please take a look at Section 2 Question 5 where I describe the grief cycle. I think it would be useful for you to understand the arc of grief. Believe me, you'll get over this, however lousy you may be feeling now. But, if you're convinced you won't and you find yourself really low and depressed, do talk to your GP or get some counselling help (see the Resource List).

Let's take a look at what is happening by completing this simple exercise:

IN TOUCH WITH YOUR FEELINGS

Answer 'Yes' or 'No' to each of the following.

Do you feel:

a) angry?
b) confused?
c) tearful?
d) ashamed?
e) abandoned?
f) frightened?
g) embarrassed?
h) lonely?
i) disbelieving?
j) a failure?

If you've answered 'Yes' to more than three, and I expect you have, you're still going through a pretty rough time. I'm going to suggest a number of things you can do that will help you to get through this horrible early patch.

Stage one – to be undertaken in this order

I. Change the focus. The more you think about how rotten you feel, the more it will become a self-fulfilling prophecy. You need to think about something different. A useful technique here is:

- Recall a past event that was good. Think of something that was really enjoyable at a time when you weren't with your husband and take yourself back there. Climb into the situation, smell the smells, capture the taste, experience what's going on around you. The better the picture you create, the more it will draw you in and give you pleasure all over again. Practise doing this every time you get a wave of negative emotion that threatens to make you feel miserable again.

- Do some exercise. Get out that aerobic exercise tape, go to the gym or local pool or jog round the park.

- Make sure you don't start skipping work by calling in sick; moping at home will only lengthen your recovery time. Keep up with your friends and get in touch again with old ones who haven't been part of your everyday life.

2. Make sure you don't make contact with your ex-partner unless you have to for practical or legal reasons connected with your separation. Every time you make contact you'll be reminded of what you're missing and feel bad. Take him off the speed dial on your mobile, don't text him,

remove him from your group mail list and any internet sites like Facebook.

3. It sounds from what you say that you're living somewhere away from the marital home. Make this place yours: don't display lots of photos of the two of you together. Of course, when you feel better, it's fine to look at them again and remember with fondness your time together but not now. If you're in the marital home and he's moved out, you need to make it different. Move things around; rearrange the bedroom; get new bedding.

Stage 2 – the order you undertake these is up to you – all have to be done

4. Once you're feeling a bit better and it's not going to take you back to square one, it can be helpful to write down all the things you'd like to say to your ex-partner, both good and bad. Let it all flow on to the paper, no holds barred; no one else is going to read it. Tell him what you liked in the relationship and what you didn't. Tell him you know that you played a big part in its demise and say how sorry you are. Allow yourself to remember that you've been loved and are capable of giving love. This will be really important when you want to start a new relationship.

Once you've said it all and taken time to write it all down (but not too long, otherwise it becomes another way to hang on to the relationship), you should start the next chapter of your life. Buy yourself a plant, either for your garden, window box or indoors. Take your letter somewhere safe and burn it: imagine all the pain evaporating into the air. Now collect the ash and dig it into the soil and plant your plant. Watch it grow from all the goodness you have taken from that relationship. This may sound odd but doing something tangible will help your brain believe that you've moved on.

5. Be aware of how you're feeling; clock the changes in your mood. What makes it better or worse? At some point, you'll find that you're feeling better and maybe for no reason other than you're getting a bit fed up with feeling down in the dumps. I know you aren't there yet but you will be. It's when that starts to happen you'll know it really is time to move on.

6. Do nice things for yourself: have a pamper day, buy new clothes that make you feel good, go and see a film, a play or a concert that your estranged husband wouldn't have gone to. Make a list of all the things you'd like to do and, even if you can't do them right away, you can think about them. What we think about affects how we feel so focus on future treats.

7. Spend some time enjoying yourself and finding out who you are again. You'll be a very different single woman from the one in her mid-thirties. Enjoy this time. It's tempting to embark on a new relationship but, if it's too soon, it won't work. Make sure you're happy with who you are before you start anything new. There isn't a fixed length of time you should wait but remember that you were with your husband for a long time so don't worry if it takes a while.

8. Set new goals and focus on them. Take up a hobby or learn a new skill. Make new friends so you expand your social circle. Take opportunities you couldn't before

because you were one half of a couple: for example, you might even think about working abroad for a time.

9. Learn the lessons from your last relationship so you don't fall into the same trap again. It's easy to say now that you'd never have another affair but you'd be surprised at how many people repeat the mistake. Focus on what went wrong and where the communication broke down that led to your affair. Write it down and consider what you could have done differently. Keep this list to look at, if it is ever needed.

10. Finally, make a list of what you liked about your ex-husband and what worked well in your relationship. Put this list away until you're ready to move on and then get this and the 'nice things to do' list out to remind yourself what you need to do and what you like in a partner.

The list above is not exhaustive; there are plenty of other things you can do so take a look in the Bibliography. Counsellors and therapists can also be very helpful; there are suggestions of where to find one in the Resource List. Also, take a look at Section 5 Question 3 where I discuss finding a good therapist. Remember, it will take time to get back on your feet again so don't be hard on yourself. This will pass and you will start to feel better.

Q5 **I'm a member of a singles group which organises a number of activities: walking, theatre, art galleries, cinema, and occasional weekends away to cities, talks and meals out. The majority of the people are in their late fifties and sixties, some working and some retired. Most are professionals and very well educated. I've done all right for myself as a builder/businessman and I have a reasonable income. My formal education was limited and what I know**

I've picked up on the way. I've met a really lovely woman and we get on well; she says I understand her. She's a senior partner in a city law firm. I'd like to see more of her and take our relationship to the next level and I think she feels the same. However, I know I can't keep up with her intellectually and sometimes find myself unable to follow the conversation at dinner parties with her friends. Am I mad to want to pursue this relationship? My children think I should go for it. I need to find my self-confidence and focus on what I can offer. I don't want to end up the handyman. How can I build up my self-esteem?

How lovely that you've met someone you like and get on well with. I think your children are spot on: of course you should continue the relationship. When we don't feel good about ourselves, it's hard to see a way forward. Our head fills up with a succession of negative messages, we put ourselves down and then we wonder why we feel unhappy. You certainly wouldn't be the first or the last to have found what you've been looking for, felt overwhelmed by the situation and sabotaged something that could have meant a lot to you. Fortunately, you're aware of this and, with a bit of a boost to your self-confidence, there's no reason why things won't go from strength to strength.

You've joined a singles group that offers certain sorts of activities; I assume they are all things you enjoy. Most of the activities you list involve brain not brawn. The likelihood, therefore, was that you'd be meeting others who wanted to pursue these types of activity. For some reason, their conversation has triggered what I believe is old thinking and you've ended up feeling inadequate. Part of you now wants to pursue this woman and rightly thinks you're just as good as anyone else while the other part is wracked with self-doubt.

In our day, doing well at school and achieving academically equalled being clever and intelligent. The opposite therefore followed: those without good grades were stupid. Yet, if we take a look at your life, you've done well, both financially and in creating a business but to you that doesn't appear to count for anything!

You will not be alone in thinking no qualifications equals lack of intelligence. Intellectual intelligence (or what I think in your case would be more appropriately labelled academic intelligence) is the ability to learn consciously, using cognitive, analytic and language skills as well as logical reasoning. The way these abilities were tested at school was through a series of exams starting with the 11+. Since the baby boomers were at school there has been a lot of work undertaken on intelligence and a new idea – emotional intelligence – has emerged. This is our ability to recognise, understand and manage emotions in others and ourselves.

These skills come from a different part of our brain: intellectual intelligence from the cerebral cortex and emotional intelligence from the limbic system. Several psychologists have defined emotional intelligence. Daniel Goleman sees it as 'the capacity for recognising our own feelings and those of others, for motivating ourselves, and for managing emotions well in ourselves and our relationships' (See Resource List). Our emotional intelligence can be learnt and developed over our lifetime. Our intellectual intelligence tends to stay the same.

In the 1950s and 1960s when you were at school, the style of teaching was very didactic and only suited one type of learner. If that wasn't your style, you were unlikely to achieve academically and the message you'll have got from your teachers was that you weren't very bright. Those who responded to this type of teaching developed a style of behaviour and thinking that went along with 'being bright' and learned to talk and discuss issues in a particular way, something they continue to do years later.

Much has been written about the academic who has a high IQ but is not able to relate emotionally to people, often being unable to make deep emotional connections but being very good at pontificating on a theory. I don't expect your new partner is looking for someone who can recite a legal textbook to her; she probably gets enough of that at work. No, what she's looking for is someone in tune with her as a person, someone to whom she can feel emotionally close and it sounds as though you could be that person!

It would be useful for you to ask yourself the following questions:

- Why does she like me?

- What attracted her to me?

- What attracted me to her?

- What are all the things I have to offer?

- What are all the things I want from a relationship?

- What are all the things I think she wants out of a relationship? (If you haven't asked her, you could start your list by listing everything she's told you she enjoys.)

One thing I do know is that, if you're going to have a successful relationship, you need to be able to talk to the other person about your concerns as well as enjoying the good bits. You also need to discuss with her your joint objectives. It's important to be clear that both of you are looking for the same thing, otherwise you could end up being disappointed. I don't expect she's looking for someone to have the dinner party conversations with; she's got friends for that! Also, I expect, if you felt a bit better about yourself, you'd stop having a problem with those conversations.

There are two key things you need to look at if you're going to make a real change inside yourself and feel good in this relationship. One is your self-belief. You believe that, because you didn't get great academic qualifications, your partner is more able than you and that she'll get bored with you or use you as a convenient handyman. I think that belief is nearly as old as you! You're stuck in the past, probably at 11 when – and I'm making an assumption – you failed the 11+ and were relegated to the C-stream. It saddens me how many 50- to 60-year-olds I meet who still define their intelligence by their success or failure in that exam. It really is time you forgot about it. Please take a look at Question 6 in this section where I discuss changing your beliefs. It's important that you work on your beliefs whether you're with her or not as this has a profound effect on how you manage your life.

Now for the other key part of the equation: your self-confidence, which is vital in almost every aspect of our lives. Self-confident people inspire confidence in others and that's what we want to see in our partners. Our level of confidence shows in the way we speak, our body language, what we say, how we say it, how we hold ourselves and so on.

I suggest you try the following exercise:

1. Think of three people you know who are very confident.

2. Write down what it is they do that lets you know they are confident. Use this as your confidence checklist.

3. Now take each of these components and think of occasions when you've used them yourself.

4. Think of a time when you want to be really confident and run the scenario through your mind as though you were there using all the positives. Go through your confidence checklist and check you've included all the components.

5. Practise this so that you become efficient at displaying confidence whenever you need it.

It's amazing how, once you 'put on' confidence, your brain responds with the appropriate message and, within minutes, you're feeling good. Your perception of yourself has an enormous impact on how others perceive you. Perception is reality – the more self-confidence you have, the more likely it is you'll succeed.

Tips to increase confidence:

1. Do what you believe is right – don't worry what others think. If you feel confident, you'll feel able to manage any challenge.

2. Be willing to take risks, not daft ones that could harm you or others but the determination to stick with this relationship, for example, even if you're a bit nervous.

3. Admit if you make mistakes and then learn from them. Admitting mistakes with humour often changes the focus.

4. Dress in a way that makes you feel good.

5. Keep physically fit. This will increase your energy.

6. Walk faster – confident people walk with a spring in their step. If you look tired or slow, you give a very different impression.

7. Sit tall and straight and attentive at dinner parties. Look interested and smile. If there are already a lot of talkers, you don't need to talk too; just show how interested you are and everyone will think you've taken part.

8. Create your own motivational speech. Write down all the things you're good at. Recall your past successes, unique skills, loving relationships and what you bring to them. Prepare a one-minute talk and repeat it to yourself ten times daily until you really believe it. If you're prepared, you won't feel tongue-tied if asked about yourself. You'll know what you have to offer.

9. Too often, we get caught up in our own concerns. We focus too much on ourselves and not enough on the needs of other people, and this can became habitual. If you become too self-absorbed with your problems, this will make you focus on the negatives. So start observing *you*. When you catch yourself at it, say 'stop' and put something else into your head.

10. When we think negatively about ourselves, we often project that feeling on to others and everyone feels bad. A good way to break this cycle is to look outwards and pay others compliments. Being able to give compliments and accept them graciously is a sign of an inner confidence.

11. When you have something to say, speak up. If you follow the first tip, you won't be worrying about what people

think. Most people are much more accepting than we imagine; in fact, most people are dealing with the exact same fears. They just hide it well.

12. Focus on what you have physically, emotionally and materially. Set aside time each day to mentally list everything you have to be grateful for.

13. Focus on your goal and what you want and stop any negative self-talk that drifts unwanted into your consciousness.

Every time you waver and think of your weaknesses, bring out that motivational speech and, metaphorically speaking, shout it from the rooftops. Just one last thought: don't neglect your strengths. Being able to do DIY is no mean feat so, if I were you, I'd dine out on it!

Q6 **My last long-term partnership ended five years ago after seven years together. I had previously been married for seventeen years and have two adult children from that marriage. I've also had a couple of very casual short relationships but nothing serious. My last relationship's ending was seriously unpleasant and the one before was pretty grim. I felt so rejected and hurt each time that I can't bear the thought of going through that again. How do I get over this fear as I know it's limiting my chances of finding a new partner? I'd really like another live-in relationship.**

You've been through a lot so it's not surprising that you're feeling anxious. We're very good at protecting ourselves from things that hurt us with a well-developed biological mechanism that comes into play when we sense we're in danger. It's called the flight or fight response. We either go into battle or we run in the opposite direction.

When it comes to your response to fear, it sounds as if your instinct is to run! I'm sure this was the right thing to do when your last serious relationship ended because it protected you from potential hurt. But I'd say it's now time for you to move on. Sometimes, however, ways of behaviour that have been useful to us in the past become a habit and, although they are no longer helpful, we continue to use them even though they prevent us from getting what we want.

Don't give yourself a hard time because you've had a five-year gap. Of course it's important to allow yourself enough time to fully get over a past relationship so you don't embark upon another on the rebound. These types of relationship often don't last and leave us with reduced self-esteem, feeding the belief that we are bad relationship material.

I think there are a few things holding you back from starting a new, fulfilling relationship. Your fear of rejection and the process of separation are chief among them but you shouldn't overlook the beliefs to which you're clinging about yourself. You also now need to consider letting go completely of memories of past relationships.

Let's start by looking at your fear of rejection. When we fear something, we usually have a number of thoughts going round in our head. For example, we fear that we won't be accepted for who we are; we fear exposing our inner feelings and desires in case they're rubbished and we are hurt again; we fear being intimate; and we fear the misery of being left and the loneliness that will follow in the wake of being rejected. And initially, of course, we fear all the nastiness connected with the end of a relationship and then the business of having to separate all our belongings.

So what does feeling fearful do for us?

1. It can make us more cautious when we're with others so we give very little of ourselves. The result, as you've found from your own experience, can be casual and fairly superficial relationships.

2. It can also result in us becoming more willing to do anything that makes us feel accepted and then we find ourselves in a relationship that isn't good for us.

3. We may find that we lose our ability to be creative and we feel constrained.

4. We lose the ability to make good choices and to be able to solve problems.

5. We find ourselves doing all the things we know will make a relationship end: being anxious, trying to over-please, watching for any sign the new partner may be irritated with us, being over-demanding and so on. In short, we create exactly what we most fear and then pat ourselves on the back and say, 'Well, that's what I expected. I knew it wouldn't last.' It leaves us precisely where we don't want to be – in a frightened state! The fear can be paralysing and leave us unable to get what we want.

So, to answer my own question: 'What does it do for us?' It doesn't help us to find a new relationship – quite the opposite, in fact!

I think you've done enough thinking about your situation. (See Section 5 Question 6). What would help you now is to address your unconscious beliefs, the messages from your past that seem to run your present even though they're outdated.

A good way to start is to think about other things in your life that have made you frightened and that are you no longer afraid of.

PAST FEARS

1. Make a list of at least five things that frightened you in the past.

2. Take the first one and run through it in your head from when you had the fear till when it was gone. Imagine you're back there in the same situation. What helped you lose that fear? For example, you might have been frightened of the dark and now you aren't. Once you know what helped, jot down the components.

3. Repeat the above step for all of your old fears.

4. You now have a list of what helped you in the past. How can you access this help now? Did you find talking to a friend helpful? Then think of a friend now who would understand and give them a call and arrange to meet. Or it may have been reading a book on the subject that drew the sting from the fear. Take a look at the Bibliography for some ideas.

Once you've completed the above exercise, try the next one. It will help you turn your fear around.

MAKING FEAR WORK POSITIVELY

1. Think about where you hold your fear in your body. It may sit in your shoulders, or give you a tight neck, or headaches. If you were to give it a colour what would it be? Does it have a sound or a taste or a smell? Identify them. And don't be frightened: making it tangible will help you conquer it.

2. Now imagine a circle in front of you. In this circle is fearlessness. Walk into the circle and think of a time you did something really well, a time when you felt confident to tackle anything put in front of you. Take yourself back to that time and be there as if it were now. Feel all those great feelings.

3. Now step out of the circle and find a new situation where you felt good and powerful and then climb in again and relive those feelings. Do it twice.

4. Now imagine yourself going on a date with a person with whom you'd like a relationship. I expect just thinking about it makes you frightened. So climb into your fearlessness circle and put on all those positive feelings you had when you were thinking about good situations. How do you feel now? Do this part of the exercise three times, or more if needed, until you feel able to meet the challenge and your fear has gone. Test your fear by trying to recreate it. What colour is it now? Does it still have a sound, smell or taste? Even if there's a bit lingering, it will have much less power.

5. Any time you feel frightened again, just get into your circle and experience that feeling of fearlessness.

Apart from fear, there can be other things that get in the way of finding meaningful new relationships. An important one is unresolved issues of resentment. As long as we harbour old resentments, we'll be unable to truly give our love to someone.

The following exercise can help you lose those resentments. It's based on one suggested by Ulli Springett in her book, *Soulmate Relationships*.

LETTING GO OF RESENTMENT

Make a list of all your partners. Go right back to your first boyfriend, however long ago that might be. Add your parent of the opposite sex as they often lay the foundation stones for your feelings.

1. Imagine each person on your list, in turn, coming to visit you now in your home. How do you feel about them? Warm or angry or fearful or low? Some you will feel very positive about.

2. Every time you feel a negative feeling towards someone, say to them in your head, 'Although I don't condone your behaviour, I will now stop disliking or hating you so we can both be free.' Imagine you're cutting the ties between the two of you with a knife. Once you can feel indifferent about a person, they will no longer influence the way you behave.

3. Write to them (you don't have to post the letter!) or speak to them, again in your head, and tell them you don't have any negative feelings towards them and wish them well. If you find yourself needing a response, go back to step two because the ties are still there.

4. Finally, make a list of all the good things you've gained from your relationships – your first orgasm, your children and so on – and thank them for what they've given you. The more positive you can feel, the more open you'll be to new relationships.

Now we need to look at your beliefs. If, as you say, your past relationships have not been totally successful, you'll have built up a number of beliefs about the opposite sex that won't be very helpful. For example, if you believe all partners will dump you and hurt you, you are going to be hesitant to put your all into a new relationship. If you believe you're lousy at relationships and you can never make them work, you're likely to get just that.

BELIEFS (THIS WORKS EQUALLY FOR MEN AND FOR WOMEN: JUST ADAPT TO FIT)

1. What generalised beliefs do you hold about men? Take a piece of paper and complete this sentence: Men are . . . Make as long a list as you can.

2. Now fill in the following sentences in the same way:
   Relationships are . . .
   I'm no good at relationships because . . .
   Good relationships are . . .
   I deserve . . .
   At my age, all I can expect from a relationship is . . .

3. Now turn these negative beliefs into something positive e.g.

   Negative belief: *I'm too old to find a new relationship* change to

Positive belief: There is no age limit to love.

Negative belief: *All men are bad at relationships* change to

Positive belief: Some men maintain long-term and happy relationships.

4. Whenever you find yourself saying something negative, turn it round. Our thinking is habitual and if you start putting positive messages into your head, this is what you'll begin to believe. To change a habit, you need to do this at least twenty times. Your aim should be to build up your positive-thinking muscle. The more you do this, the more you'll start to feel positive.

You said that the ending of your last long-term relationship was 'seriously unpleasant'. I don't know if you were just referring to the emotional side or to the practicalities. If you create a home together with someone, then everything has to be dismantled and that process in itself can be very painful.

I hope your next relationship flourishes for the rest of your days but I can't promise you that things won't go wrong. What you can do, though, is develop the skills to create a good relationship so you minimise the chance of failure.

In Section 1 Question 6, I look at the practicalities of a partnership to help you decide how you want to manage next time you live with someone. Let's hope you're now ready to find a soulmate. Once you feel secure enough to move forward, I suggest you read that answer as it will steer you in the right direction to find the perfect partner for you.

Q7 **I'm 57 and I came out of a very difficult relationship seven years ago and have now met a new partner. He was on a secondment to my place of work. We've had a fabulous six months together as a couple. I never thought I would be this happy again. He's everything I've been looking for except that he has a job at the other end of the country. I have two children, three grandchildren, lots of local friends and a job I love. He has a pretty similar set-up in his part of the world and he's really missed his family. I don't want to give up my current life and I don't want to give him up, either. What can I do?**

I wonder how you're defining the word 'couple'? I expect, if I may be so bold, in a rather limited way! As a generation, we were brought up to believe there was only one way but you, like many others, have already taken a different path. If you believe a committed relationship has to include living together, sharing a bank account, doing all the chores for each other and so on, then you're right: living several hundred miles from one another won't be enough for you. On the other hand, there's no guarantee you'd be 100 per cent happy if you were together 24/7.

Consider for a moment what makes a committed relationship. A fundamental factor must be that both parties are willing to put an equal amount of energy into the relationship and really want it to work. The key to cultivating a committed relationship is making it of primary importance. This doesn't mean that you neglect other important relationships or that you spend every minute with each other but being together does need to be high on the agenda. You also need to make sure that you create enough space for the two of you so that, when you are together, it's good quality time. A further essential is to create special couple rituals such as talking to each other on a daily basis or agreeing certain activities you'll share. The internet and mobile phones make this so much easier. For instance, you can sit in your separate homes and watch the same TV programme (although watch those phone bills!). One way to get around this is to use systems such as Skype: you can talk for free and see each other.

This type of relationship needs to worked on carefully if you're not to drift apart. You have to make a really conscious effort to keep things going although, for many, the upside is that you're always striving to show your better side. There's less rowing about whose turn it is to cook dinner or do the dishes and more opportunity to feel pleased to be able to do these things for each other.

The lifestyle I'm suggesting is not that unusual. A new demographic category has been identified to describe couples who live apart – LAT relationships or Living Apart Together. According to a survey-based study published in 2006 by John Haskey, a statistician at the Department of Social Policy at Oxford University, there are approximately a million couples in Great Britain in LAT relationships and as many as 14 per cent of all 50 to 59 year olds. This trend can also be seen in many European countries as well as in the US, Canada and Australia. David Popenoe, a sociologist with Rutgers University National Marriage Project, suggests that those figures will increase for the baby boomer generation as more of us enter our older years as divorcees. The trend will be, says Popenoe, that we'll want 'to form committed romantic relationships without sharing a residence'.

For some couples, this type of relationship is favoured as a way of keeping financial matters separate and thus reducing some of the difficulties that can arise around inheritance when both partners have their own families. For others, it means they can, like you, maintain their own individual lives, manage their family relationships and also have a committed intimate relationship. Many baby boomers who have lived for a while on their own welcome the opportunity to maintain their own space and place while also enjoying a long-distance relationship. Your LAT relationship has an added dimension as you are living a long distance apart, so popping in for a cup of tea is not possible. You need to build into the relationship the equivalent – like regular calls, texts and emails so you are part of each other's lives although not living in the same place.

I think that, if both of you see eye-to-eye on what you want from the relationship, and you arrange your lives accordingly, you'll be surprised how you can enjoy the best of both worlds.

❧ Section Four ❧

New Relationships

Q1 I divorced a number of years ago and, after having been on my own for quite a while, I met a new man and moved in and married him after a short romance. That was five years ago. Fairly early on in our relationship, I found out that he liked to wear women's clothes. At that time, it was only occasionally at home and, although I found it difficult, I accepted it. Since then, it has gradually become more important to him and he spends a lot of time dressed as a woman. He even wants me to go out with him dressed like that which I find hard. Recently, he announced that he's considering changing his gender as he wants to live as a woman. I still love him but I'm not at all sure I can cope with this. I feel as though I've lost my husband.

This is certainly not easy. It raises very fundamental issues about gender, values, beliefs and decisions about what you want from a relationship.

I'd like to start by defining some of the terms used. You will see, if you look at both the Resource List and the Bibliography, that there is some discussion at present about the terms used. Some prefer the word 'transgender' to unite people whose definition of gender is outside the generally accepted norm while others prefer to use more specific terms. There are pros and cons for both.

Almost everyone is born either as a boy or a girl, the physical differences that are manifested defining our sex. But a very small minority are intersex. These are individuals born with anatomy or physiology which differs from contemporary ideals of what constitutes 'normal' male and female bodies. Our sex is very different from our gender which is the term used for our inner sense of knowing who we are – for example, man or woman and our gender role in society. Our sexual orientation is who we are attracted to sexually. We're classified as heterosexuals if we fancy someone of the opposite sex, homosexual if we fancy someone of the same sex and bisexual if we fancy both sexes.

People who cross-dress are known as transvestite from the Latin 'trans' meaning across and 'vestire' to dress. The term was apparently coined in the early 1900s by Magnus Hirschfeld to describe people who voluntarily wore clothes of the opposite sex. The majority of transvestites are male and heterosexual; it's estimated that only 10 per cent are gay or bisexual, the same percentage as that of gays or bisexuals in the general population. Most transvestites both fantasise about women and have sex with them. Many are happy with their role as boyfriend, husband and father and enjoy being men. Most don't want to become a woman; they just want to be like them and dress like them. Cross-dressing helps them to express their more feminine side. This is part of who they are and, without being able to express this part of their psychological make-up, they find life difficult and restricted.

A transvestite has a deep-seated need to wear women's clothing and act and feel like the opposite sex. Most transvestites will tell you that they have felt like this for a long time; many say they knew when they were as young as five and dressed up in their mother's clothes or put on their lipstick. They knew deep down this was wrong and they therefore suppressed these feelings but they didn't go away. According to a survey of just over a thousand

British transvestite men in 1995 by Dr Vernon Coleman and revealed in his book, *Men in Dresses*, the age of a cross-dresser ranges from being very young to those starting in their fifties, sixties and seventies. Many are concerned about being found out and fear they will lose their jobs or destroy their marriages and therefore keep it a secret.

Coleman asked various questions in his survey including:

- Does your partner know about your transvestism? Almost three-quarters said yes.

- Does she approve? 43 per cent said yes.

- Have you been out of the house dressed as a woman? 47 per cent said they had but only at night and not with their partners.

Most transvestites, like your husband, start slowly – they may just wear women's knickers under their trousers so no one knows – and then slowly graduate to wearing wigs and jewellery. You say that you've accepted this part of your husband which is the best thing you can do, as this is part of him and won't go away, even if you forbid it. That doesn't mean you have to like it or stay in the relationship but asking him to be different will have a detrimental effect on his psyche.

There are a host of theories as to why men cross-dress. Many say it helps to reduce stress: they find the need to dress up more when they're having problems at work or at home because it helps them escape the pressures to succeed as a man. For some men, wearing silky underwear under their male clothes makes them relax while others want to dress in as feminine a way as possible, including full make-up and jewellery. Some want to spend most of their time dressed as a woman and others very little. Many develop a 'feminine self' – in other words, a cross-gender identity. Helen Boyd in her book, *My Husband Betty*, discusses her life with her husband and his feminine side and how they've managed this within their relationship. You might find this helpful to read.

Some men – and it sounds from what you've said that this is how your husband is feeling – are uncomfortable with being a man. They don't feel male inside and they want to change their sex. This is not true of the majority of transvestites who, according to Vernon Coleman's survey, are very happy to be a man who cross-dresses and have no desire for a sex change. Only 23 per cent said that they'd have the operation if they had the opportunity.

Those who want to undergo the transition from man to woman have a sexual identification entirely with the opposite sex and are defined medically as having gender dysphoria, meaning a deep and chronic feeling of discontent with their gender. A transsexual is a person who is born with all the appearances of a particular physical sex but is aware of having a different gender identity. Gender dysphoria is rare but increasing numbers of people with the condition are coming forward as it becomes more acceptable in society. It's estimated that one in four thousand people is receiving medical help for the condition in the UK at present – which means it is likely there are a lot more who have not yet sought help. Transsexuality occurs in both physical males and physical females, while most transvestites are men.

It's not unusual for someone as they approach middle age and begin to face their own mortality to feel that they can no longer repress those feelings about their gender and want to do something before it's too late. I have no evidence for this but I wonder now that we're living longer, alongside a liberalisation in societal views, whether this will be another area where we'll see many more 50+

people being able to make changes in their life that they didn't feel able to do earlier, knowing they probably still have thirty years more of active life. Some who have gender dysphoria feel that they need to undergo a complete change and submit to radical surgery, others choose to dress and live in line with their preferred gender identity and some will take hormones to change their appearance.

Being open about who we are is an essential element in a good relationship and it sounds as though you and your husband have found a way to discuss these issues honestly. Now it's really important with so major a change being contemplated by your husband that he takes full responsibility for his actions. This isn't something that you can help him decide and nor is it something for which you can be blamed if he decides against it because of your feelings.

The transition process itself takes time – the minimum is two years and it can be as long as five – so you'll have the opportunity to decide whether you can stay in this relationship as partners. It's very important that you understand the process that your partner will go through if he makes that decision and that you are well informed. It's essential you talk both with a medical practitioner and have some counselling help (see the Resource List and www.pinktherapy.com).

I'm making the assumption from your question that you don't have children but all your other relatives and friends will also be affected by your husband's decision, particularly since it sounds as if he's not 'out' as a cross-dresser. You're now being faced with something that wasn't part of the deal when you went into the relationship. You will suffer a loss and you may well already be feeling this; you'll be losing the man you chose. No doubt you'll want an intimate and close relationship with your husband if you choose to stay in the marriage but it cannot, of course, be the same.

You'll go through the grief cycle (see Section 2 Question 5). This process is particularly hard in your situation because you'll be mourning someone who's still there, someone who's going through a transition in front of your eyes. You will also have the fear of how you'll cope with your husband as he disappears and changes into someone else. It sounds to me as if the two of you have already done some of the work necessary as a couple to find a way through this as you've been faced with circumstances you hadn't planned for and survived.

If he goes ahead with his decision, your husband will be moving forward into his new life where he'll feel able to be himself in a way that hasn't been possible up till now. He may be fearful about the unknown but he won't be suffering the loss you'll be feeling. Together you need to decide how you can manage what lies ahead with each step needing to be taken at a pace that's good for both of you.

As well as the external physical changes, your husband's new identity will also alter how you relate to each other sexually. How do you feel about having a sexual relationship with a woman? Is this something that you would find possible? I heard two couples talking on a radio programme: one woman had been able to find a way to be physically intimate with her sex-change partner while another found it impossible to continue an intimate physical relationship, although the friendship and love between them remained strong enough for them to stay together.

We define our sexuality and ourselves by our interactions and responses in relation to others. This change in your partner will affect your view of yourself and how you position yourself in the world. If you continue to live with your husband after his sex change and share his bed, some people will perceive you as a lesbian and that will challenge your own identity. Whatever others say, it's imperative that you feel good in a redefined relationship. No one can know what's right for someone else and, although there are examples such as Jan Morris who in June 2008 went through a civil partnership with the woman she first married when she was a man in 1949, not everyone will feel able to do this. It wouldn't mean you didn't love your partner any more but that this was no longer the right relationship for you.

I strongly suggest you talk to a therapist who specialises in transgenderism who can help you to look at all the issues. One exercise that you could do on your own is to look at all the pros and cons for staying and for going. Discuss these with your husband and see which of these you could work on together. I can't pretend it's going to be easy but I wish you well.

Q2 **I'm 58 and I'm having a great time sexually since I came out of a long-term relationship. I'm heavily into cybersex. Some of my friends think it's perverted and they've commented that I'm not as sociable as I used to be. It suits me fine as I can stay at home, don't have to be judged physically and can have safe sex with lots of people. The drawback is I'm still on my own when the screen goes off. Is this an addiction and is it bad for me? What can I do instead?**

First of all, I think we need to define terms. Cybersex is any form of sexual expression to be found on the internet. Currently, over 60 per cent of all visits to the internet have some sexual purpose. Cybersex includes viewing and downloading pornography, playing sexual fantasy games, reading and writing sexually explicit letters and stories, emailing to meet people for sex, placing ads specifically to meet for sex, visiting sex chat rooms, online sex by engaging in sexual activity with webcams so you can see each other and, at worst, engaging with adolescents or children online. (Cybersex does not, in my opinion, include dating lines where the purpose is to make a relationship which, nonetheless, may at some point go on to involve sexual activity.)

I think the fact that you've asked this question shows that you have some concerns about your sexual behaviour. Before we discuss that, though, let's look at the internet in general, and addiction in particular, and then address your specific dilemma.

The internet has become an ever-increasing part of many people's lives. The last set of figures published by National Statistics UK in August 2008 shows that there are still less 65+ using the internet than other groups, however this is increasing by three per cent each year. In the 55–64 group nearly 70 per cent are regularly on line. The internet has transformed our culture and our way of communicating as profoundly as the introduction of the telephone in 1876.

Using the internet is not a problem in itself. It's only when it starts to affect how you live your life and conduct your relationships that there's potential trouble. It's estimated according to Michael G. Conner, a clinical, medical and family psychologist in Oregon, USA, working in the field of cybersex addiction, that about 20 per cent of us will become heavy users; that's people who spend more than 18 hours a week in non-work-related activities on the computer (source: crisiscounseling.com).

An easy way to define whether you're a heavy user and have a possible addiction is by answering the following questions:

DO I HAVE AN INTERNET ADDICTION?

1. Do you feel better when you're on the net and miserable when you stop?

2. Do you spend an increasing amount of time on it?

3. Is it preventing you from doing other things?

4. Are you finding yourself trying to limit the time spent on it because you know it's too much?

If you can answer yes to all of these, you're probably becoming borderline compulsive and it's definitely worth thinking about your behaviour and ways you can change it. If you're unable to do this yourself, there are lots of places that can help you (See the Resource List).

The internet is without doubt a great source of information; you can find out about pretty much anything instantly as well as shop for food, a huge range of goods and holidays, houses and cars. It's also a source of a wide variety of sexual information and activity and is leading a new sexual revolution in online sex.

Moreover, there are spin-offs which include phone sex with people online, online relationships and those that develop into real relationships and partnerships. The internet offers a new way to have a sexual experience. If used wisely, it's a great place to learn about people, explore new relationships and make social connections.

In a survey of 4,000 readers of the *Sun* in early 2008, the paper's agony aunt, Deidre Sanders, reported that a quarter of those who took part had used the internet to cheat on their partners by having an online 'affair', a third had used it to start a sexual relationship and 10 per cent of this group had had sex with at least eleven people they met online. She concluded that many are using the internet for casual sex and for sex via a webcam and not to meet someone for a long-lasting relationship.

Until recently, men were the more frequent users of the internet and cybersex, but this has changed over the last couple of years and women now go online more than men. It seems that the 'Men are from Mars, Women are from Venus' theory is true on the internet as well, as men and women look for different experiences while surfing the net. Men seek out more pornography than women and also look for games that offer them the opportunity to take on fantasy roles and act out their fantasies. Women look for support and relationships and a place to air their views about their lives and their 'real life' relationships.

Both men and women use the internet equally for 'cybering,' consensual discussion online for sexual arousal. Joan Sauers undertook an anonymous survey of 2,000 women when researching her book, *Sex Lives of Australian Women* (2008). She reveals that one in five women admitted to having a sexual encounter in an internet chat room with many reporting, as you imply, that the cybersex was both empowering and safe. Surprisingly, of those women polled, those in their twenties were the most avid participants in cybersex – some 26 per cent – very closely followed by those in their fifties (21 per cent). She also reported that women are getting hooked on text sex.

A whole raft of activities can be included under the umbrella of internet sex. These include chat rooms where people talk sexually and may have webcam sex, instant messaging systems and online games and/or virtual worlds where characters are created and interrelate with each other. Some people then move on from onscreen activity and seek out some of these activities for real. This can be extremely dangerous as you're meeting total strangers who might be safe to engage with when in a different 'room' but not in person.

The internet offers people anonymity: you can conceal your age, sex, marital status, race, profession and appearance. You can be whoever you want. The psychologist, Michael G. Conner says that over half of people online lie about their age, weight, job, marital status and gender.

The internet is available 24/7, your own private world you can visit to make friends and have sex without having to leave your front room; and it's always there. You don't have to be brave to go on the internet. Nobody need know you're shy; you only have to say what you choose. If someone doesn't like what you say, you can sign off and register again as someone different. It enables people to behave in ways they couldn't in real life as well as explore sexual fantasies and masturbate while looking at erotic images. When they're on the net, many people go into a disassociated state, entering a 'cyber reality'. This is really no different from when you watch too much TV and go into a semi-hypnotic state, unaware of the rest of the world going on around you. The same can happen when you get absorbed in a good book, the difference being that the book finishes but the internet is never-ending.

Cybersex allows access to a wide range of sexual material – and we're all exposed to this, whether we like it or not. When I turn on my computer in the morning, I have to delete numerous emails inviting me to partake in some sort of sexual activity or to buy some sex-enhancing drug. Anyone who is curious will at some point take a peek and, if it catches their imagination, will look further. Also, cross links can sometimes take you into areas you hadn't expected to go and you find yourself viewing something you had no idea existed. Even something unpleasant can give a rush of excitement and change your mood.

Cybersex is a specific type of internet addiction. It's thought that up to 10 per cent of users become addicts. The American Psychological Association suggests that, if a person is spending eleven hours or more online on sexual pursuits per week and/or admits it interferes with other areas of their life, this is evidence of psychological distress and compulsive behaviour.

An internet or cybersex addiction is the same as any other compulsive disorder such as drug use, alcohol, gambling, over-eating and watching too much TV. Addiction is defined as a dependence on something that can dominate your life. If you use sex sites to an excessive degree and you put other things aside in order to do so, you have some sort of addiction. Internet addiction is the source of many relationship problems and according to Dr David Greenfield, an expert in internet addiction, it is cited in many divorces. (See Bibliography).

By now, you should have a sense of whether you're addicted to cybersex and also some idea as to why you're using this as the place to have sex. As you asked about whether you're addicted, try this self-assessment test that was developed by Dr Kimberly Young. It pinpoints the common warning signs of an addiction. There are a number of other self-assessment quizzes on the internet that you can do, a good example of the fact that anything can be found online!

ARE YOU ADDICTED TO CYBERSEX?

Answer yes or no to the following statements:

1. Do you routinely spend time in sex chat rooms or via instant messaging with the sole purpose of seeking out cybersex?

2. Do you feel preoccupied with using the internet for cybersex?

3. Do you frequently use anonymous communication to engage in sexual fantasies not typically carried out in real life?

4. Do you anticipate your next online session will result in sexual arousal or gratification?

5. Do you move from cybersex to phone sex or even real-life meetings?

6. Do you hide your online activities from your partner?

7. Do you feel guilt or shame about your online use?

8. Did you accidentally become aroused by cybersex at first, and now find that you actively seek it out when you log online?

9. Do you masturbate when having cybersex or looking at online pornography?

10. Do you feel less interest in your real-life sexual partner, preferring cybersex as a primary form of sexual gratification?

If you answered yes to any of the above questions, you may be addicted to cybersex.

With the availability of adult sites and sex chat rooms, more and more people like yourself have come to worry that their initial curiosity may turn into an addiction. Addiction begins with the basic pleasure and reward pathways in the brain producing a chemical dopamine which creates an enhanced feeling, something that happens naturally during pleasurable acts such as eating.

Substances such as alcohol or activities like gambling or having cybersex can all induce this effect on the brain, the circuit which can lead to both addiction and dependence as we want to repeat this pleasurable sensation.

You said that you'd recently come out of a relationship and had found a way to enjoy yourself on the internet. At the start, I'm sure this was easier for you as you didn't have to venture out or risk being rejected or your friends trying to find you a date. However, I wonder if it's now time for you to move on and establish new real-life relationships?

It's irrelevant what your friends think about your cybersex activity as long as you're behaving responsibly and only engaging with consenting adults; that's your choice. But what those friends may have noticed is that you're withdrawing into your own private world and are no longer being as sociable as before – and that's not a very healthy sign. This must have sounded alarm bells for you, otherwise you wouldn't have written to me.

I suggest you read the other answers in this section and Section 3 Question 1 where I give lots of ideas about how to find a new relationship with someone who'd be with you whether the computer was turned on or off!

Q3 **I'm in a newish relationship and I'm feeling rather anxious about the sex. My partner is much more sexually experienced than me. I am 58 and I was married for over thirty years but, sadly, my husband died a couple of years ago. Our sex life had never been very adventurous. I was aware there were other things out there but really didn't know much about them. I went on to the internet to have a look and found myself faced with porn sites which aren't to my taste at all.**

Sex with my new partner has been all right so far but he keeps asking me what I'm into and I just don't know what to say. I've no idea what you can do. I don't want to get into something horrid or scary but I don't mind trying something new. Or am I too old for that kind of caper?

You're never too old to ... is my motto! Without wanting to sound totally unrealistic, there's very little we're too old for. We tend to use age as an excuse when the reality is that we'd never have done whatever it is at any age. I could say I'm too old to hang-glide. I've no idea if that's true or not. What is true is that I've never wanted to do it so age is just the excuse! When it comes to sex, there may be positions you find less comfortable or need to do differently (see Section 3 Question 1) but you're certainly not too old to try out new sexual activities if that's what you want to do.

The most important rule is only to do the things with which you feel comfortable. No one should try to coerce you, nor should you feel that you have to submit to his desires. The most important part of a good sexual relationship is communication. This can be both verbal and non-verbal. When we're thinking about sex with our partners or having sex with anyone, we often seem to forget about the verbal side. It sounds like you've not yet had the conversation with him about your previous sexual history and I would say this is pretty essential. It's important for you both to know what's gone before and what you might be interested in trying.

If you decide to try something new, you should make sure you feel comfortable with what's being suggested, taking things slowly. Agree also that you'll stop if either of you doesn't like it. Discuss this prior to the event so that there's no room for misinterpretation. Also, agree a signal or word that means stop. You probably won't ever have to use it but it'll make you feel more in control and more willing to try something new.

I understand from what you've said that it's your imagined ignorance that's preventing you discussing things with him. As I've commented before, it never ceases to amaze me that this is the one important area of life where we feel we should know what we're meant to do almost by osmosis and never need to ask.

In order for you to feel more confident, I'm going to give you some general information so you have a starting point. I've also listed some non-pornographic sites in the Resource List, such as www.sexuality.org or the FPA, where you can get information and some books in the Bibliography. Let's start by looking at some of the terms that are used, the meaning of which may not be clear to you. I'm not advocating, incidentally, that you pursue any of these practices, just that you have the knowledge so you can say yes or no from an informed position.

BDSM is an acronym that refers to bondage and discipline, domination and submission, sadism and masochism. Bondage involves tying, handcuffing, gagging or any other activity that restrains you or your partner. Discipline is some sort of telling off or punishment – for example, spanking, whipping or caning. Domination and submission casts one partner as the controlling influence and the other as the controlled. Often, the submissive person undertakes activities demanded by the dominant partner. Sadism and masochism refer to activities that involve pain either to oneself or another. BDSM includes for example, light spanking, the use of blindfolds, holding a partner's hands above their head during lovemaking. Some of the equipment used can be seen in high-street sex shops. If any of this sounds appealing, start gently and see what it feels like; you can always increase your sexual repertoire if you enjoy it.

Another word often used is fetish which originates from the fifteenth-century Portuguese word *feitiço* meaning sorcery, object or charm. It was the French psychologist Alfred Binet (1857–1911) who coined the term 'sexual fetishism'. He used it to describe individuals with sexual interests in objects such as clothing. A sexual fetish is when the article of desire is necessary for the person to become sexually aroused and satisfied. The article can be underwear, shoes, leather garments and so on; but, equally, some people have a fixation with breasts or feet or other body parts. This doesn't mean that, if someone is turned on by sexy underwear, they necessarily have a fetish; it may well be the person who has aroused them and the underwear is merely a prop. Fetishes have in general had a very bad press and, although extreme examples can be both harmful and illegal, in the main, they're not. However, as with any behaviour, if they become an obsession and are affecting how you manage your life and your relationship, the person concerned would probably need help. But that is by no means the norm.

There are numerous fetishes. A surprising number of men and women say they enjoy sex most when they can hear running water or be in it; thunder and lightning can also turn some people on. Voyeurism is more normally a male fetish where the man needs to see someone else having sex (watching pornography) to get aroused, often viewed together with his partner. Feet and hands are a turn-on for some people with men enjoying licking, sucking and kissing women's feet and women getting pleasure from sucking men's fingers. Others have fetishes about their partner's physical size: some get aroused by very fat people, others are turned on by taut stomachs. A pair of high heels is thought to be the most popular male fetish, according to a recent study. If one partner in a relationship has a particular fetish, it's important to talk about it – and it needn't be a stumbling block. For example, if he's turned on by shoes, work out how you could include them in your sexual activity. If your partner's fetish makes you feel uncomfortable, then say so and don't indulge in it.

Then there are sex toys that can be used to increase sexual pleasure. These include vibrators for women. Both single women and those in couples find that a vibrator can increase their ability to have an orgasm. The most commonly used vibrators are confined to the clitoris and used externally. Some women also like to use a toy to stimulate the G spot or a dildo inserted into the vagina. All of these can be used either on your own or as part of making love as a couple. If you're anxious about sex, using a vibrator can relax you and increase your confidence.

Another activity you might consider that is often arousing is your partner watching you masturbate. This can actually be very instructive as the partner who is watching can learn about what pleases the other person. A further sexual practice worth mentioning although it's a more-or-less taboo subject is anal sex. Many find this enjoyable as the anus has a number of erotic nerve endings but it's important to use lubrication. Again, if it's not something you fancy, then be sure to tell your partner (see Question 4 in this section).

Talking to each other is a vital part of good sex and that includes discussing your fantasies. According to a recent survey of British sexual fantasies undertaken by Brett Kahr and written about in his book *Sex and the Psyche* about 90 per cent of people often think about someone else during sex with their partners. A detailed study from the University of Montreal undertaken by Antonio Zadra in 2007 found that women were more likely than men to visualise current or past partners (as well as celebrities) in their erotic imaginings. Men, by contrast, veered towards imaginary people.

It's worth spending time chatting with your partner about your sexual fantasies. Choose a time when you're relaxed and fully dressed, perhaps over a glass of wine. It's a useful way of learning more about each other. Some people like to indulge in a little role-play. Pretending you're someone else can allow you to venture to places that you'd not otherwise go. You could try dressing up with one of you taking the dominant role and the other the submissive, like the boss and his secretary or headmaster and his pupil. Again, this is something that you both have to want to do for it to be enjoyable. It's no more than an adult version of playing make-believe and, as long as either of you can stop when you want, it can be good fun. And, if you don't feel like dressing up in a maid's outfit, you might want to wear some sexy underwear, suspenders and high heels.

Other people like talking dirty during sex. Our biggest sex organ is our brain so that, when someone speaks to us in a particular way, we respond automatically. For example, you can be in a room with lots of noise but, if someone mentions your name, you pick up on it even if you're engrossed in conversation. Words stimulate our brain and we respond both emotionally and physically. An erotic story can be stimulating and a good prelude to making love.

If you're going to indulge in sex talk with each other, use a sensual voice and let your partner know what you like to hear. Some couples enjoy telling each other what they're doing and how good it feels while having sex. The talking often provokes laughter and this is another excellent way of increasing pleasure. Feedback is a very useful way to improve sex for the two of you but do it in a sensitive manner so you don't make your partner feel deflated and inadequate.

Having sex in a different place can be a turn-on or even just at a different time. We all get into habits. For example, it might be that you always come home, have a shower, eat, watch TV and then have sex. Why not try doing it the other way round? Or downstairs rather than upstairs or lights on rather than off?

Touching in a sensual way is one of the most relaxing things you can do for each other. A massage can release tensions in you both and lead to very good sensual sex. Use scented massage oils and really spend some time exploring each other's bodies. Light some candles and put on some romantic music. Even if you aren't doing anything different physically, it will help both of you feel sexier.

I can't say too often how vital it is to talk to each other. Tell him that you feel inexperienced and would like to learn. Ask him what he likes doing and what he would like to introduce into your sexual activity. Explain what you're concerned about and what you like the sound of. Take it all very slowly so you get time to try things out and can see if you enjoy them.

Remember, there's no right or wrong. As long as both of you consent, no harm can come from a bit of gentle experimentation. One last thought: maybe you could agree that each of you introduces something new into your lovemaking at different points so you learn from one another. It sounds pretty exciting to me to be starting on a new sexual adventure in your fifties because, as I say, you're never too old to try something new!

Q4 **My new partner wants to have anal sex. This is something I've never done and never wanted to do. But, recently, I've been wondering if I'm not adventurous enough. Maybe it would be good? I was certainly brought up to think the only position was the missionary position by a mother whose views would largely be to lie back and think of England. I just wonder if I'm missing out. I don't even really**

know what happens and how to do it. I don't know who to talk to about it or where to find good information.

Let me start by saying I'm not a sex therapist so it would be inappropriate for me to discuss techniques. I suggest you take a look at the Bibliography which lists places where you can find more detailed information. As you've asked, I'll explain what anal sex involves and, in general terms, how it's performed as I know many people are unsure.

I want to start by saying it's really important that you're 100 per cent clear you don't need to do anything sexually you don't want to do. It's essential that you feel comfortable in your relationship and can say no about anything at any time and that you're listened to and your partner stops any activity if it doesn't feel right for you. If this isn't the case, then I think you seriously need to consider if you're in the right relationship. If you don't want to do something, that doesn't make you a prude or sexually frigid or any of the other things of which you might be accused or with which you might torture yourself.

If, however, your uncertainty springs from being faced with something new that excites and scares you in equal measure, then you might want to experiment, making sure that your partner teaches you slowly so you feel safe and good about what you're doing. There's no right or wrong as long as you're not harming yourself, being harmed by anyone else or harming others.

Many of our feelings about sex being bad come from early conditioning, both from our families and sometimes from sex-education classes. As we grew up, other influences came into play such as our friends and the media. Additionally, there are any number of myths about sex – for example, that you can't get pregnant if you have sex standing up or masturbation makes you go blind. A mix of these early influences can persist into adulthood.

It's worth thinking about your early messages:

- What ideas did you learn from your parents?

- Who else did you learn about sex from?

- Were you given a message about what was good sex and what was bad sex?

- Who told you what kind of sex you should have?

- What are the myths you were told about female sex?

- What are the myths you were told about male sex?

- What were you told about oral/anal sex and other sexual practices?

- Do you feel comfortable talking about sex?

Having answered these questions you will have more idea about your own sexual prejudices which will help you understand where your feelings come from and whether this new departure is something you want to try.

Culturally and historically, anal sex has at different times been seen as acceptable and immoral. In 2001, research revealed that approximately 12 per cent of heterosexual men and 11 per cent of heterosexual couples in the UK indulged in anal sex while two out of five heterosexual couples have tried anal sex at least once. The anus like the vagina has very sensitive nerve endings and is controlled by two powerful muscles called the sphincters. The external muscle can be contracted and relaxed at will while the inner muscle is controlled by the unconscious part of the nervous system. If you're frightened or anxious, it will contract so you can't pretend you want anal sex if your body is saying no.

The female rectum shares a wall with the vagina so that pressure on the rectum can stimulate the vagina. For men, anal penetration allows the sensitive prostate gland to be stimulated and this can be very erotic. One myth which can add to concern about anal sex is that faeces are stored within the rectum. Although there may be traces, faeces are in fact stored in the colon which is deeper within the body.

As the anal passage is not as elastic as the vagina, you must make sure that you use a lot of lubrication and your partner enters with care if you're indulging in anal intercourse. Some couples, whether heterosexual, lesbian or gay, will use vibrators or fingers to stimulate the anus. It's also important that you let your partner know how deeply you want him to penetrate. If you discover that you enjoy anal sex, then include it in your sexual repertoire. If you find out it's not for you, put it down to experience and cross it off the list.

Q5 **My marriage split up about nine months ago. I'd married very young and had missed out on my youth. My children have now left home and I thought this was my time to have some fun. I've had several lovers. Some I met on the internet and others at clubs. I didn't think about safe sex; at 53, I thought I was too old. I've just been diagnosed with chlamydia and gonorrhoea. I'm distraught; I had to go to the STI (sexually transmitted infection) clinic and sit with people my children's age. Can I continue having fun and lovers and still prevent this happening again?**

I was reminded of my biology-teaching days and my time working as a sex and relationship educator for the Family Planning Association as I had to teach about STIs. In Section 1 Question 2 I talk about sex in relation to the older person and sexual practices. I think you'd find this useful.

Interestingly, there have been very few studies till recently on older people's sexual practices. The Cambridge University Press published a paper, 'Are Older People at Risk of Sexually Transmitted Infections? A New Look at the Evidence' (2005) which raised two pertinent points about our attitudes to older people having sex.

The first is that, in two health studies commissioned in 2001 – *The National Service Framework for Older People* and *The National Strategy for Sexual Health and HIV* – sexuality or sexual health issues aren't mentioned in the former and older people don't get a mention in the latter. The second is that there had been very little research into older people's sexual habits in the UK when Cambridge University wrote their paper in 2005. A little more evidence is available in the US but, again, much less than for any other group. I wonder if this is because the researchers didn't like thinking about their parents or grandparents having sex!

A recent piece of research published in the June 2008 edition of the journal *Sexually Transmitted Diseases*, says that the rate of STIs has doubled among the over-45s in less than a decade. The research was undertaken by the Health Protection Agency by going to genito-urinary medicine (GUM) clinics in the West Midlands between 1996 and 2003. They recorded 4,445 STIs in the attendees, men and women aged 45 and older.

The most commonly diagnosed infection was genital warts, accounting for almost half (45 per cent) of the cases, with herpes next, accounting for almost one in five (19 per cent). There had also been an increase in the incidence of syphilis cases, up by 139 per cent in the 45- to 64-year-old age group. Men aged between 55 and 59 were significantly more likely to have a sexually transmitted disease than others in this age bracket. Among women, rates were highest among those aged 45 to 54.

Contrary to what might have been expected, while the number of infections identified in younger age groups rose by 97 per cent during the period of the study, those in the over-45s rose by 127 per cent. The explanation seems to be that, with an increase in separation and divorce in the older age groups, those people are more likely to be single again and making new relationships. Add in internet dating, international travel and new drugs such as Viagra® to counter erectile dysfunction and the figures suddenly seem less improbable. The researchers also mentioned that the liberal sexual attitudes which abounded when this section of the population were in their teens and twenties have stayed with them into older age. In short, we were the flower people promulgating free love and we haven't changed.

I have an alternative explanation and it's twofold. We were the generation that missed out on the sex education routinely given now to young people. Then, with the development of the pill which coincided with many of us experimenting sexually, fears of pregnancy were radically reduced and so we became less used to using a condom. Then many of us settled into long-term relationships that we believed were monogamous and we didn't worry about STIs.

Most of us who were brought up pre-HIV have remained quite ignorant about sexually transmitted diseases believing that we're too old for them. Of course this isn't the case as bacteria and viruses aren't age conscious! The Family Planning Association helpline reported that during 2007 almost 10 per cent of their callers were between 45 and 68. This is a huge increase on five years ago. As we live longer and are healthier so we'll go on being sexually active longer, too. One doctor reported that the oldest person in his clinic in the last twelve months was 93! So we do need to protect ourselves.

STIs are mainly passed from one person to another during sexual activity. There are at least twenty-five STIs, all with different symptoms. Infection is passed, vaginally, orally and anally. Most STIs will only affect you if you have sex with an infected person. Although symptoms vary, the most common are soreness, itching, pain when urinating, lumps or sores and, on occasion, discharge from the genitals.

These are the most common STIs:

Chlamydia is a sexually transmitted bacterial disease which infects the urethra, rectum and eyes in both sexes, and the cervix in women. It is easily treated with antibiotics.

Gonorrhoea is a sexually transmitted disease that can affect the urethra, cervix, and rectum, anus and throat. Sometimes there are no symptoms. It is easily treated with antibiotics.

HIV is a virus that can lead to AIDS. The virus cannot survive without human tissue and therefore can only be caught when you're having unprotected sex. It can be passed from an infected person to another through exchange of bodily fluids such as blood, semen or vaginal fluid. The virus kills cells in your immune system that fight diseases. You may not have any symptoms for years. But, once your immune system is weakened enough, you'll be susceptible to a life-threatening illness; this is the point at which you'll have developed full-blown AIDS. There are now drugs that can delay the onset of AIDS although there is, as yet, no known cure. The earlier you start a course of drugs, the better so it is really important, if you think you might have been exposed to the virus, that you talk to someone about being tested.

Hepatitis is an inflammation of the liver. Viruses are the most common cause of the illness. There are five strains of hepatitis, all causing acute illness but the long-term prognosis differs with each one. Hepatitis B is spread through sexual contact via body fluids which include blood and saliva, urine, semen and menstrual and vaginal secretions. Most people suffer flu-like symptoms, loss of appetite, jaundice and joint and abdominal pain. The treatment is rest. There is a vaccination but it's only given to those at high risk – health workers, for example. It is a very resilient virus and there are people who don't suffer the symptoms but who remain carriers and pass on the disease.

In 1989, Hepatitis C was discovered. This is passed on in the same way as Hepatitis B although many go through the acute phase with no awareness of symptoms until it becomes chronic. Treatment can be offered but is only successful in fewer than 40 per cent of sufferers.

Syphilis is a sexually transmitted disease caused by bacteria. Again, people may remain without symptoms for years, yet, if untreated, are at risk from late complications. The early stages are often difficult to recognise. The symptoms often take over three months to appear and include one or more painless ulcers on the genitals or mouth and a non-itchy skin rash. Late complications, which don't occur in all cases, cause damage to the internal organs and can prove fatal.

Genital herpes is caused by a virus called herpes simplex (HSV). There are two types: HSV1 and HSV2. Both can affect the genital area as well as the mouth and nose (cold sores) and fingers and hands. HSV2 enters through cracks in the skin or through mucous membranes. Symptoms appear two to seven days after exposure and last for two to four weeks. They include feeling generally unwell with flu-like symptoms and stinging or itchy genitals covered with small blisters filled with fluid that burst and are sore, making it painful to urinate. Drugs can be given to alleviate the symptoms. Although symptoms may then disappear, they can recur as the virus stays with you always.

Genital warts are an infection of the skin of the genital and anal area and the mucous membrane of the vagina, cervix and rectum; they are caused by human papillomavirus (HPV) and are passed by sexual contact. It causes visible warts that may disappear, stay the same or get bigger. You will remain infectious. The warts can be external or internal. A few types of wart virus that are not visible are linked to changes in the cells in the cervix and could lead to cervical cancer years later.

Crabs or lice are small crab-shaped parasites that burrow into the skin to feed on blood. Mostly, they live in pubic hair but can also be found in other body hair. They usually get transmitted through sexual activity but can be passed on by sharing towels or bedding. They're successfully treated with creams and shampoos.

I haven't described every sexual infection but there is lots of information about sexually transmitted diseases (STDs) on the internet and leaflets produced by health organisations (see the Resource List) that will give you all you need.

I hope I've said enough, though, to make you think twice about keeping yourself protected and practising safer sex. Unless you've only had one monogamous partner and so have they, you could be at risk of developing an STI. That means the man wearing a condom whether you're likely to get pregnant or not! And they do work, if used properly. If men aren't familiar with them, practise until it feels comfortable. Women can familiarise themselves with condoms by putting them on the man's penis – that can be an enjoyable part of foreplay. Check you're using the right sort of condom. For instance, if you're using a lubricant, something that becomes more common in heterosexual sex when women's vaginal secretions reduce with the menopause, make sure it's a water-based one like K-Y Jelly. Oil-based lubricants like baby oil can perish the latex within fifteen minutes. If you're having anal sex, use a stronger condom made specifically for this purpose.

It's also sensible to cover cuts and sores. Use a plaster if you're having either anal foreplay or foreplay during a menstrual period. If sharing sex toys, use the same level of protection as for penetrative sex, washing toys after each sexual encounter. If using other foreplay items where you may draw blood – whips, for instance – keep things for them strictly for personal use (see Section 3 Question 1 and Question 3 in this section for different sexual activities).

It all sounds so simple so why don't more people use condoms? One reason is that, too often, we're not prepared. But it's just as acceptable for a woman to have a condom as a man. Don't get carried away in the moment and then remember when it's too late. (Alcohol often makes us lose our inhibitions.) Neither of you can know for certain how either of your ex-partners behaved. Practise when you are on your own asking your new partner so that, by the time you do it for real, it just trips off the tongue. It's often easier to have the discussion before moments of high passion so find a time when you feel relaxed enough to talk about it.

In your question, you mentioned the uncomfortable feelings you had going to the clinic. This isn't surprising as it will be a totally new experience. A number of doctors working in sexual health clinics have recently become aware that their services are not set up for the older person and it can leave them feeling really out of place. Information and advice aimed at preventing STIs should be more inclusive of the level of sexual activity among older age groups. There is some talk about setting up clinics for older people with older staff. There is a crying need for literature that focuses on the issues that concern our age group. This is something we should be campaigning for. Knowledge is power. As long as you follow safer sexual practices, there's no reason why you can't have many more years of a healthy and fulfilling sex life.

Q6 **I started a new relationship a few months ago. My partner's great: we get on well and chat easily. However, there's a bit of a problem with sex. It's OK-ish at the weekend when we have time but he wants sex every morning and most evenings. I prefer sex at night and anyway I have to get up and out early each morning to go to work. Also I know there are things that would make the sex better but there are also some things I just don't like and I feel embarrassed to raise them with him. How do I discuss this? Unless I do, I'm worried the relationship won't last and that would be such a pity.**

Talking about sex to your partner is difficult. But that doesn't mean you should avoid it. The problem for most of us is that we just don't get enough practice at it to be skilled and therefore the conversation doesn't flow easily. Communication is the key to any healthy relationship and is essential if it's someone with whom you're intimate. If you don't talk about a problem, it becomes hidden but it doesn't go away. When it surfaces – and it always does – it's often in an inappropriate way that can cause a seriously negative response.

According to research undertaken by E. Laumann, J. H. Gagnon, R. T. Michael and S. Michaels in 1994 at the Kinsey Institute, Indiana University, 54 per cent of men think about sex every day or several times a day, 43 per cent a few times a week and four per cent less than once a month. By contrast, they discovered that 19 per cent of women think about sex every day or several times a day, two-thirds a few times a week and 14 per cent less than once a month. All in all, then, while most of us – men and women – think about sex quite a lot, it doesn't translate to talking about it.

We were brought up during a period when talking about sex and one's sexuality was taboo. It's not unusual for women in their fifties and sixties to report that they knew nothing about their bodies until they had a solitary sex-education lesson at school when they were 15 or 16. Imagine if we'd never talked about food till that age. How hard would it be to order a meal in a restaurant! And how difficult would it be to know what your partner liked to eat!

A very interesting, perhaps unique, factor about sex is that we think we should know all about it – how to do it, how to pleasure our partner – and so, if we then need help, we must be a failure! But sex should be like any skill: you should start at the beginning and take lessons, like learning to cook or drive a car or ride a bike.

A digression. When you're small, you don't know that you don't know, for example, how a cake is made and you certainly couldn't make one yourself so you're unconsciously incompetent. When you're a bit older, you may try and make one and it comes out flat. Now you're consciously incompetent. This is the point when we tend to get frustrated as we want to be able to do something and we can't, many of us deciding to give up and move on to something new.

Once we feel ready to resume our efforts, we realise we need to find ways to develop the skill, either by being shown, being told or reading a book. That's when we ask for feedback from others to discover if what we've produced is good and how to make it better. At this point as long as we follow the recipe we can do it and we are now consciously competent. A few cakes down the line, we no longer need to look at the recipe; we throw in a bit of this and a bit of that and the result is a delicious cake and we are unconsciously competent. However, if we go to stay somewhere else and we have to use a different oven, we may find ourselves making a less than perfect cake because we haven't quite adapted to the unfamiliar situation and we have to relearn and readjust.

This is much like sex. Both of you will have had sex before in long-term relationships where your partners knew you inside out. Now, you find yourself in a new relationship and you have to start discovering from scratch what it is the other person likes and then – to return to our cooking analogy – adapt the recipe accordingly.

One of the things we do when we want to please someone is give him or her either what we want ourselves or what someone else wanted. What we too rarely do is ask them what *they* want. For example, you might go out and buy your partner an expensive new watch because that delighted your previous partner when your new lover might have preferred an MP3 player! We do exactly the same with sex: we offer others what we think they want without any consultation.

If you have, as you say, a good relationship, I expect you're able to talk to him about most things. So what you now need to do is oil those 'communicating about sex' wheels.

THE SEX TALK QUIZ

Tick the answer to the question which best sums up your situation:

1. If your lover's doing something you don't like, do you:
   a) Tell him straight out?
   b) Not say anything?
   c) Praise something he does that you do like and ask for more of the same?
   d) Talk to him but never really get to the point?

2. My partner's favourite way to get affection is
   a) Not my interest
   b) I really don't know
   c) Something you have been told by them
   d) They seem to change their mind a lot

3. Have you ever faked either an orgasm or enjoyment of sexual activity?
   a) I would let them know there and then I wasn't satisfied
   b) Yes, always
   c) No, I wouldn't do that
   d) Yes, sometimes

4. You'd like to try something new sexually. Would you:
   a) Say you've always wanted to do x or y?
   b) Not say a word?
   c) Tell him what you like that he does and suggest that you add this new activity to your love-making.
   d) Keep moving his hand to the right place and hope he gets it?

Scoring.

Three or more a)s

You seem to be very concerned about your own satisfaction and not that interested in your partner's. Telling him straight like this is likely to lead to upset and rows and not good loving sex where you share your needs. While it's important to be assertive, you should be careful you don't become aggressive and ride roughshod over his feelings which could lead to your lover losing his confidence.

Three or more b)s

You're inhibited when it comes to talking about sex. You're very unlikely to get your needs met as the other person would have to be clairvoyant to know what you wanted! He will also be unsure about your response and may worry that he's not satisfying you, again leading to lack of self-confidence.

Three or more c)s

You know how to approach sexual matters with tact and diplomacy while ensuring that your needs are met. Empathising with what is good will always make your lover feel validated, they will then feel more able to really hear you and understand you when you talk about your needs.

Three or more d)s

You're trying to communicate but not very successfully which is likely to lead to confusion. Learning to talk in a straightforward manner is really important, as is giving positive feedback.

Here now are some tips for communicating successfully about sex and relationships.

1. Make sure you both have the time to talk and choose somewhere you'll both feel comfortable.

2. Don't bring up the subject just before, during or after sex. Talk about it away from the bedroom and any sexual activity.

3. Good communication is just as much to do with listening as talking. Seeing, touching, smelling and tasting are all based on instinctive responses. When it comes to listening, we're conditioned both by the way the words were used and the tone of voice. And remember, the same word can have a different meaning to different people. For example, our generation think 'wicked' means evil but our children think it means great! It's especially important when listening about sensitive subjects to check that we've understood correctly what's being said so that we don't jump to the wrong conclusions.

4. As much as 90 per cent of our communication is non-verbal. This is a double-edged sword. A sensitive lover will probably have picked up when things aren't right and may well be worried and on the defensive. On the other hand, it might be a relief to him if his partner articulates her feelings.

5. We can communicate our pleasures by the way we look and touch, not just by words. You can, without talking, guide him round your body and help him find the places you like being touched but, in the end, this is no substitute for speech.

6. If you're wanting to change the time or place you have sex:

   a) Use a soft and neutral tone and slow your voice down so you sound warm.

   b) Tell him that you really enjoy having sex with him and the time you most enjoy it is at the weekends and at night because it means you have time to stroke and cuddle him afterwards.

   c) Lighten the mood by saying you're 'too old' for sex every day or too slow at getting yourself dressed to enjoy sex in the morning as much as sex at night. Laughing at ourselves often reduces tension.

   d) Ask him when he likes having sex most and why.

   e) Agree a compromise so you both get a bit of what you want and when you want it.

7. If you're wanting to encourage something new:

   a) Make sure you don't sound bored with your current sexual activity.

   b) Modify your voice to sound soothing and sensual. Use a slightly lower tone than normal and a soft voice at a slower pace.

   c) Tell him you've seen something in a book or magazine and been fantasising about it. Show him the article, if necessary. Never mention a previous lover's technique you enjoyed.

d) You could also play a game where each of you tries to guess what the other likes most during sex.

8. If you're telling him about something that isn't arousing you sexually:

a) Sound confident and upbeat so it doesn't make him feel a failure.

b) Tell him what it is you enjoy first – for example, say you love the way he kisses your face and you'd really like it if he kissed your nipples in the same way. That way, you're able to say what you want without criticising the fact he sucks your nipples.

c) Be careful to say *and*, not *but*, as it immediately negates the first part of the sentence and makes him think he's been doing it all wrong.

9. If you're telling him about something you don't like or want:

a) Ask him, for example, how he feels about entering you from the rear? This starts the discussion in an adult fashion with no emotional overtones, which will mean he's much less likely to get defensive, much more likely to be willing to chat to you about it.

b) Listen to what he says and then offer your thoughts.

c) Always make suggestions using 'we'. Intimacy is about 'us' not 'you and me'. The more you talk about 'us', the more it will feel shared and not be heard as an attack.

10. If you're telling him about something that causes physical or emotional distress:

   a) Say it to him straight – for example, it hurts when he squeezes your nipples and you'd much prefer it if he stroked them.

   b) Tell him firmly if you've said it more than once.

   c) If he's not prepared to change, then you'll need to consider if this is the relationship for you.

Something I find very helpful when I have to have a difficult conversation is to practise in advance. One way of doing this is to imagine you're with your partner in a room with him sitting in a chair. Start by looking at the imaginary man and tell him what you want to say. Now, go and sit in his chair and imagine yourself as him hearing your words. Ask yourself if they made him feel good or cross or hurt or sad. If they raised anything negative, think what he would have preferred to hear. Armed with this knowledge, go back to your chair and try again. Repeat this exercise until you feel really confident. If you're well prepared and your intention is to make him feel good while bringing about any changes you'd like, you're sure to have success *and* an improved sex life.

❧ Section Five ❧

Blended Families

Q1 I separated from my wife twelve years ago. We've been divorced for seven of those. She's still smarting and spitting. We have grown-up children who are developing their own lives. My daughter told me last week that she was thinking about not inviting me or her mother to her wedding as she didn't want the tensions between us to spoil her day. Then she burst into tears because she doesn't want to get married without us. It just isn't fair. I've tried every which way to relate to her mother. I've supported her financially and yet she won't change her attitude. At times like this, I almost wish we hadn't split up even though life is so much better and the children don't have to listen to our daily fights.

This sounds extremely painful and, sadly, something many divorced parents go through when their differences and difficulties have not been resolved. Parents need to do the best for their children whatever they might feel about each other. When people with children separate and divorce, the most precious people in both their lives are their shared children. If you have children, you and your ex-partner will always be linked. A fantasy some have is that they won't need to ever relate to their ex, but you do, as children need both parents. Of course, if you have no children, the choice to remain in contact is yours alone.

However marvellous a step-parent might be and no matter the involvement of loving grandparents, no one cares as much about their children as the two parents. It's a relationship that will last your entire life. For many couples, this raises the problem of how to cut off any emotional involvement with their former partner while maintaining an emotional bond because of their shared children.

Let's look at how you feel. In your question, you make it clear that you feel the situation is unfair and that you've tried your hardest to make things as civilised as you can. You sound as though you believe you hold the moral high ground and that your ex-wife is in the wrong. I wonder if I were to ask her how she saw the situation whether she would see you in the way you do as the sensible, giving person? I expect not!

Separation from someone you've lived with is hard. The easiest way to break from someone is not to see them at all. But this isn't possible when you share children so you have to find other ways to break the emotional ties. If you find yourself disagreeing with me and think you're emotionally separated, tell me anyone else who makes you as cross or as hurt as her. If there is anyone, it would be your new partner or your children or your parents, all people to whom you're emotionally attached. Until you're able to see your ex-wife as just another person and not react emotionally, things will continue as they are and everyone will be tense whenever you have to be together.

We believe that, once we've got the divorce agreement, we've done the hard work and we can move forward. But, in some ways, and although it may not feel like it, that's the easy part. The difficult part of divorce comes with cutting the emotional, physical and mental ties that bind you to your ex-wife. All too often, we experience the same conflict with a former partner that we experienced within the marriage, the very things that caused the separation in the first place and which we still find impossible to manage. We just continue the same cycle. When you've lived with someone and been intimate with them, they know you inside out. Your ex-wife knows better than anyone how to wind you up and vice versa. While you go on pressing each other's buttons in this destructive way, you'll never find peace of mind and that's not good for you or your children.

One thing I've learnt over the years is that you can't make someone change. That might sound odd coming from a counsellor and coach but, in order to change, the person has got to want to do it themselves. The only person we are in control of is ourselves: we can change how we think and how we behave and how we feel. But we can't do it for someone else.

But there are ways that you can ease the situation. Behaviour breeds behaviour. If I am nice to you, you'll be nice to me. If I'm horrible to you, you'll be unpleasant back. It's the same with feelings. If I put out a negative feeling towards you and you pick it up, you'll start feeling bad. If you want things to change and for life to get easier for your children, you're going to have to start behaving differently and sending out different messages. You need to break those emotional ties that keep you in the old marriage.

I suggest you do the following 'breaking the ties' exercises. Choose the one first that appeals more and then do the other if you still feel there's any emotional connection. The exercises are based on the premise that we're all connected energetically and, when we're in a relationship with someone, we create cords of attachment between us. A good example of this is when you think of a friend who you haven't seen for years and a couple of hours later they call you out of the blue – or so it seems. We've all had those experiences. When we've been intimately involved with someone, we create many cords between us which can take some time to break.

These exercises may be different from anything you've done before but have a go. You've nothing to lose as you're in a pretty bad place in relation to your ex-wife at the moment so it can't make it any worse! When completed, you can test if the exercise has worked by thinking of something that your ex-wife does that makes your blood boil. If it still does, or even makes it warm, the ties are still there and a bit more work is needed.

BREAKING THE TIES

Option 1

1. Take yourself off to a quiet place away from everyone else.

2. Write a letter to your ex-wife, listing all the things you want to tell her that have made you so cross, resentful, hurt, sad and so on and then tell her that you're going to let these go and you forgive her for them.

3. In your letter, tell her that you're really sorry for the things that you've done that you know hurt her, made her cross, sad and resentful.

4. Read what you've written and make sure you've said everything you need to say.

5. Tell her that now you are separated the promises you made when you were together are no longer appropriate, and you no longer hold her responsible for those promises or expect her to carry them out.

6. When you're ready, take your letter to somewhere where you can burn it safely. Say goodbye to the relationship and set the paper alight. Watch it burn as the smoke goes into the atmosphere and dissipates.

7. Sit for a few minutes allowing yourself to absorb the fact that these feelings have gone.

Option 2

1. Imagine that your ex-wife and you are in a room together.

2. You're both sitting facing each other at either end of the room. Look for the cords that attach you.

3. See where they're attached and how thick they are.

4. Tell your ex-wife that it's time for the two of you to cut these ties and give yourselves the freedom to carry on your own lives, emotionally disconnected.

5. When you're ready, say whatever needs to be said to her. Speak out loud, tell her what you're sorry for and ask for her forgiveness, saying that you'll accept it. Tell her how she has hurt you and tell her that you forgive her.

6. Tell her that promises you made to each other as a married couple no longer need to be carried out.

7. Imagine that you have a sword in your hand and see yourself cutting through the ties so they're all severed. This will not hurt either of you, as they are just the cords.

8. As you do this, watch her drift away from you and say out loud: I am free!

When you've completed these exercises, try to persist with the feeling of having let go. If you find yourself drifting back in to your old habits, then repeat them until you truly feel free.

Now let's concentrate on your daughter and her wedding. The prospect of a child's wedding often reopens wounds for divorced parents that may have been partially healed. You can't help but think back to your own wedding and all the hopes and dreams you had. It's bound to make you reflect on your life and what went wrong. I'm not surprised that you're finding yourself wishing you'd stayed together as you're having to face the fact that your own dream didn't come true. It can be very helpful at this point to look at what was good about your relationship and what wasn't.

ASSESSING A RELATIONSHIP

1. Take a piece of paper and divide it in two.

2. Put positives as a heading above one column and negatives above the other.

3. Write down all the good things that came out of your marriage like children, shared holidays, meals, domestic experiences and so on.

4. Write down all the negatives – the fights, the differing sets of values and so on.

5. Now take a realistic look and remind yourself that you made the right decision to call time on the marriage.

6. Keep this list. Use the positives as a reminder before you meet her at the wedding so you feel good about her and use the negatives as a reminder if you find yourself feeling bad about the situation. Be pleased that you no longer have to have with these, so don't wallow in them!

I expect when you think about her in relation to the wedding, you have a number of negative thoughts going though your head like, 'She's pushing our daughter to have an expensive wedding and I've paid enough already' 'My new wife's role needs to be acknowledged by my ex-wife.' Now ask yourself, 'Who's central to all these thoughts?' Me, myself, I! Doesn't that strike you as a bit selfish?

Let's get one thing straight before we go any further: it's your daughter's wedding but it wasn't her divorce. She didn't divorce either of you and she has to be able to share you both equally at her wedding, whatever the circumstances of the divorce may have been and however hurt and cross you might still feel. Her needs come first. The only person who matters here is your daughter. Children of whatever age need their mum and dad and anything you do that prevents that happening is not good for them.

Tell your daughter that you were really sad when she got upset about the wedding. Explain that you know it takes two to tango and acknowledge that you've played a part in making the situation difficult. Tell her that you're going to do it differently from now. Make sure she knows that you want her to enjoy being with both her parents on her special day. Remind her that the two people who want it to be perfect as much as her are you and her mother. You know that it sometimes may not have felt like that but it will from now on.

Tell her you've done some thinking and you'd like to find out what she wants and to talk through some of your ideas. I'm going to give you a few tips to help you do this.

Firstly with your ex-wife

1. You and your ex-wife need to suspend thinking about yourselves so you can work together to make it a good wedding.

2. Tell your ex-wife that Chinese whispers about what you each want hasn't worked up till now and therefore you need to have face-to-face discussions so both know each other's views and intentions.

3. Pinpoint things that could cause a problem beforehand, like who should be in the family photos. The more prepared everyone is, the better. You all know each other's Achilles heel.

4. Agree that if any issues arise, like who are going to be ushers or how many relatives are going to be invited, that you'll discuss this with your daughter who should then talk to her mother but that, in the end, it's your daughter's decision. Go along with it, even if you don't like her choices.

And with your daughter

1. Ask your daughter when you talk with her:

   a) What are her fears about her parents on her big day?

   b) How does she want you and her mother and any step-parents to behave?

    c) What roles does she want you, her mother and her step-
       parents to play?

    d) What seating arrangement would she like?

Add your own questions to my list.

2. Remind your daughter that everyone will try their best as
   they're only interested in her. Tell her that she really needs
   to believe this so she's not so anxious that she creates a
   tension without realising it.

3. Plan with your daughter whether there are things prior to
   the wedding that you and your ex-wife have to discuss.
   Agree to meet your ex-wife with your daughter (and her
   fiancée if she wants) so that you can make the necessary
   decisions. Stick with these when they're made.

4. Remind your daughter that you're not perfect and if you do
   say something derogatory about her mother, she has
   nagging rights to tell you that she doesn't like it and wants
   it to stop.

If you allow your daughter to take the lead on this so she feels
that she's been allowed to grow up and be in charge, she'll feel
proud that she's been able to carry off her wedding with the shared
love of her parents. What better start could you give her?

Q2 **I've been on my own for a long time and brought up
my children as a single mother. They've now left home
and I've just moved in with another couple as an equal partner
in their relationship. We've been very good friends for a while
and we practise polyamory. We've pooled all our resources and**

have set up home together. It's a stable, committed relationship between the three of us. It suits me really well. The only problem is my daughters: one's appalled and won't see me; the other's keeping me at arm's length. I miss them. Should I give up my life because they disapprove? How do I help them to understand? I find it so hard to explain.

This is a really interesting question as it involves a different lifestyle from the norm which will challenge many people as well as your daughters. I should start by defining polyamory, and polyfidelity while I'm about it. I also think that my explaining the concept may help you to have the discussion you need to have with your daughters. Often when we are emotionally involved and upset we find it difficult to be clear which can lead to misunderstandings.

Before I do, I just want to share a recollection from my first job as a schoolteacher. At my very first parents' evening, I realised that two girls who I assumed were twins were in fact half-sisters. Both their mothers were present as was their father. When it was child A's turn, her father and mother came to talk to me; when it was child B's turn, the other mother and same father did the same. The first mother happily waited in the hall until it was her turn again. I remember being really challenged by this, having been brought up to think that monogamy was the only option and yet here were two well-adjusted children. Their parents practised the lifestyle you're now living – polyfidelity.

Polyamory is defined by the Polyamory Society as, 'a non-possessive, honest, responsible and ethical philosophy and practice of loving multiple people simultaneously'. Individuals in polyamorous relationships make a conscious choice together about how many partners they're going to have and how they'll live with each other. Love and intimacy are the primary goals and the relationships are equal with no dominant individual and sexual equality between each. Everyone involved agrees freely to the terms and conditions of the relationship and is committed to upholding it.

There's often a lot of negotiation when relationships are set up. It's very different from polygamy where there's a dominant male and a number of women. Polyamorous relationships can be both single-gender and mixed-gender. Another term often used for these relationships is non-monogamy but there's no reason why they can't be stable, intimate and emotionally committed.

There are a number of different types of polyamorous relationships. Polyfidelity – the situation you've described – is when there is a fixed and agreed number of people in the relationship. The partners live together and share their resources. The care of the children is shared between all the adults. A variation on this is when families are made up of larger groups of actively sexual partners although no one from outside can be admitted into the exclusive circle.

Polyamory can also be a more fluid arrangement with partners changing along the way. Often, there will be a primary relationship in which most time and energy will be invested and in which most resources will be shared. Any secondary relationship may be sparked by a sexual attraction with another person but it won't be given as much time as the primary relationship. Sometimes, the primary pair share a secondary relationship and sometimes they have their own alternative partners. I wonder, if as sometimes happens, your relationship has moved from you being the secondary relationship to you being an equal primary where all three of you live together on the same footing.

The important difference between polyamory and other relationships where there is another partner is that it is open and above board.

There are no secrets such as in an extramarital affair and nor is it casual like swinging. Swinging is defined as a recreational sexual activity or 'sport sex' where no emotional involvement is expected. It's all to do with casual sex.

Contrary to popular opinion polyamorists are not promiscuous people. They believe that you can love more than one person concurrently, both emotionally and sexually. None of us would disagree with the premise that you can love more than one person at the same time: think of your children. It's the idea of sharing the sexual part of an adult relationship that many find difficult to comprehend. This lifestyle would be an enormous challenge for most people as you'd have to be able to share without jealousy and to be truly open and honest to yourself and your partners. A multi-partner relationship is often complex and demanding so knowing yourself and your limitations is important before embarking on this type of lifestyle.

This is not a lifestyle most of us would want but that doesn't mean we shouldn't tolerate it in others. As long as you're not harming yourself or anyone else and there's full consent, it should in my opinion be fine to live in whatever arrangement that suits you. Some people believe this is the type of set-up that may well be the way that baby boomers decide to live. And why not? We already have a situation where many people are serial monogamists.

Living alone is expensive and can be lonely so sharing resources could be a good solution. Joining an already established couple would be a good move for some people while for the established couple it might add a new dimension to a not very exciting relationship. Robert J. Sternberg, a Yale psychology professor, wrote in *The Triangle of Love*, 'Every loving relationship has three ingredients: Intimacy – the baring of souls, sharing, bonding and an emotional and interpersonal involvement like a really close friendship; Passion – where there is a sexual attraction; and Commitment – a stable, dependable relationship which you stick with and work at even if you're having a rough time.'

If you look at a really close relationship where you have a commitment to each other and no sex, it would involve two out of the three components, which is more than if you were living separately. Sadly, it's also true for many couples that live-in relationships only give them one thing: the commitment. Maybe we should be more open to thinking about different ways of conducting relationships even if we end up deciding that how we have it is the way we like it.

Let's now turn to your situation with your daughters. It's interesting that a number of the questions I receive are about someone in the family not approving of how we live our lives. I discuss in Section 1 Question 6 how to talk about relationships and how to come to a mutual understanding. I suggest you read that, too, as it will give you other ideas.

I'm assuming that you've thought long and hard before you changed your lifestyle and decided that this is right for you. It's important that you now hold on to that feeling. Although it's really hard and painful when our nearest and dearest don't approve, this is not a reason for giving up what we consider to be right for us. When others are disapproving, we feel reproached and thrown into the child position even when it's our own children telling us off! From that position, it's hard to think clearly or have a coherent conversation about the issues. So I think it would be useful for you to take a few minutes on your own to think about this from your daughters' viewpoint:

- What might they be thinking?

- What might they not like about your lifestyle choice?

- Do you think it's the nature of the relationship that's troubling them or is it because you've always been there just for them and you're now in a set-up which would appear to exclude them?

- Do they feel betrayed because they knew this couple as your friends?

- Are they worried how they fit in?

- Are they concerned about what others might say, especially their friends?

- Are they worried that, as you have joined an established couple, you might end up being excluded?

Having considered these questions – and you may have others you want to add to the list – now think about what children want from their mother. I will list a few to start you thinking:

- Unconditional love

- Consistency

- Mutual respect

- Time

- The knowledge that you are secure and happy

Once you've made your list, ask yourself whether you have been offering them what they need. Have you involved them in your decisions as much as you did previously when you were on your own? Have you avoided talking about your changed situation because you thought they might not approve or did you bombard them with too many details because you were excited and then not give them time to come to terms with what was happening? Did you allow them to say what they felt and express their views? Children, whatever their age, aren't interested in hearing about their parents' sexual activity; indeed, they recoil from the very idea of it. So it would be understandable if they reacted as they did now if you've blurred those boundaries.

My hunch is you need to take a few steps back. What exactly would you like to say to them? If it's: 'I love you' and 'I miss you' and 'I want to find a way through this,' then go for it. If however you are angry and therefore want to say something negative, meeting with them is not a good idea, it won't work. You need to get rid of those feelings before you approach them. Talk through your feelings of hurt etc with someone else first, so you can then approach your daughters positively. Remember, this style of life is different and when introducing anything new to someone, the rule has to be 'go slowly and communicate clearly'.

As you're now living in your new home, I suggest that you call your daughters and say you want to meet, letting them decide where. It could be where they live or in a neutral place. Go on your own. This first meeting is just to reconnect even though your ultimate objective will be that all three of you can be happy together again. Ask them to decide the next step. The more in control they feel, the more relaxed they'll be and, therefore, the more willing to accept your new lifestyle. Don't push them; let them dictate the pace. Remember, you have the support of two other adults who can be there for you when you return home so you're not alone.

As adults, we choose to live our lives in the way that suits us best. Children sometimes forget this. On the other hand, if your daughters are going to come round to the choice their mother has made – and most people would agree that it's an unconventional one – they will only do so at their own pace and with your gentle encouragement. Impose your lifestyle on them and you'll drive an even bigger wedge between you.

Q3 **I've tried every which way to stop feeling so bad about my divorce and my ex-husband but I still veer between being angry and incredibly sad. I know my mood swings are not good for me, my family or my friends. Everyone says I should get help. I'm sure they're right and I'm pretty certain they're getting a bit fed up with me. I just don't know how to go about it. I have a friend who went to see someone but she felt worse afterwards. Other friends swear by their therapists. And I know I could go and talk to my GP. But how do I choose? There seem to be so many different sources of help out there.**

You should read Questions 1 and 6 in this section about managing post-divorce feelings. I'm going to concentrate now on pointing you in the right direction for the sort of help that would suit you best.

It always amazes me that people wait so long to go for help when they have a personal/emotional problem; were it medical, they'd make an appointment with their GP in a matter of days. Like you, most of us talk to our friends, assuming they'll be able to solve our problems. Friends are very important in good times and bad but, by definition, they can't be objective. Let's take an example. A friend talks to you on a daily basis (sometimes five times a day) about their partner. They're totally fed up, they want their partner to leave, their life is a misery, but they have to stick it out because of the children.

You've heard it all a hundred times before but, nonetheless, you bite your tongue about how boring you're finding her and make the right noises, offering a little advice along the way. And so the pattern continues. In essence you collude with her. If you recognise this scenario, please take note. As you are beginning to recognise, what's needed is professional help.

A therapist is an objective expert and stranger whose job is to enable you to find solutions to your problems. This doesn't mean they aren't interested in you because, while you're with them, you are their main focus. Once you've gone, though, they move on to someone else. Although this might sound harsh, it isn't. It's a simple statement of fact.

Many of us, for different reasons and at different times, will need to seek professional help for an emotional problem. If you are feeling really desperate, you need urgent help and should contact your GP, phone a helpline such as the Samaritans or go to A&E at your local hospital. But, in your case, you're right to want to consult a therapist. Over the years, a huge number of different therapies have emerged and there are now over three hundred different approaches. The type of person you are, the type of problem you have and the depth to which you want to tackle it will all effect who you choose.

There are three major types of therapy. Cognitive behavioural therapy (CBT) focuses on negative thought patterns and how they affect your feelings and looks at ways to break unhelpful behaviour patterns. CBT can help you to change how you think (cognitive) and what you do (behaviour). It focuses on the 'here and now' difficulties and problems, not on the causes of your distress or past symptoms; it looks for ways to improve your state of mind now. This type of therapy is often short-term and structured. Then there's psychodynamic therapy which explores unconscious patterns and, over a longer period, helps you to both understand past experiences and change negative emotions. Finally, humanistic/interpersonal therapies focus on feeling, awareness and relationships and use more experiential activities such as role playing, art therapy, Gestalt and Rogerian therapy. The energy therapies such as Emotional Freedom Technique and Thought Field Therapy would be included here.

Many experienced therapists, although trained in one field, have studied other approaches and are therefore able to offer a more wide-ranging approach. It would be useful for you to take a look at the British Association of Counselling and Psychotherapy website for more information: *www.bacp.co.uk*. Even if you choose to go to therapy privately, your GP will be able to help you look for the right type of therapist for your problems. Relate, for example, specialises in couple work and also the issues that arise from a relationship breakdown. Some organisations subscribe to an employer's assistance programme through which their employees can access counselling help. If you work, it's worth asking your HR department if this is available.

All therapists will agree a contract of confidentiality with you which means they won't talk to anyone else about you. The only time this might be broken would be with your knowledge if harm is being done to you or someone else.

I'm going to give you a list of the things I think you need to consider when finding a therapist. Some you'll need to do before you talk to them and others you should bring up on your initial contact. (Some therapists offer an initial pre-meeting in person and others do the pre-consultation on the phone.)

1. Make sure the therapist is qualified and belongs to a professional body. The BACP has a directory of therapists. An accredited therapist will be one who has shown they have experience and have met the organisation's criteria. There are a number of accrediting bodies, depending on the type of therapist.

2. Ask them about their approach in advance and make sure their way of working suits you.

3. Ask them if they have supervision. All registered therapists should be receiving supervision, which is a confidential process where the therapist can discuss their practice and maintain a high standard.

4. Check out that they are experienced in dealing with your particular issue. Some therapists are generalists but many specialise in couples, eating disorders and so on.

5. Agree practical details such as a time, place, cost, length of session and clarify in advance that they're insured. If the fees are more than you can afford, ask if they have a sliding scale. There are organisations that offer either means-tested or free therapy. Also, your GP may know a counsellor you can see or, if appropriate, refer you to see someone else in the NHS.

6. Ask if they keep notes and, if so, for what purpose; agree in advance that you should have access to them if you so wish.

7. Tell the therapist exactly what you're looking for; it's often helpful to make a list beforehand so you don't go blank when the session begins. The more open you are,

the more the therapist will be able to assess if they can help you.

8. Ask as many questions as you want; only you will know if a particular therapist is right for you. Remember, you have to feel comfortable talking to them about yourself.

9. If you decide you want to work with them, agree a contract and a regular review date.

If you feel comfortable working with a therapist you trust, then often that's more important than their therapeutic approach. It is your choice so, if you don't feel it's right for you, say so even if you've had a session. Then resume your search elsewhere. There will of course be times during the process when you're challenged and you might get a bit cross. That's par for the course. So don't expect it to all be lovely and chummy – you've got your friends for that. Do expect to be shown alternative ways to approach your problem so you can move forwards into a happier future.

Q4 **I'm 53, a mother and a grandmother, and I work nearly full-time. I lost my mother just under two years ago after a long battle with breast cancer. I was very involved in both her and my father's care. I put my life on hold for them. My father is 77 and he has just announced he plans to get married again. How can he do this? He hardly knows her. He's been very secretive about her and she's so young – just ten years older than me. It seems so disloyal to my poor mother. My brothers are beside themselves. They think she's just after the family silver and we will lose our inheritance! None of us want to go to the wedding. I feel as though all the care I've given him has just been thrown back in my face.**

Gosh! You certainly sound pretty angry and, if I may say, a bit melodramatic. I understand it's a bit of a shock and that it's raised some strong feelings but let's try and get this into perspective. You say your father has been very secretive about this relationship but who would blame him, judging by your reaction! He knows you well and knew you wouldn't be best pleased.

It's often helpful when we feel overwhelmed to stand back from a situation and try to see it from a less emotional point of view.

- Create the scenario you've outlined to me in your head. I expect you see it as a very big, colourful picture with lots of movement and probably noisy, too.

- Now reduce its size, make everyone still, turn off any sound, mute the colours and imagine the picture is sitting at the other side of the room.

- OK, now take a look as an observer. What do you see? What age does the daughter sound (that's you)? Who's acting as the parent and who as the child?

I think you will agree there's a bit of role reversal going on here. If it was your 18-year-old daughter saying she had got engaged to some unknown boy and was going to get married whether you liked it or not, your reactions would be a little more understandable.

When elderly parents become less able to look after themselves because of illness, frailty or loss of a spouse, their adult children often step into that role and become the parent in the relationship. I suspect this has been the role you've played over the last few years, ferrying your mother to hospital appointments, caring for your dad and together coping with the bereavement. Without any discussion with your father, you had, I imagine, decided that this was the role for you from now on.

Like most of us, you probably had ambivalent feelings: on the one hand, you liked it and, on the other, you felt as though you'd been dumped on. If you'd stepped into the breach unconditionally, you wouldn't now be saying that your father had thrown it all back in your face, as you wouldn't have been looking for anything in return.

It's great that you were able to support your parents through a very hard time and I have no doubt your father appreciates this. He has now come through that phase and no longer needs parenting. He's an adult and is able to make his own choices about what he wants to do with his life. When we think about our parents, we inevitably go into our inner child mode. Children want their nice mummy and daddy to live happily ever after. The fantasy is that they, like you, would never want anything different and that might well be true but, sadly, life intervened and your father was left a widower.

He has a choice now about how he lives the rest of his life again. Establishing a new relationship doesn't mean he didn't love your mother. Samuel Johnson said about second wives, 'When I censured a gentleman of my acquaintance for marrying a second time, as it shewed a disregard of his first wife, he said, "Not at all, Sir. On the contrary, were he not to marry again, it might be concluded that his first wife had given him a disgust to marriage; but by taking a second wife he pays the highest compliment to the first, by shewing that she made him so happy as a married man, that he wishes to be so a second time."' Your father understandably wants to feel part of a relationship again and enjoys being one half of a couple.

I wonder what other factors are at play here. Over the last few years, I expect you've had a lot of your father's attention. Do you worry now that he'll love you less? Are you feeling a bit frightened and abandoned? When we are bereaved, it throws many of us back into childhood feelings. It's important to recognise this and reconnect with your adult self.

Each time you leave your father and return to your own life, he's alone again. When he wakes up in the morning, he's still alone. Loneliness is a real fear for many old people. More than a million old people in the UK are suffering the misery of loneliness. Research undertaken for Help the Aged discovered that nearly half-a-million pensioners only leave their houses once a week, and a further 300,000 are entirely housebound.

I understand your concerns about your father's new friend being different and younger. But she isn't that young! Many couples have a 10- to 15-year age difference and do just fine. I had a client recently who felt much like you. Her mother had remarried someone quite different from her first husband. She had previously been fairly withdrawn, preferring to be at home. Now, she was out and about and very sociable. My client felt really saddened, as her father, a sociable man, had clearly been held back by her mother for all those years. Didn't her mother love her father enough to go out socialising with him?

When she finally confronted her mother on the subject, she said that she wanted a different relationship this time round because she didn't want to recreate her first marriage. Her first husband's death had had a profound effect on her and she had begun to see life differently. If she could choose, though, she said, she'd still like to be with her first husband with life reverting to how it had always been. Dr Emily Visher, a psychologist who studies stepfamilies, says that choosing someone different from your first spouse is common.

It may also be hard to see your father as a sexual being. We tend to asexualise our parents. This is hard to do when they fall in love, no matter our age or theirs. Seeing one's parent being flirtatious and demonstrative isn't easy. And yet, he's happy. Can't you find it in your heart to enjoy this new-found joy with him?

You mention that your brothers are worried about your inheritance. For some people, that means actual money; for others, it's represented in family possessions, items that have been part of your lives for as long as you can remember. It is important to sort this out now and discuss it in as unemotional a way as possible while your father is alive and in good spirits. Most people make provision in their wills so their children don't miss out (see the Resource List).

I think it's time you sat down and had a chat with your dad. But first, list all the plus points connected with him having found someone he wants to marry:

1. He won't be lonely

2. He's likely to be healthier if in a stable relationship

3. He'll have someone to share his everyday life

4. He'll have someone to look after him 24/7

5. You are freer now to get on with your life, which you say you had put on hold.

Who knows – when things settle down, you might find that she becomes a friend.

When you talk to him:

- Start by saying you're pleased he's found someone to share his life.

- Explain how you're finding it difficult to adjust.

- Suggest you meet her soon and begin to establish an adult relationship with her.

- Invite her round to introduce her to family members.

- Tell him that you and your siblings have some concern about certain family belongings and that you'd also like to discuss the whole question of inheritance.

- Be as positive as you can about her. I'm absolutely sure he wants your approval as much as you wanted his when you married. If you really feel this woman is bad for him, then you need to say so but you should be specific about the person, not the general business of him marrying again.

I don't usually give direct advice but, in this instance, I think it's time you and your siblings moved on, just as your dad has done. It sounds to me as though all of you need to renegotiate an adult relationship with your father, otherwise you could end up with a divided family and that's something that would have made your mother very sad indeed.

Q5 **I'm a desperate stepmother. I have three children of my own who are now in their mid and late teens. Their father and I divorced a number of years ago and I was on my own for a while. They still see their father regularly and he is a big part of their lives. I've recently remarried a man whose**

wife died two years ago from breast cancer. He had his children when he was in his forties and they are still young, six, eight, and eleven. I'm trying to do a good job but I'm really struggling. Half the time I feel put upon and the other half I don't feel I'm a good enough mother in his eyes. What can I do to be a better mother?

Being a step-parent isn't easy and, although it's now a common family form, it wasn't so when most of us were growing up. Therefore, we have little experience of it. And there's little doubt that it's hard to create a second or third family. It would also be wrong of me to make it sound as if first families don't struggle, too. They do. But they usually experience fewer pressures, particularly in the early days.

Stepfamilies involve households in which one or both of the adults has a child or children from a previous relationship. The adults may be married, living together or in civil partnerships and any sexuality. Many terms are used for these types of families: reconstituted, reconstructed, bi-nuclear and blended. Personally, I prefer 'blended' as it conjures up for me what families are aiming to achieve. Some stepfamilies are more complicated than others and many involve extended family relationships, including non-resident biological parents who are hugely important, plus all the grandparents and aunts and uncles of the children.

Very often, when people become part of a stepfamily, they bring with them some of the myths that they've heard and internalised and therefore believe at some level.

Myth 1: It's easy to adjust to stepfamily life. WRONG!
The adults want it to be easy. They've met someone new, fallen in love and want it all to be lovely. Prior to this, they'll have been

through a tough time and they want it all to be better. However, as you're discovering, stepfamilies are complicated and it takes time not only to get to know each other but to respect and trust one another, too.

Myth 2: Everyone will love each other instantly and love each other's children as much as if they were their own. WRONG!
It takes time to make really deep loving relationships. The bond between a natural parent and child and a step-parent and child will always be different and, if people pretend otherwise, there can only be problems.

Myth 3: A stepfamily isn't as good as real family; only first families are true families. WRONG!
They're different. Simple as that. If you have an idealised view of the family, then a stepfamily will always be second best. And, if that's what you believe, that's what you will get. It's really important as adults that you see the stepfamily as a good nurturing place for children – yours and his – where they can grow and develop and thrive. What's more, you should let them know you genuinely believe this.

Myth 4: Step-parents are wicked and the natural parent is kind and generous. WRONG!
We all know the stories of Snow White and Cinderella and David Copperfield. We were brought up on them. This can colour how we see our partner behaving towards our children and make us fearful to truly parent our stepchildren in case they find fault with us.

Myth 5: Children of divorce, bereavement and remarriage are damaged forever. WRONG!
Children go through a painful period of re-adjustment. They need to be allowed to express and come to terms with their hurt. Research

has demonstrated that in time most children recover their emotional balance to be no different from children in first-marriage families.

Stepfamilies have lots of similarities to first families. However, there are also some factors unique to stepfamilies. For a start, they only exist because something else has ended: either a relationship has broken down or a death has occurred. Both are very painful experiences. The new family has developed out of the wreckage and will inevitably bring with it stresses and strains. Adults and children both grieve the loss of their first family; children will do this even if family life was difficult.

If, as in your situation, one of the parents has died, this parent can often be idealised by both the children and the bereaved parent. Many times, stepmothers in this situation say that it feels as if they were meant to be a clone of the late parent and obviously this isn't possible. Whatever they do doesn't seem good enough and they feel they're in the shadow of the deceased parent. The vast majority of children of divorced couples still fervently wish their parents would get back together again. The creation of a new stepfamily ends that fantasy for them once and for all and can leave them angry and hurt and wanting to lash out at the step-parent. Whatever the cause of the ending of a marriage – whether it be divorce or death – there will always be some unfinished business for all concerned.

Both of you have come to this relationship having had the experience of sharing parenthood with someone else. You bring with you the knowledge of both the things you liked and the things you found difficult in your previous relationships. You also bring all the fears about suffering another loss, either because the relationship might not work out or because your new partner might die, as well as the excitement of having found another relationship and the start of a new life. Children also come with fears; for example that it isn't worth getting close to a new person because the previous one didn't last.

Unlike with your first marriage, when you had some time on your own and then the experience of adjusting to parenthood, in stepfamilies it all happens in one great rush. You and your second husband had to find a way to blend a new family out of two already existing families. There are eight of you, six who didn't choose for this to happen and may be very unsure whether it's what they want. No wonder it hasn't been easy!

Your children still have a father who's involved with them. They now belong to two households and will need to learn how to negotiate the differences between the home they had with you, their father's home and the new home. They may, for example, find themselves with less space and having to relate to younger children. Perhaps your youngest has lost his or her position as the baby of the family. Your children may feel that they never have you on your own any more as their step-siblings always seem to be around. They will have a bolt-hole at their father's where they can cool off if they fancy a break and, as they get a bit older they'll be able to make more choices about when they go there. Your stepchildren have no such escape route when they're fed up with the situation. They only have one home. They will rarely get their father on his own. And then there will be times when you may feel like the outsider when your children are at their dad's and you are 'stuck' with this new family.

Having outlined some of the issues and difficulties, which I hope will enable you to see why you feel like you do, let's look at what can be done to ease the passage.

I. The feelings, concerns and joys from the past cannot be ignored. However much you hope to move forward, things will come up that need to be talked through as a family. Relationships are messy: they don't follow a neat set of rules. Tackle issues as they arise. The process can't be rushed.

2. Make a good co-parenting plan with your partner. Agree what you both think is important and how you want to relate to the children. This of course isn't static so it should be discussed regularly. Don't take sides against each other; appear united in front of the children. If you must argue, do it in your own time in your own private space.

3. Have minimal expectations. Make your goals small and achievable. For example, if your goal is that everyone will have polite conversations at mealtimes with no one interrupting and everyone being interested in everyone else, you're likely to feel disappointed. In time, you can modify your goal to encourage each family member to say what they've been up to that day and so you will slowly progress to your ideal.

4. Accept that the bond between you and your children as opposed to you and your stepchildren is different. You do not have the biological link and unquestioning commitment which most people feel for their natural children. You'll be much less likely to love them unconditionally although your feelings will of course grow. Having said that, make sure you treat them all equally in relation to disciplinary matters and treats.

5. Spend time alone with both your own children and your stepchildren. As they are all different ages, they will require different things. It's important the older ones don't miss out on more grown-up activities, while the younger ones should be given time to play. It's especially

important for your stepchildren to have time alone with their father.

6. Make sure all the children know that the step-parent is not a replacement for their real parent but is a significant adult who will bring something different to their lives.

7. Try not to take things personally (easier said than done, I know). This is a difficult, complicated and new family structure which will have tensions however great a mother you are.

8. Discuss with your new husband how you want to manage the children's discipline. It's essential that you have a good relationship with them before you take this on yourself. It often helps if the disciplining is left to the natural parent. However, don't run to your husband and ask him to do it on your behalf; this will only seem like telling tales behind your stepchildren's backs and can't fail to be divisive. Always suggest that you are there when your husband is talking about something in which you're involved. This way, you'll avoid the 'he said/she said this' scenario. If it's an argument between your children and your stepchildren, ensure that both you and your husband are present to sort it out together so no one thinks one is siding with the other.

9. Remember, it takes a lot of time, patience and love to create a stepfamily. Research shows it can be anywhere between two and five years and even as much as ten so you're only just beginning!

Last, but not least, remember the two of you. You need time alone to strengthen the bond between you and your husband as you develop your joint family. It's a huge task to take on children who aren't yours and to parent them but, if you work together on this, there's absolutely no reason why you won't have as stable and loving a family as anyone else's.

Q6 **I'm no good at this. My wife and I divorced very acrimoniously nine years ago. The children split their time more or less equally between both of us. My wife and I still don't speak. I hate it when my kids spend time with their mother and her new partner. It always feels as though I might lose them. I know they should see her but I don't find it easy. I find myself minding when they pop round to see her when I'm out or phone her for advice. My behaviour at those times is not good. I have remarried and my new wife gets on brilliantly with my kids and I'm delighted this is the case. How do I manage my feelings?**

You said it and you're right! I'm not saying that it is surprising or unusual that you mind your children going to see their mother. But letting it affect how you behave and how you relate to them certainly isn't good for any of you. I know you know that, so let's look at what's going on for you and how this could change.

You're having to share your children who are extremely important to you with someone who has hurt you and who you don't like, someone who may well feel the same way about you. Perhaps you believe your ex-wife is not a good parent, or not as good as you, while you may also believe that your children's stepmother is making a better job of parenting them. But the reality is that you and your ex-wife created these lovely young people together. And, when you're thinking rationally, you know it's really important that the children maintain a good, loving, supportive, open and honest relationship with both their parents.

It was you and your ex who fell out, who fought and/or cheated on each other, not the children. No one's suggesting you should now have a close relationship with her but you do need to allow your children to do so. You have to let them go to her with as much joy as when they go to a friend's for a sleepover or to summer camp. You need to find a way to be civil to her so you can co-parent effectively, not least because there'll always be events you have to share (see Question 1 in this section). I know it isn't easy, otherwise you'd have done it by now.

I'm now going to look at one particular aspect of your situation – your jealousy, the feelings it creates and how to manage them. You may not consider your feelings as such but read my definition and see if you agree.

Jealousy is the fear of losing something that one possesses to another person. It's often used interchangeably with envy which is the pain or frustration caused when someone has something you don't and you want it. From what you say, your children's relationship with your wife threatens you and that, in my view, makes you sound jealous of the relationship they have with her. An example of envy would be if you minded that your ex-wife had a better car than you. Very often, both emotions are present in the type of situation you are describing.

Jealous feelings are not based on a rational assessment of the situation. We can feel extremely jealous without there being any real justification for it. Jealousy is made up of a mixture of things:

- Emotions, including anger, sadness, guilt, envy, fear, grief and humiliation.

- Thoughts, including blame, self-pity, concern about self-image and anxiety about being upstaged.

- Behaviour, including sarcasm, perceived nagging, aggression, sulking and martyrdom.

Unlike anger, jealousy can last much longer. Being jealous is a normal emotion in our lives and we'll all have experienced it at times. Like any emotion, it can vary in intensity from slight irritation to an all-consuming high state of anxiety usually linked to feelings of deep insecurity, a preoccupation with oneself, paranoia and inappropriate behaviour in an attempt to control the situation.

I'm going to offer you two ways to tackle these feelings. Try both.

First, I'd like to introduce you to an idea that comes from Cognitive Behavioural Therapy (CBT). The basic premise is that 'you feel the way you think'. If something happens to you – your children going to see their mother, for example – you may feel they're doing something to hurt you and therefore you lash out at them. CBT looks at the thought or belief *behind* the feelings – for instance, 'I believe they'll have a better time there' or 'She doesn't deserve them.'

It is the meaning we give to our thoughts and beliefs that creates the emotion and behaviour that we then exhibit. This is true for both negative and positive feelings. If you think positively about something and give it a positive meaning, you will feel good. If I bring you bunch of flowers, you think I must be pleased to see you and you feel good. On the other hand, you could wonder what I wanted from you. Then you might start feeling bad and a little paranoid. Sometimes, the meaning we attach to something is not the true one.

CBT encourages people to break down their problem into three parts: the ABC of the problem.

A is the activating event – in other words, what has taken place.

B is your beliefs, which include your values, thoughts, attitudes and expectations of yourself.

C is the consequences, which include your emotions, behaviour and any other feelings you may have.

Both your beliefs and your feelings have an effect on your behaviour and this in turn will affect how you see the external world.

ABC THINKING

(NB Only do this when you're not in the midst of feeling bad.)

1. Take a sheet of paper and divide it into five columns.

2. Head one Activating Event, the second Beliefs, the third Consequences.

3. Write down the event that upset you and then fill in the Beliefs column with all the thoughts you had.

4. Now fill in the Consequences column to include all your emotions, feelings and behaviour.

5. Now go to the fourth column and head it Errors. Write down your thinking errors, by which I mean alternative explanations for your reaction to a particular event. For example, is my thinking a bit over-the-top? Am I playing clairvoyant and predicting the future? Am I using past history as though it was a fact? Am I telling myself that I can't bear it?

6. Next go to column five and head it Alternatives. Write down any other thoughts you could have instead. If stuck, it can sometimes help to ask yourself what you'd have said if this were happening to a friend. Even if you don't come up with a convincing alternative, it's always helpful to question your habitual behaviour.

You can now test yourself and see if your emotions feel different when you think of the event in question. But the greatest test, of course, is when you're next faced with the same situation. Don't be hard on yourself if your reactions don't change immediately. These thoughts and feelings can take a bit of time to shift. If you're interested in CBT, take a look at the Resource List and the Bibliography.

Now to my second way of tackling this problem:

THINGS TO CONSIDER AND CHANGE

1. Observe what triggers the jealousy. What are the images that come into your head when jealousy strikes? Are they particular colours? Do they have sounds associated with them? Can you feel them in a particular part of your body?

2. Think about your jealousy. Ask yourself the following questions:

   a) Why do I feel jealous?
   b) What am I afraid of?
   c) What makes me feel insecure?
   d) Where and when have I felt like this before?

3. Think where this feeling came from. Have you always been jealous? Or do you know when it happened first? You

may just be falling into old patterns of behaviour, which it is possible to reverse (see Section 3 Question 6).

4. Recognise that your jealousy is creating a self-fulfilling prophecy. When you behave jealously, you're responding to what you believe the children's behaviour means. You have no evidence they don't love you. The more you respond badly, the more they'll feel they have to avoid telling you what they are doing; you'll then feel they have secrets and round it goes.

5. Stop thinking you can have their attention all the time and that their life revolves around you. One of the by-products of a divorce is that you'll see less of your children. As they grow up, they will want to spend time with their friends and later they'll have partners of their own. Unless you learn to let go with love, you'll find yourself feeling jealous and hurt when they spend time with other people. I can guarantee that, if you make them feel bad, you'll be storing up problems for the future. You'll reap what you sowed.

6. Bite your tongue when you feel jealousy taking over; don't react in a destructive way. Make sure you don't go quiet and withdraw or accuse others or shout or do whatever you normally do on these occasions. Hold on to yourself.

7. As I said earlier, jealousy often results from low self-esteem. It can also be due to a deep-seated fear of abandonment, that someone will leave you or withdraw their love and attention; it's often as a result of something that happened in your childhood. As a child, it's understandable to feel hurt if you're left out but, as adults, we need to be aware that, more often than not, how people

behave doesn't revolve around you, nor is it a reflection of how they feel about you.

8. Comparing yourself to your wife and counting how much time your children spend with her isn't productive; it just detracts from what you have and makes you bitter and sour. Focus on all the good things you have in your life. Be grateful and celebrate that you have a loving relationship with your children and so does your new wife.

9. If you're going to move forward, you need to forgive your ex-wife and genuinely mean it. You both made mistakes, you were both responsible for the marriage ending and you need to let go. Unless you truly forgive, nothing will change. (See Question 1 in this section, especially 'Breaking the Ties' exercise.)

Changing your behaviour, thoughts and feelings requires hard work. It won't be easy so give yourself time and forgive yourself if you make mistakes. Don't wallow in negative thoughts.

Here are some tips for what you can do which will help:

1. Change what you do when the children go to visit your ex-wife. One person we haven't talked about much is your new wife. How do you think it makes her feel to witness all that anger and upset spent on a past relationship? Concentrate on her and spend some really good quality time when you're alone.

2. Do some activity that makes you feel good and proud of yourself.

3. Make sure your time is filled even if it's just catching up

on the chores that you can't do when you have a house full of children.

4. Trust your children to know how to love both their parents and not one at the expense of the other.

5. Let go of controlling your children's lives; let them make the decisions. As they get older, they'll need to be able to choose where they spend their time.

6. Say goodbye nicely! Be warm and loving and wish them a good time, letting them know that you'll be having a good time, too.

I think you'll be amazed, as you start to change, how different life will look and how much happier everyone will be all round. If you do find yourself unable to shift your jealous thoughts, then get some professional help. CBT is one form of therapy that can be very useful in these situations but there are others. Take a look in the Resource List and see what appeals to you. (See Question 3, which has information on how to find a therapist.)

⁕ Section Six ⁕
Significant Others

Q1 My son and his wife split up a few months ago. I've always been very close to both of them. My son is devastated although I think he is partly to blame and is struggling to cope, but, in truth, I don't think either of them has behaved very well. They have four children aged eleven, seven, four and two who I saw very regularly. The children are living with their mother and my son has moved in here while things are being sorted out financially. My daughter-in-law is refusing to let me come round as she's so angry with my son. It means I have virtually no contact with my grandchildren. I'm finding it particularly hard as my husband left me which makes the past feel very present. How do we find a way through this?

As age expectancy increases, it is predicted that the average person in the UK will spend 35 years as a grandparent – that's longer than they'll have had their child living at home. As an involved grandparent, you'll have had a significant influence on your grandchildren. How to manage the situation now with all its potential difficulties will be a real challenge.

A survey undertaken by the Future Foundation for Saga magazine in 2005 examined the modern roles of grandparents and identified five types.

Racy – join in all activities for fun; Hearts of Gold – kind and caring and happy to help with childcare; Adventure Seekers – affluent, with their own lives but enjoy time with the grandchildren; Traditionalists – more formal and often older but still willing to lend a hand; and Quiet Reminiscer – mostly keep their distance. (See the Resource List for more information.)

I preferred the four more tongue-in-cheek descriptions identified by a San Francisco newspaper:

1. Spoils the grandchildren like crazy, always arrives with gifts, over-indulges them and is the complete opposite to how they brought up their own children.

2. Loves the grandchildren but doesn't want them too close or to make a mess of their perfect house with beautiful ornaments on low shelves.

3. Loves kids but finds babies more difficult. Becomes more involved as the children grow up and wants to share in their activities. (This more usually applies to men.)

4. Believes they know more about childrearing than the parents. Usually very involved on a regular basis but minds if things aren't done their way. (This more usually applies to women.)

The problem you raise is sadly not uncommon and is likely to increase while divorce rates rise. A significant number of the baby boomer generation have themselves been through a divorce so, as well as having to help their children through this difficult phase of their lives, they're also having to deal with emotions that recall painful personal memories.

Past experiences will inevitably have an effect on our present lives. This is of course no bad thing: it's the way we learn and move on. Where it can cause a difficulty is when a situation transports you to your past and you start to behave from *that* place and not from today's situation. Imagine a timeline with the past behind you, the present right in front of your nose and the future stretching out before you. Take a look at that line and then try to move forward with only the occasional backward glance, if you must. But dwelling on too many negative feelings won't do you any favours.

If that's what's happening right now, try the following exercise:

HOW WAS IT THEN?

1. Tick the adjectives that apply and add in any of your own. When I think of my separation, I feel:

   a) Happy
   b) Frightened
   c) Unsafe
   d) Angry
   e) Disrespected
   f) Lonely
   g) Relieved
   h) A bad person
   i) Abandoned
   j) Positively challenged
   k) Jealous
   l) Exhausted
   m) Lacking in self-confidence

2. Take a look at your list. How many of the words are positive? Not many, I expect. If you allow yourself to

dwell on the past, you'll feel bad and powerless. Your self-esteem will take a knock.

Below are a couple of exercises to change your emotional state so you feel positive and more able to cope with the situation.

IDENTIFYING THE CRITIC AND THE FRIEND

1. Take a piece of paper and divide your page into four columns.

2. Head column 1: Feelings (e.g. **I felt angry.**), column 2: What was happening? (i.e. the fact: **He had left me.**), column 3: Self-Criticism (e.g. **I did take control over the children.**) and Column 4: What a good friend would say (e.g. **You were a good mother.**)

You now have alternatives to say to yourself every time one of those negative thoughts goes through your head. It will take practice to change the message but it's worth doing as it will make you feel stronger.

1. Write down all the things you've learnt through your earlier experience for example, self-sufficiency, budgeting, increased self-esteem, DIY skills.

2. Then write down how these new skills and abilities could come in useful now: the ability to negotiate, for instance, which you once had to do with your ex-husband will be helpful in the current situation.

3. Keep this list with you if you ever waiver and wonder whether you have the relevant skills to cope.

Having done this, if you still find that you're reacting as though it's you who's been going through this split, I would recommend that you get some support from a relationship coach or counsellor who will help to root you in the present, enabling you to be both a good support for your son and daughter-in-law and a hands-on grandmother.

The reasons why a grandparent might be denied access to their grandchildren at the time of a separation are rarely to do with the grandparent as an individual. It's related to the grandparent's connection to the spouse, as you have said, and the difficulty for the other partner/parent in separating this from their role as a grandparent. Anyone who's been involved with a family when they break up knows that there are ripples felt way beyond the immediate inner circle.

The split and loss of the close relationship with your daughter-in-law will have affected you deeply and you will have to come to terms with your grief. You need to find time to do this away from your family, as they will have no emotional capacity left over to support you. Although there has been much written about the effect on children and their parents when there's a family breakdown and its impact on parental rights, there has been little research undertaken on the effect on the grandparents involved and their rights. However, a number of organisations have been set up in the last few years aimed specifically at grandparents. Please take a look at the Resource List and Bibliography.

Parents have joint parental responsibility for their children if they are married at the time of their children's birth. This is not automatically the right of the father, if the couple are unmarried. Parental responsibility is defined as 'all the rights, duties, powers, responsibilities and authority which, by law, a parent of a child has in relation to the child and their property'. Only in exceptional circumstances do grandparents have any legal rights or responsibilities in relation to their grandchildren which means that it's the parents who decide who sees their offspring. I think one of the greatest fears for paternal grandparents is that, if the children's parents split up acrimoniously, you're likely to be the ones who will miss out.

In order to change the situation, you're going to have to talk to your daughter-in-law. Although you say you're not impressed with the way that either of them has behaved, I'm sure as his mother you'll be feeling for your son. From your daughter-in-law's perspective, it will look, even if that isn't the case, as though you've sided with your son, not least because he's now living with you.

The most important thing is that you don't take sides. It isn't your battle. That doesn't mean you can't be supportive to both of them but your daughter-in-law really needs to believe you're neutral otherwise she'll continue to want to keep you away. The people to ally yourself with are your grandchildren: they're the ones who need you. A close relationship with a trusted adult to whom they can express their feelings is really important for children. They'll be confused and unsure how to talk to either parent about the situation. Who better to be that sounding board than you? The problem, though, is how to achieve this.

Talk with your son about the situation and tell him how sad you are that your relationship with the children has become a casualty in the crossfire between him and his estranged wife. Make sure he knows that your relationship with him and your relationship with your grandchildren is separate. One way to do this is to write to both parents telling them of your continued intention to be there for your grandchildren in exactly the same way as you were before the marriage broke down. If you saw them twice a week in the old days, then that's what you should suggest doing now.

Ask if you can come and talk to your daughter-in-law about what's happened and see if you can work out a solution. Tell her that you really want the relationship to survive and you're happy to do whatever it takes. Be willing to rearrange things to accommodate her and be as calm and warm as you know how. She is the key to your grandchildren. Even if you're not invited to visit them at home, there's no reason why you can't write, send presents and emails or chat on the phone.

Keep away from discussing any legal conflict that's going on with the parents. Allow your son and daughter-in-law to deal with this themselves. Of course, your son will want your advice but make it clear you're giving it to him as your son and not as the father of your grandchildren. If your daughter-in-law thinks you are siding with him against her, it will immediately lead to a withdrawal of cooperation. And make sure you *never* become the go-between or you'll run the risk of destroying your relationship with both of them.

If talking and negotiating with your daughter-in-law don't work, you could suggest mediation but, in order for this to happen, both parties must be willing to get involved. If you're still being denied access to your grandchildren, the final resort is to put in an application to the court. This is not an easy process because, in law, contact with your grandchildren is not seen as a given. If one parent objects, you then have to make a case to show that, prior to the split, you had a meaningful and ongoing relationship with the children. If, finally, you're given access, the parent – in this case, the mother – could still make it really difficult and it's a ruling that is not easy to enforce.

All of this will sound pretty difficult and painful and, once you're into that kind of battle, it certainly isn't going to be good for your grandchildren. So, make sure, if you were to go down this route, that it's for the right reasons. Sometimes, if we're fuelled by our own past, we find ourselves motivated by misplaced anger which won't benefit anyone.

Once your son is living in his own home, though, things will begin to settle down. The stronger you can be for the two of them, while remaining neutral about their relationship and loving and caring for your grandchildren, the more likely you'll be to find a way through this difficult and distressing time.

Q2 **My father died a few years go and my mother fairly recently. My father was ill for a short time but my mother had Alzheimer's for a number of years. It was a huge strain on me. The physical effort of driving over to see her, liaising with the carers and lately the residential home and also dealing with my four brothers and sisters took its toll. The funeral and clearing our parents' house was a nightmare. I had a neck ache for months which is finally beginning to clear. I now don't know what to do about my siblings. We used to see each other reasonably regularly when our parents were well and we had to deal with each other and argued continuously through our mother's illness. If I'm honest, I have very little in common with them although I like some more than others. Should I reinstate the family get togethers or is it OK to let those relationships just drift apart? I know I'd be really sad if my kids didn't keep up with each other after I've gone.**

So many of my friends and clients have raised this as an issue. It's one of the consequences of improved medicine and life expectancy that many baby boomers have to find a way to manage elderly relatives. It was only when my mother, who's suffering from vascular dementia, went into residential care that I started to sleep properly again after three anxious years of worry. It's no wonder you've been feeling tense and unwell. It may seem simplistic to suggest that you probably felt you had the world on your shoulders and that's what caused your neck ache but I expect that was certainly a contributory factor.

Most of us aren't very good at looking after ourselves and we don't listen to our bodies. We wait until we have a raging temperature or can't stand up or have severe stomach pains before we take any notice. A recent study in the *Journals of Gerontology* (May 2008) looked at 8,234 diary entries of 119 adults who were helping older parents while maintaining their own lives. Some spent just a couple of hours a week on parental duties; others were involved each day.

Both psychologically and physically, all the mid-life children involved reported some stress on days of contact. Question 6 in this section has more information on looking after elderly parents. I know this no longer directly affects you, but for anyone reading this who is currently looking after ageing parents, it's important you realistically assess what you can do and find help for the things you can't manage, otherwise you risk the possibility of making yourself ill.

Now let's turn to you and your siblings. The relationship between our siblings is often complicated. As children, we shared the two people most important to us. We had to find a way to share their love and whatever else was on offer. No wonder many of us become competitive! We spent a lot of time with our siblings, particularly in our early years, more than with anyone else. As a result, they know us really well. They learnt about who we were, our strengths and weaknesses, and about how to get the better of us.

Dorothy Rowe in her book, *My Dearest Enemy, My Dangerous Friend: The Making and Breaking of Sibling Bonds*, discusses this unique relationship. Our birth order has an influence on who we become and how we relate to other people. Eldest children frequently feel displaced by the next sibling. A younger child can feel that they'll never catch up and compete with the older one, something which is undoubtedly true when they're small. A middle child can wonder where they fit into the family and that they have no special place. We love our siblings while at times feeling intense hatred and envy of them and it is this combination that is at the base of a complex relationship.

Not everyone will behave in the way I'm about to describe but many will recognise it. Eldest children tend to take the surrogate parent role. The others see them as the leader – not difficult to understand since they got there first and therefore reached every milestone ahead of the rest. They tend to be responsible, logical, perfectionist, law-abiding (in wanting to please the parents, they tend to follow the rules), driven, authoritarian and critical.

The middle child grows up with no firm position. Many parents, when introducing their children, especially when they're a same-sex family, say, 'X is my eldest, Z is my youngest and this is Y,' a child with no label attached. The middle child is usually insightful, observant, creative, independent, the negotiator and peacemaker. He or she can be passive and a loner. The youngest, meanwhile, is often seen by the parents as sweet and adorable and not having to take much responsibility even when they're in their fifties! They're usually very sociable, creative, laid back and unconventional although they can be manipulative and dependent.

Many of us continue throughout our lives to have a predisposition to these roles in all our relationships but we mostly manage to keep a perspective. Within the family, however, we become uncontained and revert to early behavioural patterns. Dorothy Rowe suggests that a belief the majority of children have is that the role of their siblings is 'your task in life is to make up for whatever your existence deprived me of'. Most of us also feel that there is an expectation that we should be close and keep in touch with our siblings whether we want to or not.

I will hazard a guess that you're the eldest in your family or have certainly taken the dominant role of sibling team leader. It sounds like you felt you needed to manage all of the parent care so that you now feel you have to continue the relationship with your siblings. You probably believe that no one else can or wants to do anything; they just leave it to you to organise things. The result is that you are resentful.

Now that your mother is dead, perhaps you have assumed her role, however unwittingly. Some of your siblings will feel relieved about this while others may rebel. But it needn't be like this. You're all adults so you can decide how you want to relate to one another over the coming years. You also need to ask yourself some important questions about why you want a relationship with your brothers and sisters and what kind it should be.

It isn't easy to shrug off patterns of behaviour but it's essential if you want to create something new. This may be the last time that you play sibling team leader so let's make sure it gets you the outcome you want. A few words of caution: the sibling who has taken the organiser role very often forgets to ask others what they want, they just tell them. Now is the time to ask them about future family dynamics and then wait for the response. It doesn't need to be you who does all the running. In my experience, if you practise a little patience, others will be spurred into action.

You mention your children. None of us, however hard we try and whatever insight we may have, will have created a family devoid of sibling rivalries. All we can do is be aware if we're labelling our children and assigning them pre-determined roles. Who, for example, will you appoint as executor of your will? Will it automatically be the eldest? In short, make sure you don't create for them the problems you've been experiencing with your own siblings. We can't change our parents but we can change how we parent.

Q3 **Life isn't how I expected it to be. My father-in-law is ill and in hospital. He's lived on his own for years and been totally independent. Now that will no longer be possible. My husband is an only child and he thinks that we should ask him to move in with us. I can see the sense in it but I know I'll end up doing the lion's share of the caring and I don't want to. He doesn't want to go into a home and I don't think it would be very kind of us to make him do so. I work full-time in a job I enjoy; quite apart from anything else, it's essential financially as we're still supporting two children at university. At the moment, I'm just too exhausted to think about anything as almost all our spare time is taken up by going to visit my father-in-law. I know we'll have to make a decision sooner or later but I don't know what it should be. I'm so confused.**

If I had a pound for every time someone over 50 said to me that life hadn't turned out how they'd expected, I'd be a very rich woman! We baby boomers were brought up believing that all would be easy when we reached this age. It was the myth created by our parents who had lived through the war, had children born into a post-war era of hope and expectation and who wanted more than anything to believe that the bright new future had come and all would be well. I am not saying that their hopes have proved far-fetched but life has almost certainly turned out differently from most of our expectations.

For a moment let's indulge ourselves and take a look at how it was meant to be:

- Sit quietly and conjure up a picture of where you thought you'd be living and what you thought you'd be doing. Imagine your immediate family and then your parents and extended family. For those of you who like to draw or paint, you might want to literally create a picture.

- Now put that on one side and draw or visualise how it is today for you and all the family.

- Look at the two pictures you have created, on paper or in your mind: Where are they similar? It's important to note the bits that are how you imagined they'd be.

- Now look at the parts that aren't the same and make a list of them. Based on your question, I'm assuming they'll be the majority.

- Examine how you feel when you hold the dream picture.

- If there are elements you feel you could still achieve, even if it will involve some effort, write them down so they become personal goals.

- Now dump the old picture! It's doing you no good and is just dragging you down.

If we spend our lives hankering after an impossible dream which bears no relation to reality, we're bound to be disappointed. However, if our vision and the reality coincide, we can achieve our goals and feel good about it. And if, as sometimes happens, our life exceeds our vision, then we need to celebrate this unlooked-for bonus.

I worked recently with a woman whose parents had died when she was young. Life had sometimes been hard for her as a result and it was not, of course, what she had hoped for but it was the reality. Whenever she thought about how her life could have turned out, she had a mental picture of two lovely elderly parents, adoring her, being supportive, the perfect grandparents. This was not the slightest bit useful as it left her feeling sad and abandoned. Coming to terms with the reality and acceptance of her situation was her first step to feeling different. She was then able to look at how she could deal with her life as it was, not how she wished it could be. She didn't need to look very far. She had aunts and in-laws who could certainly fill the gap when it came to help with childcare and babysitting. They'd always been there but now she was accepting of them, happy for them to step into the gap her own parents would have filled.

Now let's turn more specifically to the problems that are facing you. You're a fully-fledged member of the sandwich generation, the group who are the layer between ageing parents and their own children. Let's be clear here: it's not easy either to become elderly or a 'parent' to your own parents. However, as more and more people live into their eighties and nineties and medical science helps them to overcome their physical ailments, a growing number of elderly people will inevitably need help with the demands of everyday life. As baby boomers, we'll probably be in this position ourselves one day so, as well as finding a way to cope with the generation above us now, we need to create a blueprint for our children. I'm sure that's more important in the legacy stakes than an extra few thousand that might come their way.

Whatever anyone may tell you, it's usually women – whether daughters, daughters-in-law or nieces – who are left to care for the elderly while also trying to meet the needs of the next generation. Like you, many of us are still at work, enjoying it, perhaps even at the peak of our careers, when we're faced with having to make difficult choices about parental care.

A report entitled *The Cost of a Parent* was published in 2007 following a survey commissioned by Liverpool Victoria, Britain's largest Friendly Society. It revealed that one in eight adults has elderly parents or in-laws who need assistance, with grown-up children spending on average more than eight hours a week visiting and running errands for their parents and with a fifth spending more than double that time on parental care.

Let's now move to the options available to you and your husband. This is without doubt a shared problem to be agreed upon by both of you; you also need to involve your father-in-law, something people in your situation sometimes forget. While our parents have their mental faculties it's really important that they're part of the decision-making process when it comes to choices in their declining years. They may have to compromise as they can no longer be fully independent but that doesn't mean they should be removed from the equation. Too often, I talk to people who seem to have forgotten this and start treating their parents as children and then wonder why there's a family fall-out.

You've found yourself suddenly faced with a crisis that could have been partially avoided if you, your husband and your father-in-law had planned in advance. For most of us, parents and children alike, it's hard to bear the fact that the roles will reverse and the power will shift. It may explain why so few of us plan ahead. The conversations you need to have now won't be easy: you'll need to talk about wills, living wills, power of attorney and how your father-in-law wants to be cared for when he comes out of hospital. These are delicate matters and need to be handled as sensitively and non-emotionally as possible, otherwise everyone's likely to get upset (see Section 1 Questions 7 and 8 for more on this).

As parents get older and need more care, there are four options available (some of these will no longer be an option for you). The elderly parent can:

- Live with you

- Live in their own home

- Live in residential care

- Live in sheltered accommodation

On the face of it, living at home may seem the best option because the elderly person will be in familiar surroundings being visited by carers, either paid for by themselves or by social services, depending on their financial circumstances. The disadvantages are that full-time care is very pricey and the care offered by social services may not be enough. There is also the danger of isolation and loneliness as many of their peers will have passed away be in a similar position. Their house will probably require some modification to take account of the elderly person's physical frailties (see the Resource List for information on where you can get help and advice).

Living in sheltered accommodation is ideal if the person is fit enough. They're able to be independent but, with a warden on the premises, there is always someone to hand if they need help. There are a number of different types of sheltered accommodation, both private and state-run, so again look at the Resource List for more on this. The accommodation often has communal facilities, a place to meet others, and activities are offered on site. This can be an ideal first move from the elderly person's own home. The disadvantages are that they still have to do all their own household chores and, if they do deteriorate, they'll be forced to move if they require more care.

Residential care offers a safe environment where the elderly can have their own room and therefore some privacy and independence and also be with peers with whom they can share time and activities. There will be care available round the clock which will give everyone peace of mind. It's important that you find a home that suits the person and is occupied by like-minded people.

One of the factors that often stops families suggesting or agreeing to their parents going into a care home is guilt. I talk about this in the next question in this section. Also, for those who are looking for a home for both parents, there is real concern that they might be split up. This is by no means always the case. More and more homes have double rooms and some have suites so couples can spend time together.

The final option available is living with you. I wonder if this option has arisen because you're faced with a crisis or if this has always been on the cards. My hunch is that it's the former and, although it might be a short-term solution while you decide what to do next, unless it's what you all want, it will be fraught with problems.

Let's take a look at living with you from your father-in-law's perspective. He will have to move from his familiar area to yours where he won't know many people, if any, independently of you. He will have given up all his independence and will have to live by your rules. Your father-in-law and your husband will have to negotiate a way to relate to each other so they don't fall back into old habits. He will know that most of the care – doing the washing, cleaning his room, looking after him if he's ill and so on – will fall to you and, however long you've been part of the family, you aren't his child and it could feel intrusive. If he needs a lot of care and you're still working, you will have to employ extra help during the day which would reduce any potential discomfort he might feel. He'll want to contribute in some way so he doesn't feel a financial burden and this needs to be discussed in advance; he may also wish to help by doing the odd chore.

For all the difficulties, sometimes living with an elderly relative is the right thing to do because it's a comfort to know that he or she are safe in the bosom of the family. They will probably sell their property and can add to the value of yours as you'll now have extra money to spend on adaptations such as, say, an extra room and bathroom. This will also offer a measure of independence.

If this is the route you plan to go down, you and your husband need to do some serious thinking and make some decisions before you broach the possibility with your father-in-law. He then needs to decide if this is the best solution for him.

I've listed below the things I think you should consider and the best way to approach them. They would need to be agreed before he moved in.

1. Discuss everything together and then with your father-in-law.

2. Both you and your husband should make a list of the issues you think would be difficult and resolve these before the arrangement starts; I expect there would need to be some compromise on both sides.

3. Repeat this exercise with your father-in-law.

4. Agree 'house rules' beforehand. You may want to agree, for example, that you only eat together once a week or that certain places remain private. Also, you should discuss in advance a code of dress when walking around the house.

5. We all need some privacy: don't assume that everyone wants to spend every waking hour together.

6. Include your children in the discussion, even if they do mostly live away from home.

7. Decide how you would manage the changed situation financially. Perhaps he would contribute regularly or give a lump sum for house adjustments – or both.

8. Think of things he can do to maintain independence, groups he could join, chores he could do and so on.

9. Agree you will have occasional 'house meetings' where everyone is given five minutes to say how they feel with no interruptions from anyone else. Once you've each had your turn, you can look at ways to solve any problem.

10. In case he is ever unwell, make sure there's an emergency system to call you if you're there, or for someone external if you're not.

11. Don't agree to take on all the extra tasks yourself: divide them between you and your husband. It's his father, after all. And make sure you don't become the 'bad guy' because you are always the one who says when there's a problem.

12. Ensure you get enough help from social services and healthcare professionals so there would be enough time for you and your husband, as well as proper weekend breaks and holidays.

This is a very difficult decision and a major step. One way to ease the situation is to try it on a trial basis. Maybe agree that he stays for the first three months after he comes out of hospital and then you can all assess the best way forward. Also never forget: there are lots of people out there who can help.

In researching this book, I met a group of gay men who talked about the fact that they, as some heterosexual men and women, don't have children who they could go and live with, even if they wanted to. They raised two important concerns: one was that they'd need to be somewhere where they felt able to be 'out' as gay men, not wishing to end their days pretending in the way many had started their adult life; the other was to fantasise about the ideal place and the ideal carers! They're not alone as people often talk about wanting to be either in sheltered accommodation or a residential setting with their pals. If that's what you want when your time comes, you need to start planning now.

Q4 **I am 62 and I have four adult children. We downsized when the youngest went to university. We now have two, in their mid to late twenties, back living at home while they try to get decent jobs. This leaves us no spare room. My eldest child's relationship has just split up and he wants to come home, too. There's no room. I feel dreadful that we can't accommodate them all and feel now that we should never have moved. I don't know whether to tell one of the others to go to make space for the eldest. My husband thinks they should all go and it's time we had a life for just the two of us, particularly after a year on our own which we both enjoyed. What can I do to keep everyone happy? This isn't how I expected life to be at my age. I'm the one who gets upset and feels guilty. How do I solve the situation?**

Your question focuses on the other half of the sandwich discussed in the previous question and answer. Do take a look at that as many of the same principles apply. I discuss this and the 'never expected it to' phenomenon which our generation seems to be experiencing!

Let's start by looking at guilt which is a universal emotion although some of us are much more prone to it than others and particularly, I think, if you're a parent. Guilt is the feeling we have when we've done something we think we shouldn't have done or we haven't done something we think we should have done. It can leave us feeling sick to the core and anxious, too, as well as unable to move forward and make rational decisions.

Psychologists have defined two sorts of guilt: 'healthy' and 'unhealthy' guilt. Healthy guilt is an appropriate feeling (although the strength of it can sometimes be out of proportion to the event) because it alerts you to the fact you may have done or said something that wasn't very sensitive and you need to apologise and behave differently in future. An example would be spending too much time working and not giving your family enough attention and then being snappy with them because you are over-tired. Your guilt alerts you to this and gives you an opportunity to do something about it. It's only useful, of course, if you identify why there's a problem and then rectify it. If we feel bad but don't change our behaviour, we just add to the 'pile of guilt' and wear ourselves down.

Unhealthy guilt is what we usually get from outsiders or from our own 'internalised parent' who tells us something is wrong and that we're not living up to the required standard; in other words, the part inside ourselves that ticks us off. An example of this would be feeling guilty because you only vacuum the living-room carpet once a week. You know that's sufficient but you also know your mother would disapprove so you give yourself a hard time. Or it can be when someone tells you that they're happy having their six children living at home and would never dream of downsizing. Instead of listening with detached interest to how they manage their life, you immediately compare yourself to them, decide you're falling short and feel terrible as a result.

This type of guilt does us no good; it lowers our self-esteem and general sense of wellbeing. Often, when others say something that makes you feel guilty, it's because they want you to do it their way and act like them. If you are aware of this, you won't internalise the feeling but accept they have a different point of view and carry on doing things the way that suits you best.

One method of checking out whether your guilt is healthy or unhealthy is to ask yourself the following questions:

- Does this feeling make me want to behave differently?

- If I do behave differently, will it make me feel better?

Take my first example – too much time working. You'll obviously feel better if you spend more time with your family and are less snappy. So if the answer to the questions is yes, your guilty feeling was useful, assuming you acted on it.

When it comes to the vacuuming example, you'll simply feel resentful if you're motivated by what your mother might say were she there. So that is unhealthy guilt and not useful at all.

Now let's look at your family and the situation you find yourself in. What exactly do you feel guilty about? There are a number of possibilities. I'll start the list for you:

- Your husband isn't getting enough of your attention?

- Your eldest child isn't getting the space he currently needs?

- Your two youngest aren't taking responsibility for their own lives?

- Downsizing because it was the right thing for you and your husband left the children without a bedroom each?

- Your own parents wouldn't have behaved like this?

  a) They'd never have asked us to leave home.
  b) They'd never have let us live at home just to save money.

I'm sure you can add to this list! Once you've finished, ask yourself the two questions about each statement and make a decision about which ones are 'healthy guilt' that will prompt you to change your behaviour and which ones are 'unhealthy guilt' and need to be dumped without further ado.

You're certainly not alone in having adult children at home. Figures from the Office of National Statistics in 2007 revealed that 57 per cent of men and 38 per cent of women aged 20–24 are still living at home. By their late twenties, more than one in five men still live with their parents, twice as many as women of that age. The number of children who return home has doubled since the late 1950s. More than half of today's 25-year-old men have never married or lived with a girlfriend, an increase from a third in the 1970s, while the number of unattached 30-year-old men has doubled. The charity Parentline has recently called for more government support for parents of adult children in their report, 'Will they ever fly the nest?'

Many young people return home after university, some moving only when they get a job, others waiting until they can get a deposit together to buy a property of their own. In the present economic climate where mortgages are harder to obtain, young people are going to have to be realistic about where they choose to live, otherwise they could be with us for many years. Some parents are now reducing their own retirement savings to help their children on their way which, although well-intentioned, may leave the older generation with difficulties later on. Some children are already finding themselves having to help their elderly parents financially.

The new phenomenon some baby boomer parents are facing is children returning home sometimes two or three times. This was not the case when we were young: once we'd left home, it was for good. And it seems that there's more impact on parents when their children return home after being away rather than from those who never left in the first place. This is probably what your husband is responding to. Even though many parents find it hard when their children first leave home, they usually readjust well and their lives move on to the next chapter. Understandably, when children return, the children themselves may feel a mixture of resentment, disappointment, lack of privacy and guilt about being a financial drain. It seems from the available research that mothers often see this as a time to create a new bond with the young person while fathers find it harder. Joanna Trollope's *Second Honeymoon* is a novel on just this subject.

If living with adult children is going to work, agreements need to be made and adhered to. This is a different stage in all your lives. The following are suggestions for parents to consider and agree upon, ideally before anyone comes back home. This way, the ground rules will be established in advance. It's essential that both of you agree and uphold these rules otherwise it will have a negative impact on your own relationship:

- Children should always let you know if they'll be away for the night or have friends to stay.

- Agree in advance about rent or payment in kind, such as performing household chores, cooking meals a couple of nights a week, buying food, doing their own washing and so on.

- Helping them manage their money. Not charging rent may not do them any favours in the long term as they could get used to living at an inflated level. If you don't feel comfortable about this, you could charge rent but save it for them so they can add it to a deposit for either rental or purchase when they move out.

- Agree areas where you won't interfere – for example, how late they stay out and who they go out with.

- Have an exit plan. Agree for how long they'll be living with you. It's a good idea to agree this prior to their moving in so they work towards independence.

Once they're installed, it's important to:

- Communicate – talk to each other when things get tricky, otherwise small niggles will fester and lead to big rows.

- Help them with their plans to move out so they're able to achieve their goals.

- Don't suffocate them or you'll end up having the equivalent of adolescent rows.

You ask what you can do to keep everyone happy. Impossible! But what you *can* be is fair and consistent. And don't, for heaven's sake, blame yourself for having moved into a smaller house when your fourth child went off to university. On the other hand, it's good to be able to help out in a crisis so having a spare room or a bed settee available with a time limit on its occupancy is a positive way of helping in times of stress – like now. My suggestion would be that you all sit down as a family and see how you can help the one who's going through the tough time. One of the others may decide it's time to move on or to double up while they make their exit plans.

Q5 **I have two children and I separated acrimoniously from my husband a couple of years ago. Several of my close friends rallied round him at the time and so I lost some people who'd been dear to me. This caused me a lot of sadness. I've recently moved in with a new partner and again friends are causing a problem. When I was on my own after our separation, I saw a lot of my mates but now I don't have as much free time to see them. How do you balance friends and partners? Women's friendships and men's seem so different. My new partner finds all this hard to understand especially when friends phone late at night and want an hour's chat.**

I'm going to focus on friendships and relationships and not on your separation or new partner as these subjects are covered elsewhere, e.g. in Section 3 Question 5. So, let's start by looking at what happens to friendships when there's a separation. It's an old and not so funny joke that a couple's assets include their friends and that these, too, are divided when a separation or divorce occurs. This is often something that's not foreseen and can create a lot of upset.

Many people going through separation and divorce assume that the friends who knew them first will stick by them. But it isn't that easy because friendships evolve – and, from the moment you and your original friend acquired partners, the dynamic was bound to change.

If you've been in a long-term relationship, as many of us have by our age, who was whose friend first is pretty irrelevant by now.

It's very hard when there's a conflict to stay impartial and non-judgmental. If the splitting partners are fighting – and you say yours was an acrimonious split – it's almost impossible for friends to know what to do and how to get it right. One partner may feel wronged or betrayed if the other partner is mentioned to them by a friend; it's difficult for mutual friends to even say they've seen or spoken to the estranged partner. In the end, it's easier to see the friend who makes the least fuss.

When you're having a tough time, it is not always possible to accept that, although our friends really care about us, they also want to get something out of the relationship. If it's relentless hard work, they'll no longer want to see us with the same frequency. The problem is that, at the point of separation, people feel very vulnerable, often adding to their pain and loneliness by making it hard for their friends, either by constantly complaining about their situation or moaning about the ex, and being self-absorbed and therefore less sensitive to their friends' needs.

An added problem is that before a separation most things are talked about together, certainly concerns about children, and sometimes these concerns will have been shared with friends. Now, however, the couple may not be sharing anything and therefore friends may know something about a child that one parent doesn't. If friends are to manage this minefield, it's really important they are very clear and mindful of the new boundaries. It's all too easy to tread on toes unwittingly, causing upset not only to the couple but to their children as well.

A by-product of a couple splitting up is that other couples begin to examine their own relationships and it sometimes shows up problems. Some couples will choose to avoid their separated friends simply for fear of a contaminating effect on their own marriage. For others, the loss of the relationship they had with their friends is too great to bear so they drop them and look to other couples to fill the gap.

Let's now turn to friendship in general. It is by no means a new phenomenon. Early philosophers such as Aristotle and Cicero talked about friendship. Aristotle believed that there were three forms of friendship, one genuine, one based on usefulness and one on pleasure. The first lasts forever but the other two are less enduring. Cicero built on this, adding that we should 'ask from friends and do for friends only what is good'. He also suggested we should offer our help freely and not wait to be asked, giving open and honest advice without embarrassment. Things really haven't changed that much!

Before we look at your friendships, I suggest you do the following quiz:

FRIENDSHIP QUIZ

Think of ten people you know – family member, partner, oldest friend, work colleague and so on – and then answer the following questions about them, circling the answer that fits each one best:

I. a) I can spend hours with them and still enjoy it

b) I meet these people at shared activities e.g. work, the gym, an evening class

c) I am happy to pass some time with them

d) I'm always pleased to see them

e) I used to know them really well but distance means we don't see each other as often

2. a) I would be happy to see them as often as I could

   b) I would wave and say hi if I met them in the street

   c) We share things in common – for example, we have children of the same age

   d) I call them every so often

   e) We've had some good times together

3. a) I always find something to really laugh about with them

   b) I know very little about them

   c) They're part of my wider circle

   d) I would suggest lunch at work to them if I was going in a group

   e) We can talk fairly intimately

4. a) I can often shorthand the conversation because they understand me

   b) I wouldn't have coffee or lunch with them by myself

   c) I tend to see them when one of their friends invites them round

   d) I'd invite them to a party I was giving

e) If I had more time, I'd know them better

5. a) I only have two or three of them I can talk to about anything, including my deepest feelings

b) I know them as an acquaintance

c) I have known them for a while but not well

d) They're great to be out with in a small group

e) I like them a lot but our friendship hasn't developed further

Take the first person on your list and add up the number of times they scored a, b, c and so on. Then do this for the other nine.

Mostly a) These are the people closest to you, the ones who are privy to your inner feelings. These relationships are based on mutual giving and receiving. You don't hold back on what you say to each other. These friends often have high expectations of us. Your partner should be in this group.

Mostly b) These are acquaintances you know because you share a setting, typically the workplace. You're happy to see them there but not elsewhere. You know little personal information about them. You would only invite them if you were putting on an event, e.g. a charity ball and you needed a lot of people to come.

Mostly c) You know these people quite well, often going out in a group with them but rarely individually. If you're alone together, you won't be lost for words but your conversation would be quite superficial. This category may include people from your past.

Mostly d) These are people you work with or live near to and whose company you enjoy. You'd invite them if you were having, say, twenty people to your house but they are by no means in your inner circle of friends.

Mostly e) These are people you really like but who you don't know as well as you could, although that might change one day. Or, perhaps, you know them well but they just aren't around much.

So, are you someone who has mainly a-type friends? They'll have been used to seeing you alone, to calling you at all hours of the day and night, you being there for them and they for you in your time of trouble. They need to take on board and respect that things have changed for you. The other types of friends are much less likely to demand your time except if there is a serious crisis.

It's been said that there are good friends and toxic friends – the ones who cause us grief and pain. Tim Melville-Ross, when he was Director-General of the Institute of Directors, talked about two types of people. 'Radiators' are the ones, he said, who give out and are enthusiastic about life. 'Drains' are those who are needy and sap you. When your marriage broke up, it would be perfectly understandable if you had gone from being a 'radiator' to a 'drain'. Surely your close friends understood that. Equally, your new life is giving you different priorities, again something your old friends should understand.

An interesting piece of research was undertaken by Dr Gindo Tampubolon, a sociologist at Manchester University. Some 10,000 British individuals were studied over the ten years between 1992 and 2002. His overall findings were that the friendship amongst women and men is fundamentally different. He came up with the following, sometimes less-than-surprising findings:

1. Women make 'deeper and more moral' friendships; men's are more 'calculating'.

2. Women's friendships are about the relationship itself.

3. Women keep their friends despite geography and social mobility and are likely to maintain a friendship for longer.

4. Women stand by their friends through thick and thin.

5. Women's views of friendship are connected to how they see themselves.

6. Men are more likely to base their friendships on activities and social relationships like football and drinking.

7. Single and older people and white-collar workers were better at pairing up.

8. Middle-class people were more likely to have a broader network of friends while working-class people had most of their friends in the same socio-economic group.

9. Three-quarters of best friends were of the same sex.

It's only fair to point out that women also hope to get something for themselves from their friendships – for example, someone with whom to share an experience, like bringing up children. I don't believe any of us are completely altruistic but women in the main talk more about themselves and the relationship than men do.

It's understandable, based on the findings of this research, that your new partner worries about your friendships. I think it would be helpful if you talked to him about the different types of friendship

I've outlined above; it might help if he also did the quiz. It sounds to me as if a number of your friends believe that regular contact is what makes a good friend and quantity as well as quality is part of the deal. They need to know that, if there were a crisis in their lives, you would drop everything for them but that you can't be at their beck and call every day. If you did, you'd end up with a partner who felt he wasn't a priority in your life which would inevitably lead to problems.

One last thought: a piece of research undertaken at the Centre for Ageing Studies in Adelaide, Australia, over the ten years between 1992 and 2002 looked at how a range of social, health and lifestyle factors affected the survival rates of more than 1,500 people over 70. Those with good social networks were found to be 22 per cent less likely to die during the following decade than those without. The conclusion was that a good close friend is more likely than a close family member to promote longevity and that, of all the social interactions, 'friends are the most important in terms of survival'. So, if your partner does complain, I'd send him out to find some pals of his own rather than agree to give up yours!

Q6 **My parents split up many years ago and both married again. I have good relationships with my step-parents and get on OK with my stepsiblings. Up until now, that is. All four parents are elderly and all do or will need care. My mother is physically very frail and my stepfather has early dementia as does my father, although his is more advanced. My stepmother is totally on the ball and finds it hard to cope with him. I now have to negotiate with my own siblings as well as my stepsiblings. It's a minefield and all the issues about being a reconstituted family are coming to a head. Am I supposed to look after my step-parents as well?**

You raise a very interesting question. Most of the stepfamily research to date focuses on younger children and doesn't answer the questions that are being faced by you and will be faced by many more as the baby boomer generation move into later adulthood. We grew up at a time of changing social values when divorce became much more prevalent (see Section 1 Question 6) with the result that re-marriages and step-parenting inevitably increased. So you're something of a pioneer, for all the comfort it will bring you. Many people of your age who have step-parents will have experienced the death of a parent. Re-marriage of widowed parents is not uncommon, either. But to have two sets of elderly parents is still reasonably rare.

Stepfamilies with adult children fall into two categories: those that were formed when the children were young but are now adults and those that were formed when the children were already adults. Even if the children were adults when their parents re-married it's still possible with the increase in life expectancy for a step-parent to be around for thirty-plus years.

There are a number of issues that arise in stepfamilies, which are different from first families. I have addressed this in Section 5, Question 5 and you may also be interested in reading other questions in that section. Financial worries when illness sets in or age tightens its grip can become a source of tension between parents and siblings.

I can't tell you what to do but I think it would be helpful if we looked at what's being said by the few researchers who have done studies in this area and, in a moment, examine the stepfamily cycle created by Patricia Papernow and written about in her book *Becoming a Stepfamily*. This will help you to understand your two families better and how to tackle the issues increasingly facing you. For ideas on how families can negotiate the care of elderly parents, take a look at my previous book, *Who's That Woman in the Mirror?* as well as at some of the other books in the Bibliography.

Lawrence Ganong and Marilyn Coleman published an article in the *Journal of Gerontology* in 2006 reporting on their research study, 'Obligations to Stepparents Acquired in Later Life'. They found that most people when asked would say that looking after older parents is a familial responsibility. The parents looked after the children when they were young and now it was time for the children to repay that debt, not least because of the sacrifices the parents made.

I have a different take on this. It is without doubt an obligation for parents to look after their children until they're young adults and able to look after themselves. But I don't think it's necessarily an obligation for children to look after their parents. It was the choice of the parents to have children in the first place. But the reverse isn't true. Of course, if children want to look after their parents because they have a close emotional bond and they make a conscious free choice to do so, that's great and what everyone would wish. For this to happen, though, parents need to create the kind of relationships where children feel good being with them. Sadly, from my experience, that isn't always the case although it doesn't stop those parents still having these expectations.

Ganong and Coleman's research showed that adults felt less obligated to support step-parents than their biological parents for perhaps understandable reasons. Others were happy to help because their parent had chosen the step-parent as a partner and therefore indirectly they were supporting their biological mother or father. However, the decision to support step-parents was more likely to be based on the closeness and quality of the relationship between the stepchildren and their step-parent. A close step-parent is often seen as more worthy of help than a biological parent who's been absent. That said, Adam Davey, a developmental psychologist at Temple University, Philadelphia, found in his research published in 2007 that ageing step-parents were only half as likely as biological parents to receive care from grown children.

Patricia Papernow describes a cycle that all stepfamilies go through if they're going to create a good familial relationship. She divides it into three main stages – early, middle and later, and seven sub-stages: The early phase has three stages. During these, the family is still bound and divided by its biological lines. All the members of the old family behave as they've always done in regard to each other. They adhere to all the old rules and ways of caring for one another with connections remaining really strong between the original family members.

Early stage

Stage One is the fantasy stage. The adults are very keen, perhaps unrealistically so, to make everything better, to heal all past hurts. They are also looking for their new partners to provide what the last one didn't, if the first marriage ended in divorce, and to fill the gaps if the first partner died. The new partners are in love and believe that this is enough to make the children similarly love one another and get on well with the new step-parent. There is high expectation and hope all round. The children, meanwhile, may often still hold on to the fantasy that their biological parents will get back together again one day.

Stage Two is the assimilation or 'immersion' stage. This is when reality begins to hit. It isn't all as everyone had hoped. Step-parents who had expected to just fit in find themselves as outsiders as their partner retains an intense connection with their children. The children often also have a strong relationship with their biological non-resident parent. Step-parents experience a period of considerable disorientation, confusion and anxiety, with negative feelings of jealousy, resentment, shame and self-blame. The two adults will also be experiencing difficulties, the biological parent wondering if this was the right thing to do and whether the step-parent truly wants to connect to the children. The step-parent, as a result, may well feel unsupported by their partner, busy nurturing his/her own children. When two existing families join forces, each adult will have to cope with being both parent and step-parent.

Stage Three is the awareness stage when the parents begin to make some sense of what's going on. It should by now be possible to start discussing feelings. When step-parents start to see that they're the outsiders in the other family and that it's the situation not them that's the issue, they are likely to gain back some of their self-confidence. The biological parent becomes more aware of their role in relation to their children and the potential tensions faced by the step-parent. Both partners need to let go of the fantasy that this will be easy and begin together to create some realistic structures for their new family.

Middle stage

Stage Four is mobilisation, the beginning of the middle stage where restructuring really starts to take place. Step-parents begin to express their needs, raising differences of opinion and generally making their demands known. It is almost inevitably a period of conflict. The step-parent is relieved they can say what they feel and the biological parent becomes even more uncomfortable about having a foot in both camps. The two adults are also striving for time alone together to be a couple.

Stage Five is all about action when the family starts to negotiate and new boundaries are drawn. Relationships have to be realigned and changes made. The family group begins to move away from being bound by the original biological family's way of operating towards being a stable stepfamily. Step-parents are creating their own relationships with their stepchildren that are not dependent on the other parent.

Later stage

Stage Six is less intense as things settle down and life becomes easier. Agreements have been made and can be put into practice. There is much less competition and parents and step-parents can make pair relationships both with the children and each other. Now, people have good one-to-one relationships which become more real, intimate and satisfying. Step-parents and biological parents are able to share parenting issues with each other and the children will not automatically try to divide and rule. The role of the step-parent is clearly defined and everyone feels easier about it.

Stage Seven is resolution time when the family is finally stable and solid. The newly configured family has begun to create its own history with its rules and modes of behaviour. Of course, like any family, there will be ups and downs but nothing that will threaten the core of the stepfamily. The step-parent feels as though they belong, albeit as an 'insider outsider'. They are fully involved in family life, as well as being able to be outside enough to discuss issues that might be difficult to share with the biological parent.

It will usually take from four to seven years for a family to go through this process. When there are two families coming together, as in your case, it's obviously a more complex business.

Step issues will continue to arise whenever there is a significant event: choice of school, moving house, a different stepchild coming to live in the house and join the family, college, graduations, weddings, illness and bereavements. As you're finding, managing parents as they get older will present new and additional problems. At stressful times, the family may re-experience the whole of the cycle in miniature but this won't seriously threaten the step-parent or the step-parent/child relationship, even if it does lead to upsets, confusion and arguments. New agreements and ways of behaving need again to be agreed.

As you're currently experiencing difficulties, I suspect your family has moved back into an earlier stage. You may find it helpful to look at the exercises suggested by Patricia Papernow where she offers tips to help you through these tricky times (see Bibliography). If you continue to be really stuck, seeking some professional help would be a good idea (e.g. parentlineplus.org.uk or for fathers, www.dad.info).

Right now, you're faced with a big problem as you have four elderly parents and step-parents. You will, I think, have to make some choices as to where your help is needed and how much time you can give. (See Question 3 in this section.) One thing that would be very helpful is for you to see each of the two families to which you belong as individual entities. They will both have their own needs, operate uniquely and be made up of different people with their individual characteristics, demands and behaviour. You will have a different role in each family and different expectations will be made of you. I suggest you identify where it is that you hold the more primary role and who needs you most. You only have so much time and energy you can give so decide what has to be done first, who else can help you and always remember that it's possible to say no!

Last Thoughts

Since I wrote the last book only fifteen months ago, my postbag has quadrupled and the enquiries and comments that we've received at Experience Matters have surpassed any of our expectations. We are in the business of educating, through coaching, workshops and a virtual community of question writers and experts who have between them a wealth of knowledge. Do take a look at what we offer.

At present, we're developing our site further to offer more information. There are many places where you can find holiday and travel information and financial advice but few where you can gain the knowledge, insight and support to manage your home and working lives.

The more we hear from you the more we can offer that meets your needs. Please go to the website: www.experiencematters.org.uk or join as a member and receive regular updates. You might like to come to our workshops which cover a wide number of topics including love and sex and meet other like-minded people who want to find the best way to enjoy this next stage of our lives.

Resource List

General Resources

www.adviceguide.org.uk
Advice guide from Citizens
Advice Bureau

Provides information on rights,
benefits, housing, family
matters, employment, debt,
consumer and legal issues.

www.ageconcern.co.uk.
Age Concern – the UK's largest
organisation working with and
for older people

Local services, books, shops,
fact sheets, telephone
information on housing,
income, pensions, wills,
lasting power of attorney etc.

www.bacp.co.uk
British Association for
Counselling and Psychotherapy –
a charity working towards the
promotion and regulation of
counselling and psychotherapy

Information, training and
directory of therapists for
counselling and psychotherapy.

www.bbc.co.uk
BBC website

Information and links to many
areas, including ageing, health,
relationships etc.

www.channel4.com/health
Channel 4 television website

Information on sex, health and relationships.

www.direct.gov.uk/en/over50s
Government website offering services for the 50+

A very useful portal site for the over-fifties. Covers all areas including wills, advanced directives, lasting power of attorney etc.

www.experiencematters.org.uk
Experience Matters Ltd. Coaching and consultancy for the 50+

A consultancy that specialises in issues affecting the 50+ and management solutions for organisations. Workshops and coaching to enable individuals to find solutions to a variety of problems.

www.fpa.org.uk
UK Family Planning Association – a registered charity working to improve sexual health and reproductive rights for all people

Information about sexual health, sexually transmitted infections and clinics.

www.businessballs.com
Free ethical training and development resource run by Alan Chapman

Information on many topics and personal development, self- and organisational development.

www.ivillage.co.uk
An online site offering information for all age groups

Features, articles, forums and quizzes on a wide variety of issues including health, relationships, parenting and work.

www.kinseyinstitute.org
The Kinsey Institute – research in sex, gender and reproduction

Information and research into human sexuality, gender and reproduction.

www.laterlife.com
UK website for the 50+

Information on a variety of topics, ideas and features to help enjoy retirement and later life to the full.

www.maturetimes.co.uk
The Mature Times – online newspaper

Articles and news on a wide variety of topics affecting the 50+.

www.netdoctor.co.uk
Net Doctor – a comprehensive site for all health issues

Information on a wide variety of topics; men's and women's health, sex, grief etc.

www.nhsdirect.nhs.uk
NHS Direct – National Health Service website

Information and advice on health issues, online self-help guide, 24-hour telephone service. General information on health and emotional issues.

www.oneplusone.org.uk
One Plus One – Supporting family relationships

Comprehensive site with information on all aspects of couple and family relation-ships. Puts research into practice.

www.parship.co.uk
Parship – Europe's largest online
matchmaking service

Dating, information,
testimonials, research and
articles.

www.patient.co.uk
Patient UK

Health information and advice
for patients and carers.

www.relate.org.uk
Relate – the largest relationship
counselling organisation in
the UK

Advice, relationship
counselling, sex therapy,
workshops, mediation, consul-
tations and support
face-to-face, by phone and
through the website.

www.retirement-matters.co.uk
Retirement Matters

Comprehensive website for the
50+ including health and
sexual matters.

www.saga.co.uk
SAGA – magazine and
organisation for the 50+

General information including
health, travel, insurance, and
Saga Zone online social
community.

www.sexuality.org
Society for human sexuality

Positive and helpful information on all forms of human
sexuality.

www.statistics.gov.uk
The UK Statistics Authority

Data on economy, population and society at national and local level.

www.womenbloom.com
Women Bloom – inspiring and supporting women to make the most of mid-life

An American website with articles, forums, news and information for women of 50+.

⊰ Section One ⊱

Additional resources

www.alzheimers.org.uk
Alzheimer's Society – a leading care and research charity for people with all types of dementia, their families and carers

Information about different forms of dementia, help for carers, news and events.

www.basrt.org.uk
British Association for Sexual and Relationship Therapy

National specialist charity for sexual and relationship therapy, plus list of therapists.

www.bma.org.uk
British Medical Association

Information on health and ageing, including sexual health for the older person.

www.caregiver.org
Family Caregiver Alliance

Public voice for caregivers. Information, education, services, research and advocacy.

www.divorcebusting.org
Divorce and relationship website links

A site that links to other websites dealing with marital/couple issues.

www.funeral-service-spain.com
Natural burials

Range of different places for ashes to be scattered, including sky burials.

www.greenburialcouncil.org
Green Burial Council

A non-profit organisation founded to educate the public about burials that are sustainable for the planet.

www.ipm.org.uk
Institute of Psychosexual Medicine

Education, training and research into psychosexual medicine.

www.iwf.org.uk
Internet Watch Foundation

UK hotline for reporting illegal content, specifically child sexual abuse.

www.marriagebuilders.com
Marriage builders – successful marriage advice

Answers to questions on love, adultery, marriage and counselling and love.

www.mceu.gov.uk
Marine Consents and
Environment Unit

Now part of the Marine and
Fisheries Agency. Information
on burial at sea.

www.naturaldeath.org.uk
The Natural Death Centre

Independent funeral advice for
the UK. Funeral Choices,
living wills, advanced health
directive advice and support.

www.ncdv.org.uk
National Centre for Domestic
Violence

Support for victims of
domestic abuse. Offers 24-
hour helpline.

www.publicguardian.gov.uk
Office of the Public Guardian

Information on making and
registering a lasting power of
attorney.

www.respect.uk.net
Respect – UK charity association
for domestic violence perpetrator
programmes

Information for those
experiencing domestic
violence, and associated
support services.

www.womensaid.org.uk
Women's Aid

A key national charity
working to end domestic
violence against women and
children.

❧ Section Two ❧

Additional resources

www.cancerbackup.org.uk
Cancer Backup and Macmillan
Cancer Support merged
information service

Europe's leading cancer
information service providing
accurate, up-to-date and
authoritative cancer information, resources and support.

www.civilpartnershipguide.com
Civil partnership guide

An online resource for gay
and lesbian people who are
thinking about or planning
their civil partnership.

www.familyequality.org
Family Equality Council

Works to ensure equality for
lesbian, gay, bisexual transgender families.

www.gaypsychotherapy.com
Michael Shernoff – psychotherapy

Information on gay relationships, articles and counselling.

www.gaystheword.co.uk
Lesbian and gay bookshop

An independent bookshop for
independent thinkers.

www.geocities.com/Str8_Spouse
Straight spouse support

An organisation that provides nationwide support for individuals whose spouse or partner is gay or lesbian.

www.gmfa.org.uk
The gay men's health charity

Links to useful websites on a wide variety of gay issues, including groups.

www.grieflink.asn.au
Bereavement information resource

An Australian information resource on death-related grief for individuals and professionals.

www.lesbian.org
Promoting lesbian visibility on the internet

Links to lots of useful sites for lesbians.

www.lesbilicious.co.uk
Lesbilicious – online lesbian magazine

Offering information on a variety of lifestyle topics.

www.marriedgay.org
General website for lesbians, gays and bisexuals

Information for married men and women who are gay, lesbian or bisexual and for their partners.

www.pinktherapy.com
UK's largest independent therapy organisation working with gender and sexual minority groups

Promotes high-quality therapy and training services for people who are lesbian, gay, bisexual and transsexual.

www.retirementexpert.co.uk
Retirement issues

Advice, features and tips from experts on a variety of retirement aspects.

www.straightspouse.org
The Straight Spouse Network, an American organisation set up for straight spouses with gay, lesbian, transgender or bisexual partners

Online support, features, advice.

✺ Section Three ✺

Additional resources

www.belladepaulo.com
Bella DePaulo – social scientist website

Information for single men and women, with Links to singles studies.

www.danielgoleman.imp
Emotional intelligence (EI)

Updates and information on his thinking and EI model.

www.ezinarticles.com
Ezine articles

Numerous articles from numerous experts on all sorts of subjects.

www.separateddads.co.uk
Resource for separated dads

Help and advice for separated fathers.

www.sexualityadvice.com
Sexuality and advice

A gateway to sites full of information and education about sex, relationships and sexual health.

www.therelationshipgym.com
Relationship and dating advice

Relationship help and advice, whether you are single or not.

www.thirdage.com
Third Age online information site

Mid-life health, relationships, career advice and more.

www.ivillage.co.uk
Online site for women

Where women can exchange views and advice and support on a range of issues.

❧ Section Four ❧

Additional resources

www.avert.org
Avert – international AIDS charity

Information on sexuality and sexual health.

www.askmen.com
Men's online free magazine

Information on relationships and health, dating and love.

www.beaumontsociety.org.uk
The Beaumont Society

A support group for transsexuals, those that cross-dress, transvestites and their family friends and colleagues.

www.crisiscounselling.com
Website offering help for internet addiction

Information on cybersex and internet addiction.

www.kinseyinstitute.org
The Kinsey Institute for research into sex, gender and reproduction

Sexuality information, advice, links, help, reports and data.

www.netaddiction.com
Center for Internet Addiction Recovery

Offers help and treatment services, resources and information.

www.ozabis.info
Abis – information on BDSM (Australian website)

Resources and information on Bondage and Discipline, Dominance and Submission, Sadism and Masochism.

www.pinkpractice.co.uk
Counselling and psychotherapy for sexual minorities

Information site, plus lists of UKCP registered psychotherapists and BACP registered senior counsellors for lesbians/gays/and bisexuals.

www.pinktherapy.com
Therapy organisation working with gender and sexual minority clients.

A source for information, therapists, self-help videos and training for gender issues.

www.psychologicalscience.org
Association for Psychological
Science

Publications, journals, links
and the advancement of scien-
tifically orientated psychology.

www.sexualrecovery.com
Sexual Recovery Institute

Provides assessment and
treatment of sexually addictive
behaviours for the individual
and their family.

www.vernoncoleman.com
Vernon Coleman, campaigner and
author

Books, ideas and information
from former GP. Survey on
cross-dressing.

www.transgenderzone.com
UK-based support website

Information on transgender
law, medical articles, and
advice and support.

❧ Section Five ❧

Additional resources

www.babcp.com
British Association for Behavioural
and Cognitive Psychotherapies

A leading organisation for the
theory, practice and development of cognitive behavioural
therapy (CBT) in the UK.

www.divorce.co.uk
Divorce and separation resource

Information and advice for families on marriage breakdown, the divorce process and how to cope.

www.divorce360.com
Divorce 360.com website

Help, advice and community for people going through or recovering from a divorce and the issues around it.

www.fnf.org.uk
Families Need Fathers

Help with shared parenting issues arising from a relationship breakdown for mothers and fathers married or not, grandparents and extended families.

www.kidsinthemiddle.org
Divorce hurts. Kids in the Middle® helps

A non-profit American agency providing support, counselling, group and individual therapy education for kids and families coping with separation and divorce.

www.polyamorysociety.org
The Polyamory Society

A non-profit organisation which promotes and supports the interests of individuals of multi-partenered relationships and their families.

www.repsych.ac.uk
The Royal College of
Psychiatrists

Improving the lives of people
affected by mental illness. Has
useful information on CBT
and other therapies.

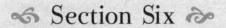

❦ Section Six ❧

Additional resources

www.boomerangkidshelp.com
Boomerang Kids contracts

Articles, advice and a contract
for those with older children
living at home.

www.careforthefamily.org.uk
Care for the Family charity

A national charity which aims
to promote strong family life,
information and support.

www.dorothyrowe.com.au
Dorothy Rowe

The website of Dorothy Rowe
– a world-renowned psychologist and writer, with numerous
articles and podcasts.

www.elderlyparents.org.uk
Elderly parents support

Organisation with advice and
information on the welfare of
elderly parents.

www.futurefoundation.net
Future Foundation – online trends
and consultancy

Independent commercial
think-tank whose work is
strategic and future focused.

www.grandparents-association.org.uk
The Grandparents' Association

Provides support and information to enable the relationship
between grandchildren and
grandparents to flourish.

www.grandparentsplus.org.uk
Grandparents Plus – a national
charity for children and
extended families

Promotes the vital role of
grandparents and the
extended family in children's
lives: training and information.

www.helptheaged.org.uk
Help the Aged – an international
charity supporting older
people's needs

Offers advice and information
on a wide variety of issues
that affect elderly people and
their carers.

www.housingcare.org
Options for older people

Information about sheltered
housing, care and residential
homes and all forms of elderly
care in the UK.

www.infed.org
Resources for adult education

Resource for community
education, informal adult
education, lifelong learning
and social action.

Bibliography

Abbott, Deborah and Farmer, Ellen *From Wedded Wife to Lesbian Life*, USA: The Crossing Press, 1995

Adelman, Marcy, R. *Midlife Lesbian Relationships: Friends, Lovers, Children, and Parents*, Routledge, 2000

Baldwin, Guy *Ties That Bind: SM/Leather/Fetish/Erotic Style*, Daedalus Publishing Company, 1993

Block, Joel D. with Susan Crain Bakos *Sex over 50*, Prentice Hall, 1999

Blood, Imogen *Older Women and Domestic Violence*, London: Help the Aged, 2004

Blue, Violet, *The Ultimate Guide to Sexual Fantasy*, Cleis Press, 2004

Boyd, Helen *My Husband Betty: Love, Sex and Life with a Crossdresser*, Seal Press, 2003

Boyd, Helen *She's Not the Man I Married: My Life with a Transgender Husband*, Seal Press, 2006

Brass, Perry *How to Survive Your Own Gay Life*, Belhue Press, 1998

Brown, Paul and Kell, Christine *The Good Sex Book: The New Illustrated Guide*, Courage Books, 1997

Cohn-Sherbok, Dan and Lavinia *What Do You Do When Your Parents Live Forever?*, O Books, 2007

Coleman, Dr Vernon *Men in Dresses: A Study of Transvestism/Cross-dressing*, A European Medical Journal Special Monograph, 1996

Culbreth, Judsen, *The Boomers' Guide to Online Dating*, Rodale Books, 2005

DePaulo, Bella *Singled Out: How Singles Are Stereotyped, Stigmatized and Ignored, and Still Live Happily Ever After*, St Martin's Press, 1999

Diamond, Lisa M *Sexual Fluidity*, Harvard University Press, 2008

Morgan Disney and Associates with Cupitt, L. and Associates, and

Council on Ageing, Partnership against Domestic Violence (Australia) *Two Lives, Two Worlds: Older People and Domestic Violence*, volumes 1 and 2, 2000

Dooley, Michael and Stacey, Sarah *Your Change, Your Choice*, Hodder Mobius, new edn 2006

Frith Powell, Helena *To Hell in High Heels*, Arrow Books Ltd, 2008

Ganong, Lawrence and Coleman, Marilyn 'Obligations to Stepparents Acquired in Later Life', *Journals of Gerontology*, 2006

Gilchrist, Cherry and Owen, Lara *Love Begins at 40*, Hay House UK, 2008

Godson, Suzi with Agace, Mel *The Sex Book*, Cassell Illustrated, 2002

Goleman, Daniel *Emotional Intelligence: Why It Can Matter More Than IQ*, Bloomsbury, new edn 1996

Gottman, John *The Seven Principles for Making Marriages Work*, New York: Crown, 1999

Gottman, John *Why Marriages Succeed or Fail and How You Can Make Yours Last*, Simon & Schuster, 1994

Greenfield, David *Virtual Addiction*: *Help for Netheads, Cyberfreaks, and Those Who Love Them*, New Harbinger Publications, 1999

Greer, G. *The Female Eunuch*, Flamingo, re-issue 1999

Grever, Carol *My Husband Is Gay*, USA: The Crossing Press, 2001

Grollman, Earl A. *Living When a Loved One Has Died*, Beacon Press, 1997

Grove, Walter, and Shin, Hee-Choon 'The psychological well-being of divorced and widowed men and women', *Journal of Family Issues*, 10, 122–144, December, 1989

Harrison, Barbara *50+ and Looking for Love Online*, USA: The Crossing Press, 2000

Hayman, Suzie *Relate Guide: Stepfamilies, living successfully with other people's children*, Vermilion, 2001

Hayman, Suzie *Stepfamilies: Surviving and Thriving in a New Family*, Simon and Schuster, 2005

Hendrix, Harville *Getting the Love You Want*, Pocket Books, 2005

Hooper, Anne *How Was It For You?* Carroll & Brown Publishers, 2005

Hooper, Anne *The Ultimate Sex Book*, Dorling Kindersley, 1992

Jones, Maggie *Marrying an Older Man*, Piatkus Books, 1993

Kahr, Brett *Sex and the Psyche*: *Revealing the True Nature of Our Secret Fantasies from the Largest Ever Survey of Its Kind*, Allen Lane, 2007

Kirshenbaum, Mira *When Good People Have Affairs: Inside the Hearts and Minds of People in Two Relationships,* St Martin's Press, 2008

Kubler-Ross, Elisabeth *On Death and Dying*, Simon & Schuster, 1997

Laumann, E., Gagnon, J.H., Michael, R.T., and Michaels, S. 'The Social Organization of Sexuality: Sexual Practices in the United States', Chicago: University of Chicago Press, 1994

Liverpool Victoria Friendly Society. 'The Cost of a Parent' report survey, 2007

Lucas, Richard F. and Donnellan, M. Brent 'How Stable Is Happiness?' *Journal of Research in Personality*, 41, 1091–1098, October 2007

Manuel, Lisa 'Does caregiving lead to abuse?' newsletter 2004, *www.womanabuseprevention.com*

Marshall, Andrew G. *I Love You but I'm Not in Love with You*, Bloomsbury Publishing, 2006

Morris, Jan *Conundrum*, Faber and Faber, new edn 2002

Neuberger, Julia *Not Dead Yet*, Harper Collins, 2008

Papernow, Patricia L. *Becoming a Stepfamily*, Jossey-Bass Inc, 1993

Peele, Stanton with Brodsky, Archie *Love and Addiction*, Abacus, 1977

Robbins, John *Still Healthy at 100*, Hodder, 2008

Rowe, Dorothy *My Dearest Enemy, My Dangerous Friend: Making and Breaking Sibling Bonds*, Routledge, 2007

Sauers, Joan *Sex Lives of Australian Women*, Random House, 2008

'Sexual behaviour in Britain: early heterosexual experience', *The Lancet*, 358, issue 9296, December 2001

Scott, Marsha et al. 'Older Women and Domestic Violence in Scotland', Centre for Research on Families and Relationships, 2004

Shernoff, Michael *Gay Widowers: Life After the Death of a Partner*, Hawarth Press, 1997

Simring, Steven, Simring, Klavans Sue, Busnar, Gene *Making Marriage Work for Dummies*, John Wiley and Sons, 1999

Smith, Terri and Harper, James M. *When Your Parent Remarries Late in Life*, Adams Media, 2007

Spezzano, Chuck *If It Hurts It Isn't Love*, Mobius, new edn 2001

Springett, Ulli *Soulmate Relationships*, Piatkus Books, 2003

Spurr, Pam *Sinful Sex*, Robson Books, 2002

Stanko, Professor Elizabeth, *Domestic Violence Data*, Economic and Social Research Council, 2000

Sternberg, Robert J. *The New Psychology of Love*, Yale University Press, 2006

Sternberg, Robert J. *The Triangle of Love: Intimacy, Passion, Commitment*, Basic Books, 1988

Stewart, Susan D. *Brave New Stepfamilies*, Sage, 2007

Strock, Carren, *Married Women Who Love Women*, 2nd edn, Routledge, 2008

Talbot, Nicci, ed: Denise Robertson, *Get Over Your Break-Up*, Hodder Arnold, 2007

Tampubolon, Dr Gindo, 'Fluxes and constants in the dynamics of friendships,' report, *Social Networks*, Manchester University, 2007

Tennov, Dorothy *Love and Limerence*, Scarborough House, 1999

Tessler, Stacy et al. 'A Study of sexuality and health among older adults in the USA' *New England Journal of Medicine*, 357, for the National Institute of Ageing, August 2007

Trimberger, E. Kay *The New Single Woman*, Beacon Press, 2005

Trollope, Joanna *Second Honeymoon*, Bloomsbury, 2006

University of Sheffield 'Are older people at risk of sexually transmitted infections? A new look at the evidence' *Reviews in Clinical Gerontology*, 14, Cambridge University Press, 2004

Walby, Professor Sylvia, and Allen J. 'The cost of domestic violence', University of Leeds, 2004

Weiner Davis, Michele *The Sex-Starved Marriage*, Simon & Schuster, 2004

Weinman Lear, Martha *Where Did I Leave My Glasses? The What, When and Why of Normal Memory Loss*, Wellness Central, 2008

Weinstock, Jacqueline S. and Rothblum, Esther D. *Lesbian Ex-Lovers: The Really Long-Term Relationships*, NY: Harrington Park Press, 2004

Williamson, Marianne *The Age of Miracles: Embracing the New Midlife*, Hay House, 2007

Wilson, Rob and Branch. Rhena *Cognitive Behavioural Therapy for Dummies*, John Wiley & Sons, 2006

Wilson, Trish *Pfizer Global Study of Sexual Attitudes and Behaviours*, Report, 2006

Woodall, Karen and Woodall, Nick *Putting Children First: A Handbook for Separated Parents*, Piatkus Books, 2007

Zadra, Antonio 'Sexual Activity Reported in Dreams of Men and Women', American Academy of Sleep Medicine, *Science Daily*, 2007

Index

ABC thinking 232–4
Abis 290
addiction, Internet 168–9, 171–4
Adelman, Marcy 106
adoption, homosexual couples 91
Adult Industry Trade Association 45
advance directives 66–7
affairs 14–21, 135–43
Affectionate Regard 53, 54
Age Concern 279
alcohol 25, 27, 40
Alzheimer's disease 56–64
Alzheimer's Society 57, 58, 61, 283
American Psychological Society 38
anal sex 178, 180–3, 189
Aristotle 265
askmen.com 289
assimilation stage 273–4
Association for Psychological
    Science 291
Avert 289
awareness stage 274

BBC website 279
BDSM 176, 290
Beaumont Society 290
Binet, Alfred 177
bisexuality 71–8, 162

    see also homosexuality
    friends' advice 79–80, 82
blended families 199–237
Block, Joel 10, 113
Blood, Imogen 34
Boomerang Kids Contracts 293
Boyd, Helen 164
brain, three parts 136
"breaking the ties" exercises
    201–4
British Association for Behavioural
    and Cognitive Psychotherapies
    (BABCP) 291
British Association of Counselling
    and Psychotherapy (BACP) 216,
    217, 279
British Association for Sexual and
    Relationship Therapy 283
British Medical Association 283
burials 64–70, 284
businessballs.com 280
Buxton, Amy 73

Cancer Backup 286
Care for the Family Charity 293
carers
    see also parents, caring for
    Alzheimer's disease 56–64

Census 121–2
Center for Internet Addiction
    Recovery 290
Centre of Ageing Studies 270
cerebellum 136
cerebral cortex 136
Channel 4 website 280
Cheney, Patricia 77
children
    Alzheimer's disease 61
    bisexual partners 74–5
    disapproval of parents 207–14
    divorced parents 199–207, 230–7
    domestic violence 31, 35
    ex-partners' new partner 130,
        132
    grandparents after divorce 238–
        45
    leaving home 49
    lesbian couples 89–96
    looking after parents 12, 218–23,
        245–6, 249–57, 270–6
    moving back in 257–63
    parents' death 65
    step-parents 223–30
chlamydia 186
Cicero 265
Citizens Advice Bureau 279
Civil Partnership Act 90, 101
civil partnerships 89–96, 101, 286
cognitive behavioural therapy
    (CBT) 215–16, 232–4, 237
Coleman, Marilyn 272
Coleman, Vernon 163, 164, 291
commitment test 92–4
common-law partners 90
Complan Active survey 112
compliments 149
condoms 188–9

confidence, increasing 148–50
Conner, Michael G. 168, 171
Council of Europe 31
counselling 56
    affairs 18
    depression 86
    domestic violence 36
    grandparents 242
    mood swings 214–18
    sex change 165–7
    websites 279, 282–3, 286–7,
        290, 291–3
crabs 188
cremation 68, 69–70
crisiscounselling.com 290
cross-dressing 161–7
cybersex 167–74

Davey, Adam 273
death
    see also grief
    burials 64–70, 284
    parents 65
    partner 96–104
DePaulo, Bella 122–3, 288
depression 40, 85–9
diabetes 27
Diamond, Lisa 82–3
diaries 14–15
diuretics 25
divorce 11–12, 48–56, 73
    see also marriage
    effect on children 225–6
    ex-partners' new partner
        127–35
    feelings towards ex-partner
        230–7
    friends relationship 263–70
    mood swings 214–18

ongoing bitterness 199–207
websites 284, 292
Donnellan, Brent 123
drugs 22–3, 28, 40

ejaculation
less 28
premature 27
elastic band effect 43
elderlyparents.org.uk 293
elderly *see* parents
emotional intelligence 145, 288
energy therapies 216
erections
dysfunction 26–7, 40
sex quiz 114, 115
Experience Matters 277, 280
Ezine 288

Families Need Fathers 292
Family Caregiver Alliance 284
Family Equality Council 72, 286
Family Planning Association 176,
280
fantasies 178–9
fantasy stage 273
fear
making it positive 154–5
past 153
fetishism 177–8
finances
Alzheimer's disease 60
retirement 88
flight or fight response 150–1
focus, changing 140
foreplay 116–17, 189
friends
advice 78–84
as family 108

friendship quiz 265–8
ok to be single 120–7
ex-partners 104–11
partner balance 263–70
post divorce 214–15
support 138–9
Future Foundation 238–9, 294

Gagnon, J. H. 191
gametophobia 94
Ganong, Lawrence 272
gaypsychotherapy.com 286
gaystheword.com 286
gay 71–111, 162
children 89–96
ex-partners as friends 104–11
friends' advice 78–84
older singles 96–104
partner's death 96–104
widowers 100–1
gender dysphoria 164–5
genital warts 184, 188
Global Study of Sexual Activities
and Behaviours 113
Goleman, Daniel 145
gonorrhoea 186
Gottman, John 16–17, 54
Government website 280
grandparents
divorced parents 238–45
ex-partners' new partner
132–3
Grandparents Association 294
Grandparents Plus 294
Green Burial Council 284
green burials 68–9, 284
Greenfield, David 172
Greer, Germaine 82
Grever, Carol 74–5

grief 97–100
  bereavement website 287
  cycle 72, 98–9, 139, 166
Grove, Walter 123
guilt
  caring for parents 254
  children moving back in 257–63
  healthy/unhealthy 258–60

Haskey, John 159
healthcare proxy 66
healthy guilt 258–60
heart attacks, sex quiz 116
Help the Aged 34, 221, 294
hepatitis 187
herpes 184, 187–8
Hirschfield, Magnus 162
HIV/AIDS 186–7
housingcare.org 294
humanistic/interpersonal therapies
  216

illness, partners 96–8
incontinence, orgasm 26
infed.org 294
inheritance 222
in-laws, friendship after divorces
  131–2
Institute of Psychosexual Medicine
  284
intellectual compatibility 143–50
Internet
  addiction 168–9, 171–4
  affairs 16
  cybersex 167–74
  long-distance relationships 159
  pornography 44–8
Internet Watch Foundation 46, 284
ivillage.co.uk 280, 289

jealousy
  divorced parents 231–7
  ex lovers 104–11
Johnson, Samuel 220

Kahr, Brett 178
Kegel exercises *see* pelvic floor
  exercises
Kids in the Middle 292
Kinsey Institute 281, 290
Kübler-Ross, Elisabeth 98
Kurokawa, Nobou 87

lasting power of attorney (LPA)
  67–8
laterlife.com 281
Laumann, E. 191
law, pornography 45–6
lesbian.org 287
Lesbilicious 287
limbic brain 136–7
limerence 52
Liverpool Victoria Friendly Society
  252
Living Apart Together (LAT) 159–
  60
living wills 60, 64, 66–7, 252
long-distance relationships 158–60
Loving Attachment 53–4, 55, 56
lubrication 24, 28, 118, 178, 183
Lucas, Richard 123

MacLean, Paul 136
Macmillan Cancer Support 286
Manuel, Lisa 34
Marine Consents and Environment
  Unit 285
marriage 14–70

see also divorce
  affairs 14–21, 135–43
  bisexual partner 71–8
  cross-dressing 161–7
  domestic violence 29–37
  elderly parents 218–23
  ideal myth 55, 121–2, 124
  leaving 48–56
  low desire 37–44
  physical sexual difficulties 21–9
  review 50–1
  step-parents 223–30
  timeline 51–2
marriage Alzheimer's disease 56–64
Marriage Builders 284
marriedgay.org 287
Marshall, Andrew G. 52, 53, 54–5
massage 180
masturbation 25, 178
Mature Times 281
Melville-Ross, Tim 268
menopause 23–4, 39
Michael, R. T. 191
Michaels, S. 191
mobilisation stage 274
Monette, Paul 97
Morris, Jan 167
Morris, Wendy 122

National Centre for Domestic
  Violence 285
National Survey of Sexual Attitudes
  and Lifestyles 15
natural burials 68–9, 284
Natural Death Centre 285
negative feelings
  changing 156–7
  letting go 155
Net Doctor 281

new relationships 161–98
  conversations about sex 190–8
  intellectual compatibility 143–50
  sexual variety 174–80
NHS Direct 281

oestrogen 23–4, 25
Office of National Statistics 11, 12,
  49
Office of the Public Guardian
  (OPG) 67, 285
One Plus One 281
oral sex 117, 118
orgasm
  difficulty 25–6
  inability 27–8
  oestrogen effect 23
  sex quiz 115, 117

Papernow, Patricia 271, 273–6
parental responsibility 91, 96,
  242–3
parents
  caring for 12, 218–23, 245–6,
    249–57, 270–6
  children of divorcees 199–207
  children moving back in 257–63
  elderly, remarriage 218–23
  lesbian children 107
  step-parents 223–30, 270–6
  support 138
Parship 282
Patient UK 282
pelvic floor exercises 25
Perpetrator Programme 36
pinkpractice.co.uk 290
pinktherapy.com 287, 290
polyamory 207–14
Polyamory Society 208, 292

polyfidelity 208–14
polygamy 209
Popenoe, David 159
pornography, websites 44–8
power of attorney 60, 66, 67–8, 252
Pratchett, Terry 57, 63
premature ejaculation 27
Pritchard, Jacqui 34
progesterone, falling levels 23, 24
psychodynamic therapy 216

rejection, fear of 151–2
Relate 10, 216, 282
resentment
    affairs 19
    letting go 155–6
    low desire 42
    retirement 85–9
residential care 253, 254, 257
Respect 285
Retired Husband Syndrome 87
retirement
    resentment 85–9
    websites 282, 288
role-play 118, 179
role reversal 219
Rowe, Dorothy 246–8, 293
Royal College of Psychiatrists 293

SAGA 282
Sauers, Joan 170
Sanders, Deidre 169
Scott, Marshall 34
seesaw effect 43
self-esteem
    building 143–50
    retirement 86
self-image 40

separateddads.co.uk 288
sex 10–11
    Alzheimer's disease 62
    conversations about 37–8, 42–3, 55–6, 178–80, 190–8
    low desire 37–44
    over-fifties expectations 112–20
    physical difficulties 21–9
    quiz 113–17
    variety 174–80
sex change 164–6
sex talk 179
sex talk quiz 193–4
sex toys 178, 189
sexual fluidity 82–3
sexualityadvice.com 289
sexuality.org 176
sexually transmitted diseases 73, 74, 183–90
Sexual Recovery Institute 291
shame, bisexual partners 73
Shared Residence Order 91
sheltered accommodation 253, 257
Shernoff, Michael 100–1, 286
Shin, Hee-choon 123
siblings 245–9
singles 12, 112–60
    convincing friends 120–7
    ex-partners' new partner 127–35
    fear of painful separations 150–7
    long-distance relationships 158–60
    older homosexuals 96–104
    safe sex 183–90
sky burials 64, 68, 70
smoking 27
social services 59, 253
Society for Human Sexuality 282
Statistics Authority 283

stepfamily cycle 271, 273–6
step-parents 223–30
caring for 270–6
Sternberg, Robert J. 210–11
Straight Spouse Network 71–2, 73, 288
Strock, Carren 81
swinging 210
syphilis 185, 187

Tampubolon, Gindo 268–9
Tennov, Dorothy 52
Tessier, L. J. 'Tess' 105
testosterone 23, 24
    falling levels 26–8, 39
    replacement therapy 25
Third Age 289
timeline 51–2
transgender 161–7
transgenderzone.com 291
transvestites 161–7
Trimberger, Kay 127
Trollope, Joanna 261

unhealthy guilt 258–60

vaginal atrophy 23, 25
vaginal dryness 23, 24–5, 28, 115
values, shared 125
Viagra 27
vibrators 25, 178, 183
violence 29–37
Visher, Emily 221
voyeurism 177
vulvodynia 26

Weiner Davis, Michele 43
Weinstock, Jacqueline 106, 108
wills 66–7, 222, 252
    living 60, 64, 66–7, 252
Women Bloom 283
Women's Aid 285

Young, Kimberley 172

Zadra, Antonio 178

Now you can buy any of these other bestselling non-fiction titles from your bookshop or *direct from the publisher*.

FREE P&P AND UK DELIVERY
(Overseas and Ireland £3.50 per book)

Who's That Woman in the Mirror?   *Keren Smedley*   £7.99
'Age is irrelevant, unless you happen to be a bottle of wine' – Joan Collins. In this book you'll find all the answers to your questions about mid-life change and reinvention.

If Not Now, When?   *Esther Rantzen*   £7.99
An inspirational life guide for the baby boomer generation from well-loved TV personality, founder of Childline, writer and broadcaster Esther Rantzen.

By Myself and Then Some   *Lauren Bacall*   £8.99
A remarkable story of the life of the iconic, award-winning American actress whose career has spanned over six decades.

Living History   *Hillary Clinton*   £8.99
America's former First Lady reveals what really happened during her eight years in the White House.

Send Yourself Roses   *Kathleen Turner*   £7.99
The iconic leading lady reveals her astonishing trajectory from struggling New York actress to household name – a result of passionate ambition, powerful instinct and unwavering self-belief.

Wonderful Today   *Pattie Boyd*   £8.99
The drop-dead gorgeous model, photographer, and ex-wife and muse of George Harrison and Eric Clapton speaks out in this compelling and moving autobiography.

The Kindness of Strangers   *Kate Adie*   £7.99
The former BBC Chief News Correspondent describes her courageous career reporting from the frontline of the world's trouble spots since 1969.

TO ORDER SIMPLY CALL THIS NUMBER

01235 400 414

or visit our website: www.headline.co.uk

Prices and availability subject to change without notice.